SmartSuite Millennium

═fast & easy™

Send Us Your Comments

To comment on this book or any other Prima Technology title, visit Prima's Reader Response page on the Web at **www.primapublishing.com/comments**.

How to Order:

For information on quantity discounts, contact the publisher: Prima Publishing, P.O. Box 1260BK, Rocklin, CA 95677-1260; (916) 632-4400. On your letterhead, include information concerning the intended use of the books and the number of books you wish to purchase. For individual orders, turn to the back of this book for more information, or visit Prima's Web site at **www.primapublishing.com.**

SmartSuite® Millennium

fast & easy™

Diane Koers

PRIMA PUBLISHING

Prima Publishing and colophon are registered trademarks of Prima Communications, Inc.
Fast & Easy is a trademark of Prima Communications, Inc. Prima Publishing, Rocklin, California 95677.

Publisher: Matthew H. Carleson

Managing Editor: Dan J. Foster

Acquisitions Editor: Jenny L. Watson

Project Editor: Kevin W. Ferns

Technical Reviewer: Pamela Palmer

Copy Editor: Judy A. Ohm

Interior Layout: Shawn Morningstar

Cover Design: Prima Design Team

Indexer: Emily Glossbrenner

ISBN: 0-7615-1699-9

Library of Congress Catalog Card Number: 98-66622

Printed in the United States of America

98 99 00 01 02 HH 10 9 8 7 6 5 4 3 2 1

To Gloria.

You're always there for me when I need you.
May we be friends for life!

Acknowledgments

I am deeply thankful to the many people at Prima Publishing who worked on this book. Thank you for all the time you gave and for your assistance.

To Jenny Watson, for the opportunity to write this book and for her confidence in me. To Pam Palmer and Judy Ohm, for their help in making this book technically and grammatically correct, and to Kevin Ferns, for all his patience and guidance.

Lastly, a big thank you to my husband, Vern, who kept me supplied with my "working chocolate!"

About the Author

Diane Koers owns and operates All Business Service, a software training and consulting business formed in 1988, which services the central Indiana area. She specializes in word processing, spreadsheet, and graphics software, and provides training and support for Peachtree Accounting Software. Diane's authoring experience includes Prima's *Lotus 1-2-3 97 Fast & Easy*, *WordPerfect 8 Fast & Easy*, *Windows 98 Fast & Easy*, and *The Essential Windows 98 Book*. She has also developed and written software training manuals for her clients' use.

Active in her church and civic activities, Diane enjoys spending her free time traveling and playing with her grandson and her three Yorkshire Terriers.

Contents
at a Glance

PART IV
USING FREELANCE 187

PART V
USING ORGANIZER 223

PART VI
USING APPROACH 281

APPENDIXES 319

Contents

PART II
USING WORD PRO 25

PART VI
USING APPROACH.............. 281

Introduction

This new *Fast & Easy* book from Prima Publishing will help you use the many and varied features of Lotus's popular SmartSuite product. SmartSuite is designed to answer most of your personal and professional computing needs. It provides you with a word processor, spreadsheet, database manager, personal calendar and contact management system, and presentation graphics program.

Fast & Easy books teach you with a step-by-step approach, clear language, and color illustrations of exactly what you will see on your screen. *SmartSuite Millennium Fast & Easy* provides the tools you need to successfully tackle the potentially overwhelming challenge of learning to use SmartSuite. You will be able to quickly tap into the program's user-friendly integrated design and feature-rich environment.

WHO SHOULD READ THIS BOOK?

The easy-to-follow, highly visual nature of this book makes it the perfect learning tool for a beginning computer user. However, it is also ideal for those who are new to this version of SmartSuite, or for those who feel comfortable with computers and software, but have never used these types of programs before.

In addition, anyone using a software application always needs an occasional reminder about the steps required to perform a particular task. By using *SmartSuite Millennium Fast & Easy*, any level of user can look up steps for a task quickly without having to plow through pages of descriptions.

In short, this book can be used by the beginning to intermediate computer user as a learning tool or as a step-by-step task reference.

ADDED ADVICE TO MAKE YOU A PRO

You'll notice that this book uses steps and keeps explanations to a minimum to help you learn faster. Included in the book are a few elements that provide some additional comments to help you master the program, without encumbering your progress through the steps:

✦ **Tips** often offer shortcuts when performing an action, or a hint about a feature that might make your work in SmartSuite quicker and easier.

✦ **Notes** give you a bit of background or additional information about a feature, or advice about how to use the feature in your day-to-day activities.

In addition, the two appendixes will show you how to install SmartSuite and use a fascinating new feature called ViaVoice Gold. With ViaVoice, you can dictate right into your computer!

Read and enjoy this *Fast & Easy* book. It is certainly the fastest and easiest way to learn Lotus SmartSuite Millennium Edition.

PART I
Discovering SmartSuite

February

$27,540.0

$31,212.7

$18,400.0

$11,235.5

$88,388.2

0.00 | $12,000.0

1 Getting Started with SmartSuite

SmartSuite is designed to meet the majority of your everyday software needs. Using SmartSuite, you can perform a multitude of tasks including creating letters, generating reports, tracking your budget, producing a slide show presentation, and designing a database to track your videotape collection. SmartSuite is versatile, yet powerful enough to be useful to both the office professional and the home user. Before you start, you'll want to familiarize yourself with the components that make up SmartSuite. In this chapter, you'll learn how to:

✦ Open and view the various components of SmartSuite

✦ Use the SmartCenter

✦ Explore the SmartCenter drawers

UNDERSTANDING THE PARTS OF SMARTSUITE

SmartSuite is not just one application—it is a group of several different applications. Each application in SmartSuite is designed to have a specific function. The following sections explain what these functions are.

SmartCenter

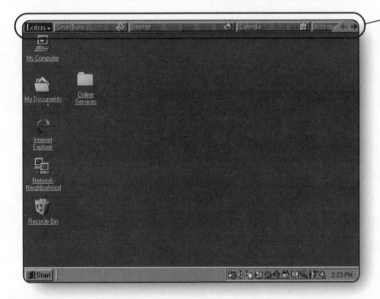

SmartCenter acts as a hub for the SmartSuite applications. You can organize your work by using SmartCenter's drawers and folders.

Word Pro

Word Pro is SmartSuite's word processor. This is the tool you'll use when you need to work with text. Word Pro can create a wide range of documents, including letters, memos, faxes, reports, newsletters, and calendars. Word Pro is a WYSIWYG (What You See Is What You Get) word processor. This means that the document on the screen looks like the printed document. You can immediately see the impact, for example, of making text bold or changing its font. Word Pro also includes support for ViaVoice Gold, which will allow you to dictate directly into your Word Pro document.

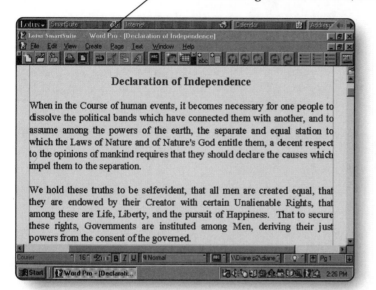

1-2-3

Lotus 1-2-3 is an easy to use, powerful spreadsheet application. Whenever you need to work with numbers, 1-2-3 is the application to use. Some of the uses for 1-2-3 include creating budgets, proposals, financial statements, and charts. Using 1-2-3, you can enter the numbers you want to work with, perform calculations with them, and, if you want, create a chart from them.

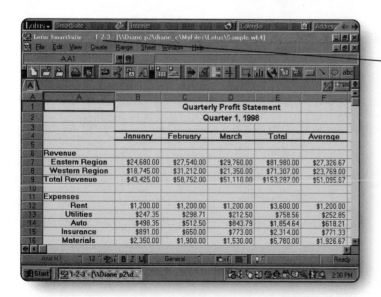

Freelance Graphics

Freelance Graphics makes creating quality presentations a simple matter of using your mouse to select format options and using your keyboard to enter the text of the presentation. If you have never created a presentation using a computer before, you're going to love using Freelance Graphics!

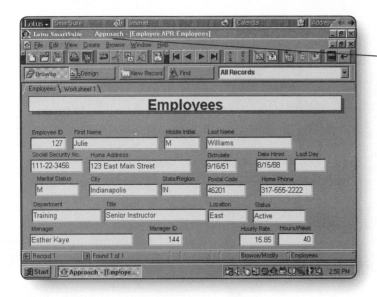

Approach

Approach is SmartSuite's database application. A database application is used to store and organize information. Examples of database uses include keeping a home inventory, managing a collection such as videos, baseball cards, or books, and tracking employee information.

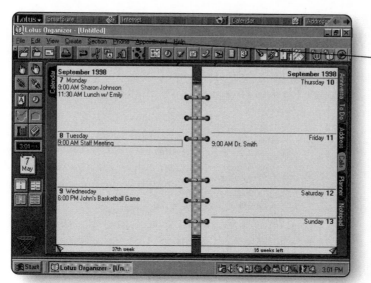

Lotus Organizer

To keep yourself organized, you may have one book to track your appointments and another to track names, addresses, and telephone numbers. You may have a to-do list as well. Organizer lets you manage all this information in one location on your computer. Using Organizer, you can track appointments, store contact information, do tasks, and make telephone calls.

USING SMARTCENTER

SmartCenter automatically starts when you turn on your computer after you have installed SmartSuite. SmartCenter allows you to do a variety of tasks, including starting SmartSuite applications, opening files created with SmartSuite applications, accessing the Internet, opening and using your calendar and address book, and working with reminder lists.

NOTE
SmartCenter is organized like a file cabinet. The first level of organization is the drawer. Just like drawers in a real file cabinet, SmartCenter drawers hold folders.

Using Drawers

You may not see all the available drawers. This is because they can't all fit on your screen at the same time. To view the other drawers, use the scroll buttons found on the right end of the SmartCenter bar.

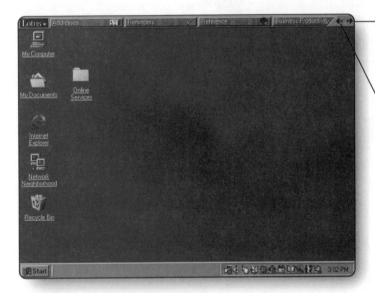

1. **Click** on the **right scroll button**. Additional drawers will be listed in SmartCenter.

2. **Click** on the **left scroll button**. The drawer listing will be scrolled back to the left.

Each of these drawers contains folders. To view the folders in a drawer, you must first open the drawer.

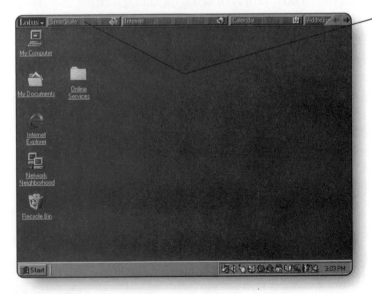

3. **Click** on the **drawer handle**. The folders in this drawer will appear. Folders come in different colors, and each folder has its name listed on its tab.

4. **Click** on the **drawer handle**. The drawer will close.

TIP

You can also click on the bar located at the top of the opened drawer to close the drawer.

Working with Folders

Each SmartCenter drawer has several folders in it. Some of the folders act like those found in real file cabinets because they store documents. Others have specialized designs so they act as calendars or address books, and some of the folders are actually tools that allow you to work with the Internet and use the Thesaurus. The steps for accessing all these types of folders are identical.

1. **Click** on the **drawer handle** of the drawer where the folder is located. The folders located in that drawer will appear.

2. **Click** on the **folder tab** of the folder you want to work with. The folder will open.

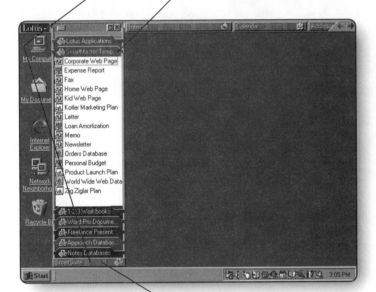

NOTE
After you open the folder, the folder type will determine your action. For example, if the folder contains documents, you can double-click on the icon representing the document to open the document. If the folder is a calendar folder, you can click on a time slot to enter an appointment.

3. **Click** on the **drawer handle**. The drawer will close.

TIP
After you are finished working with the contents of a drawer, close the drawer so that your desktop will not become too cluttered.

2 Getting Help

Although you'll find many answers to your questions in SmartSuite, sometimes you need additional information. Lotus supplies you with several types of assistance. In this chapter, you'll learn how to:

✦ Use the Help Contents and Index

✦ Ask the SmartSuite Expert for advice

✦ Get help on the Web

ACCESSING HELP TOPICS FROM THE SMARTCENTER

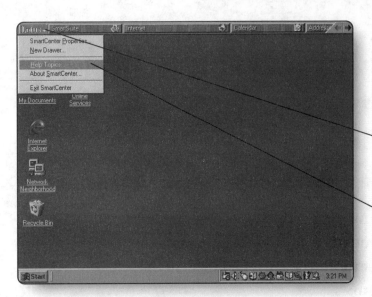

Help with the SmartSuite products is available several ways. One method, using the SmartCenter, shows you that help is only a mouse-click away.

1. **Click** on the **SmartCenter menu button**. The SmartCenter menu will appear.

2. **Click** on **Help Topics**. The Help Topics dialog box will open.

ACCESSING HELP TOPICS FROM A SMARTSUITE APPLICATION

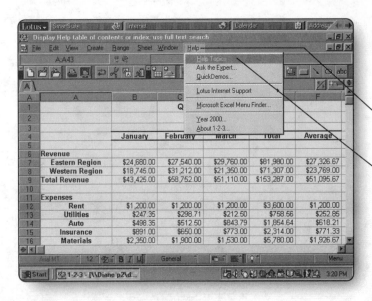

When you are working with any of the SmartSuite applications, you can access help through the Help menu.

1. **Click** on **Help**. The Help menu will appear.

2. **Click** on **Help Topics**. The Help Topics dialog box will open.

USING HELP TOPICS

The Help Contents page of the Help Topics dialog box presents help information in a book-like format so that you can browse available topics.

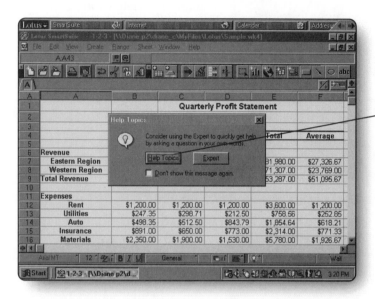

1. Open the **Help Topics** using one of the two methods just listed. A Help Topics dialog box will appear.

2. Click on **Help Topics**. The Help Topics dialog box will appear with the Contents tab displayed.

3. Click on a **general topic**. The topic will be highlighted.

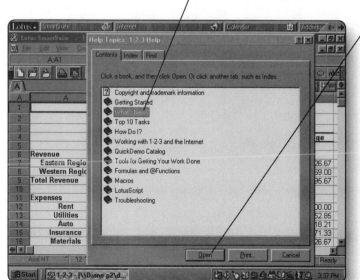

4. Click on **Open**. Additional topics will appear, and in some cases, books.

NOTE

A *general topic* is signified by a small book, whereas a *specific topic* is indicated by a paper with a question mark on it. Some general topics may have other general topics listed under them.

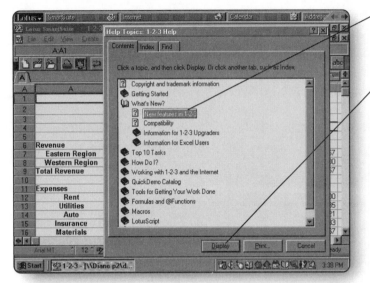

5. **Click** on the **specific topic** you want to view. The topic will be highlighted.

6. **Click** on **Display**. The SmartSuite Help window will appear.

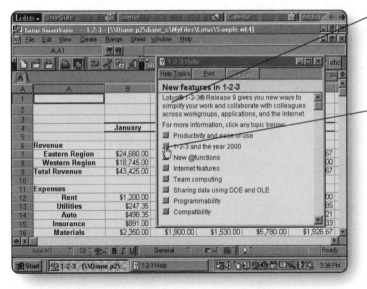

7. **Read** the **information** presented. The help information may have several additional sources of information for you.

8. **Click** on a **button** to display additional information.

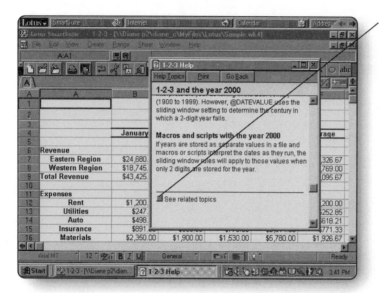

9. Click on the **See related topics button**. The Topics Found dialog box will open.

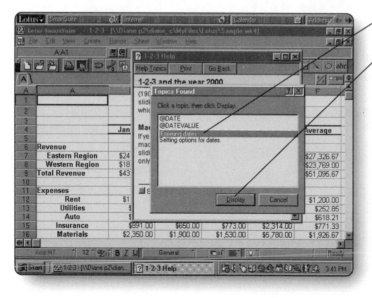

10. Click on a **topic**.

11. Click on **Display**. The SmartSuite Help window for that topic will appear.

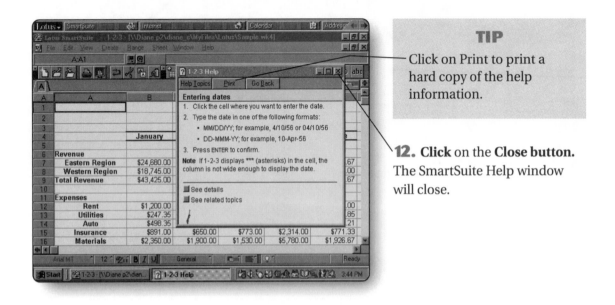

TIP

Click on Print to print a hard copy of the help information.

12. **Click** on the **Close button.** The SmartSuite Help window will close.

USING THE HELP INDEX

SmartSuite's help features also include an index of topics. You can search through an extensive list to find just what you're looking for.

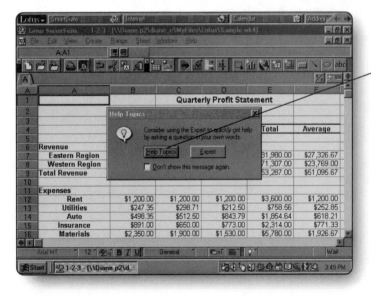

1. **Open** the **Help Topics.** A Help Topics dialog box will appear.

2. **Click** on **Help Topics**. The Help Topics dialog box will appear with the Contents tab displayed.

3. **Click** on the **Index tab**, if necessary. The Index tab will come to the front. The topics are listed alphabetically with some topics displaying a list of subtopics.

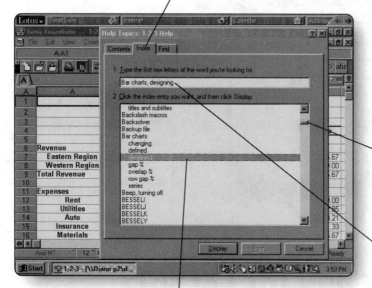

4a. **Scroll** through the **list of topics** until you find the topic you are looking for.

OR

4b. **Type** the **first word** of the topic you are looking for. The topics will jump alphabetically to the word you type.

5. **Double-click** on the desired **topic**. The information will be displayed on the right side of the screen.

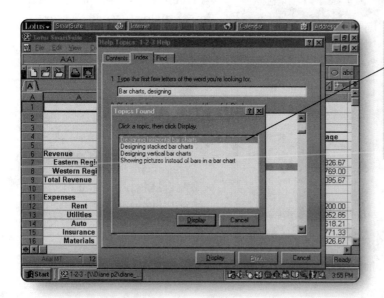

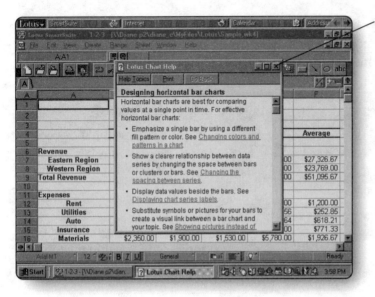

6. Click on the **Close button.** The SmartSuite Help window will close.

USING THE EXPERT

Got a question? Ask the SmartSuite expert! It's ready and willing to assist you wherever it can.

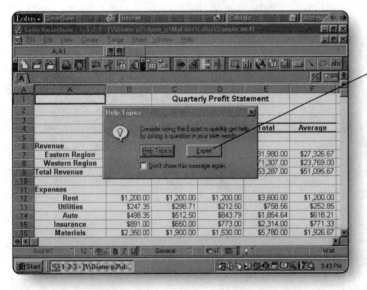

1. Open the **Help Topics.** A Help Topics dialog box will appear.

2. Click on **Expert**. The Expert dialog box will appear.

TIP

You can also access the Expert from any application by clicking on Help and then clicking on Ask the Expert.

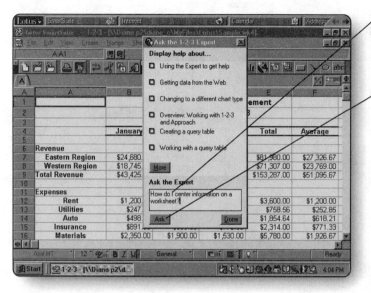

3. **Type** your **question** in the Ask the Expert box. Your text will appear in the box.

4. **Click** on **Ask**. A list of possible solutions will appear.

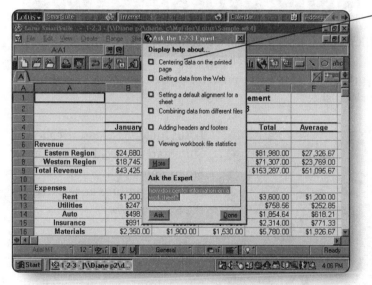

5. **Click** on the **solution** most likely to answer your question. The help topic will appear.

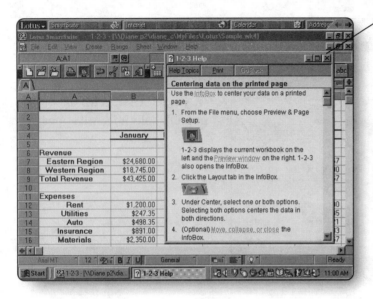

6. **Click** on the **Close button**. The help topics window will close.

FINDING HELP ON THE WEB

There are many sources of assistance supplied with SmartSuite. You've already seen several good resources. Another one is the World Wide Web. Lotus includes technical support for you at its Web site.

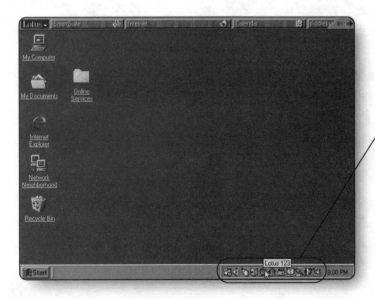

Lotus includes a feature called SuiteStart to quickly launch any SmartSuite application. The SuiteStart buttons are located in the System Tray.

1. **Open** any **SmartSuite application** by clicking on a button from the SuiteStart icons.

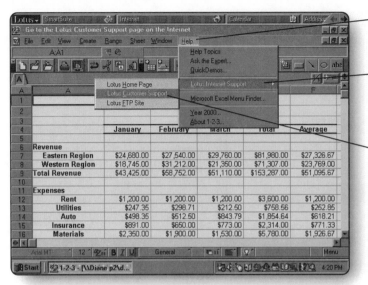

2. Click on **Help**. The Help menu will appear.

3. Click on **Lotus Internet Support**. A submenu will appear.

4. Click on **Lotus Customer Support**. If you are not already connected to the Internet, your Web browser will launch and you'll be prompted to connect.

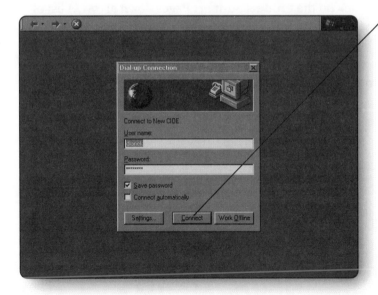

5. Click on **Connect**. Your Internet connection will be established and the Lotus Customer Support Web Page will be displayed.

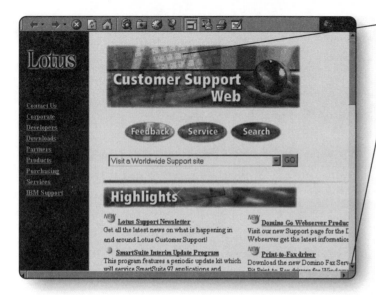

This Web page will change periodically; however, Lotus places several possible locations through which you can continue searching for information.

6. **Click** on the **Scroll down arrow** to view the various support options.

7. **Click** on the **Product Support Pages down arrow**. A list of Lotus products will be displayed.

8. **Click** on the **Lotus product** you want to investigate. The product will be displayed in the list box.

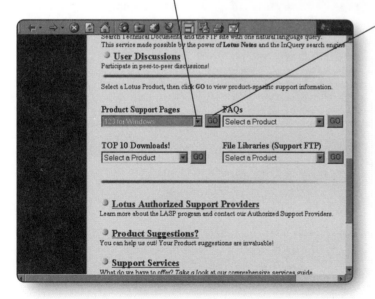

9. **Click** on **Go**. The support Web page for the selected product will be displayed.

NOTE

You may be prompted with one or more Security Alert or Redirect dialog boxes. Click on Yes.

Several options will appear on this screen.

✦ **Search KnowledgeBase**. Click on this to search through Lotus technical documents.

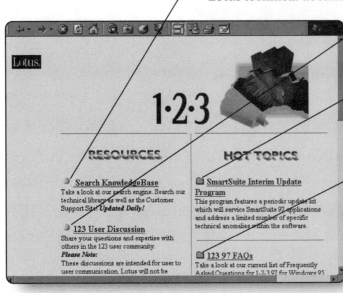

✦ **User Discussions**. Click on this to join in discussions with other Lotus users.

✦ **Interim Updates**. Click on this to keep your application up to date with the latest patches and fixes.

✦ **FAQs**. Click on this to look for Frequently Asked Questions on any Lotus topic.

10. **Scroll** through the **Web page** to view additional topics and **Click** on the **Lotus resource** you want to use. Follow any instructions that appear on that screen.

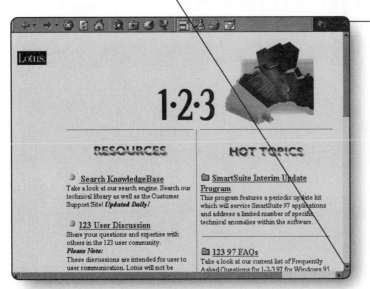

11. **Click** on the **Close button** to exit the online help.

NOTE

You may be prompted to close your Internet connection. Click on Yes if you want to disconnect.

PART I REVIEW QUESTIONS

1. **What is SmartCenter?** *See "Understanding the Parts of SmartSuite" in Chapter 1*

2. **What kind of a word processing program is Word Pro?** *See "Understanding the Parts of SmartSuite" in Chapter 1*

3. **What type of application is Approach?** *See "Understanding the Parts of SmartSuite" in Chapter 1*

4. **What should you do when you are finished working with the contents of a SmartCenter drawer?** *See "Working with Folders" in Chapter 1*

5. **What are the two ways to access help in SmartSuite?** *See "Getting Help" in Chapter 2*

6. **What icon signifies a general help topic?** *See "Using Help Topics" in Chapter 2.*

7. **How are topics listed in the Help index?** *See "Using the Help Index" in Chapter 2*

8. **How can you get answers from the SmartSuite Expert?** *See "Using the Expert" in Chapter 2*

9. **What is KnowledgeBase?** *See "Finding Help on the Web" in Chapter 2*

10. **What are interim updates?** *See "Finding Help on the Web" in Chapter 2*

PART II

Using Word Pro

$27,540.00
$31,212.75
$18,400.00
$11,235.50
$88,388.25

0.00 $12,000.00

Page 1 of 1

3 Creating a Simple Document

When you need to create a document, use Word Pro. Word Pro is great for everything text-based, from the simplest letter to a professional-looking report. You'll become comfortable using its text editing capabilities, including adding text formatting such as bold, italic, and a variety of fonts to your documents. You'll use features such as tables or the spell-checker to save you time and add polish to your documents. In this chapter, you'll learn how to:

✦ Start the Word Pro program

✦ Create a document

✦ Insert the current date

✦ Move around in a Word Pro document

✦ Select and delete text

✦ Undo your mistakes

STARTING WORD PRO

The SmartCenter makes it easy to start Word Pro and all the SmartSuite applications.

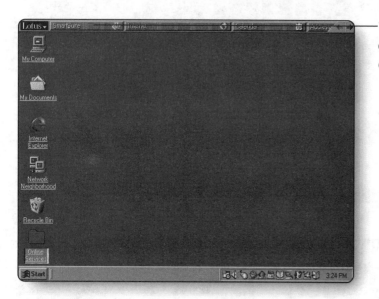

1. **Click** on the **SmartSuite drawer handle**. The drawer will open.

2. **Click** on the **Lotus Applications folder tab**. The contents of this folder will be displayed.

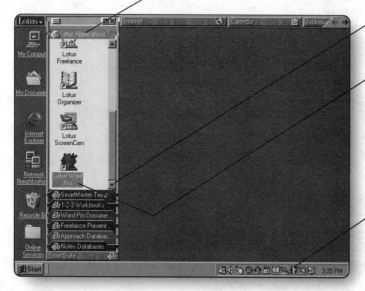

3. **Click** on the **down arrow** until you see the Lotus Word Pro icon.

4. **Double-click** on the **Lotus Word Pro icon**. Word Pro will start and the Welcome to Lotus Word Pro dialog box will open.

TIP

Another way to start the Word Pro program is to click on the Word Pro button in the System Tray.

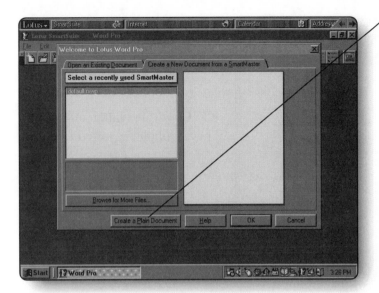

5. Click on **Create a Plain Document**. A blank document will appear on your screen.

CREATING A DOCUMENT

When typing in Word Pro, press the Enter key only when you get to the end of a paragraph or when you want an extra blank line between paragraphs. Word Pro takes care of the rest. If the word you are typing does not fit entirely on the current line, Word Pro will go to the next line. This is called *word wrap*.

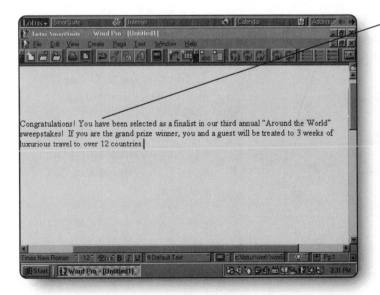

1. Type some **text**. The text you type will appear at the location of the insertion point.

NOTE

If you make any mistakes while typing, you can press the Backspace key to erase any letter to the left of the blinking insertion point.

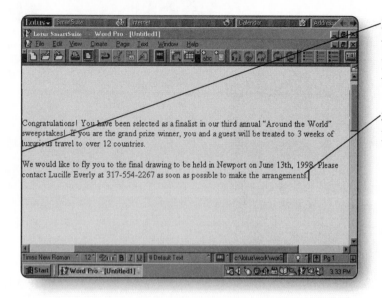

2 Press the **Enter key twice** when you have completed a paragraph. The insertion point will move down two lines.

3. Continue typing until you have completed your document.

INSERTING THE DATE AND TIME

Instead of fishing around your desk looking for your calendar, let Word Pro put today's date in your document for you.

1. Click on the **insertion point** where you want to insert the date. The insertion point will blink at the location you selected.

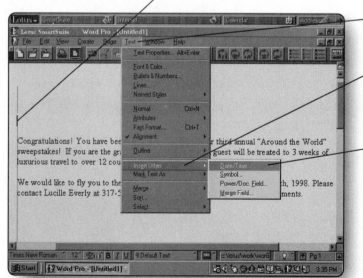

2. Click on **Text**. The Text menu will appear.

3. Click on **Insert Other**. The Insert Other submenu will appear.

4. Click on **Date/Time**. The Insert Date/Time dialog box will open.

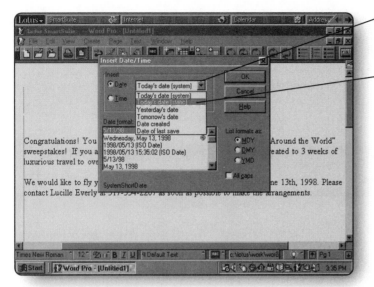

5. **Click** on the **down arrow**. A list of date choices will appear.

6. **Click** on a **date type**. The selected date type will appear in the list box.

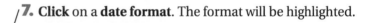

7. **Click** on a **date format**. The format will be highlighted.

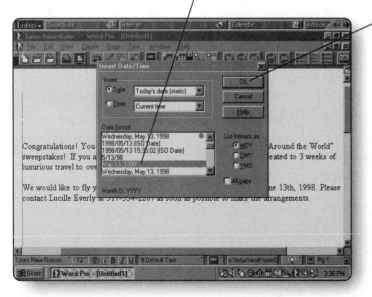

8. **Click** on **OK**. The date will be inserted into your document at the location of the insertion point.

NOTE

A system date is *dynamic*, which means the date on the document will change according to the actual current date, whereas a *static* date does not change the next time your document is opened.

MOVING AROUND IN A WORD PRO DOCUMENT

Word Pro provides several ways to move around a document quickly.

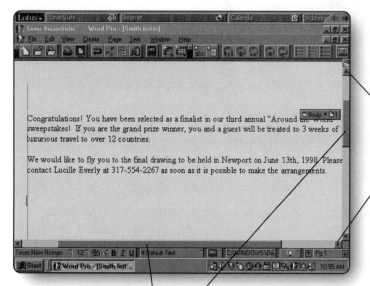

Moving around Using the Scroll Bar

1. Click on the **arrow** repeatedly at either end of the vertical scroll bar to move the document up and down in the window.

2. Click on the **arrow** repeatedly at either end of the horizontal scroll bar to move the document left or right in the window.

3. Click on the **vertical scroll box** and **hold** the **mouse button** while you drag the scroll box up or down. Notice that when you move the scroll box, an indicator box will appear telling you which page you're scrolling over.

4. Click on the **horizontal scroll box** and **hold** the **mouse button** while you drag the scroll box left or right.

> ### NOTE
> When moving through a document using the scroll bar, the insertion point does not move—only the screen display moves. You must click in the document to move the insertion point to a new location when using the scroll bar.

Moving Around Using the Keyboard

You may prefer to use your keyboard to move around in your document. This mini-table illustrates these shortcut keys.

To Move	Do This
Right one word	Press Ctrl + Right Arrow
Left one word	Press Ctrl + Left Arrow
To the beginning of a line	Press Home
To the end of a line	Press End
To the beginning of the paragraph	Press Ctrl + Up Arrow
To the next paragraph	Press Ctrl + Down Arrow
Down one screen	Press Page Down
Up one screen	Press Page Up
To the beginning of the document	Press Ctrl + Home
To the end of the document	Press Ctrl + End
To a specified page number	Press Ctrl + G

INSERTING TEXT

Word Pro begins in *insert* mode. This means that when you want to add new text to a document, any existing text will move to the right to make room for the new text.

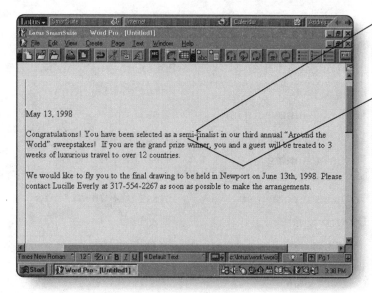

1. **Click** to place an **insertion point** where you want to add additional text.

2. **Type** the **new text**. The new text is inserted into the document.

SELECTING TEXT

In order to move, copy, delete, or change the formatting of text, you first need to select it. When text is selected, it will appear on your screen as light type on a dark background—just the reverse of unselected text. You can only select a sequential block of text at a time; not bits of text in different places.

NOTE

You can select a word, sentence, paragraph, or the entire document by using the shortcut menu.

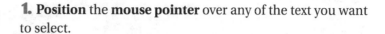

1. Position the **mouse pointer** over any of the text you want to select.

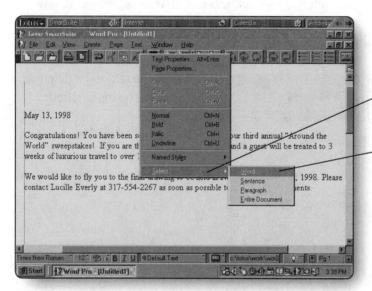

2. Click the **right mouse button**. The shortcut menu will appear.

3. Click on **Select**. The Select submenu will appear.

4. Click on a **selection** from the Select submenu. The text will be highlighted.

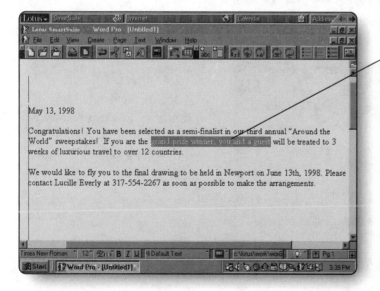

TIP

Alternatively, you can select a block of text by clicking at the beginning of the text. Then press and hold the mouse button and drag across the text until you get to the end of the text you want to select. Release the mouse button.

NOTE

Text can be deselected by clicking elsewhere in the document.

DELETING TEXT

You can delete unwanted text one character, one word, one paragraph, one page, or any combination of the above, at a time.

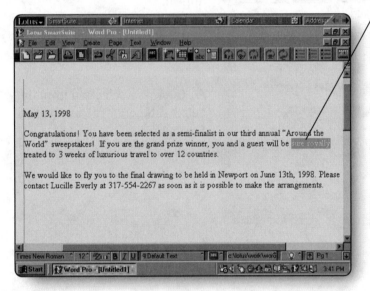

1. **Select** the **text** to be deleted. The text will be highlighted.

2 **Press** the **Delete key**. The text will be deleted.

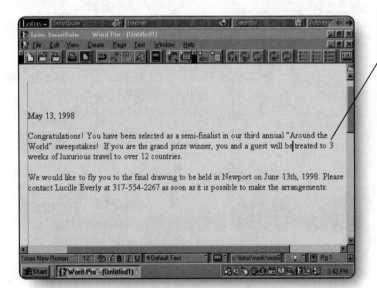

NOTE

As soon as the deleted text disappears, any text below or to the right of the deleted words will move up to remove blank spaces.

UNDOING MISTAKES

Word Pro has a feature called *Undo*. This feature will reverse the last step or steps you performed. The default setting allows you to undo the last four steps you've taken in the document.

1. **Click** on the **Undo button**. The last action you took will be reversed.

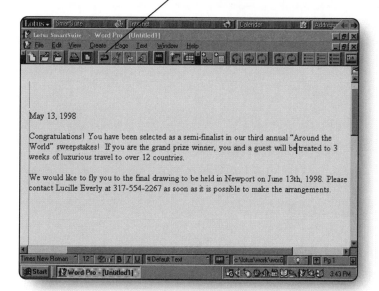

TIP

You can control the number of steps Word Pro can undo by choosing File, User Setup and then Word Pro Preferences. The Undo levels can be set between 1 and 32768.

2. **Click** on the **Undo button** again to reverse another step.

4 Formatting Word Pro Documents

Appearance is everything when it comes to word processing, so Word Pro offers several ways to improve the appearance of your document through formatting. Formatting allows you to change the look of your document by changing the look of the text. In this chapter, you'll learn how to:

✦ Work with text properties

✦ Set paragraph alignment and indentation

✦ Work with bullets

✦ Set and delete tabs

✦ Insert special symbols

WORKING WITH TEXT ATTRIBUTES

You can change the appearance of text in a variety of ways. For example, you can change the font or make the text bold or underlined.

Making Text Bold

Applying the bold attribute to text makes the text characters thicker and darker.

1. Select the **text** you want to make bold. It will be highlighted.

2. Click on **Text**. The Text menu will appear.

3. Click on **Attributes**. The Attributes submenu will appear.

4. Click on **Bold**. The selected text will be in bold.

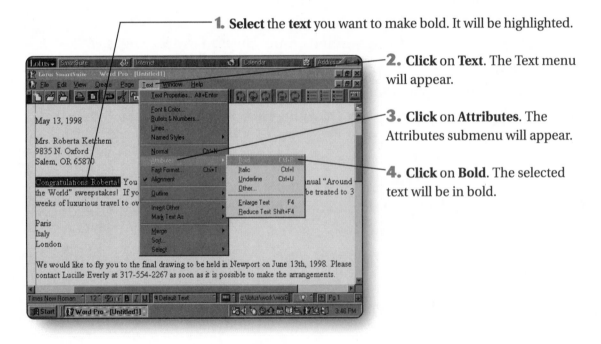

Underlining Text

Using the underline attribute can call special attention to parts of your document.

1. **Select** the **text** you want to underline. The text will be highlighted.

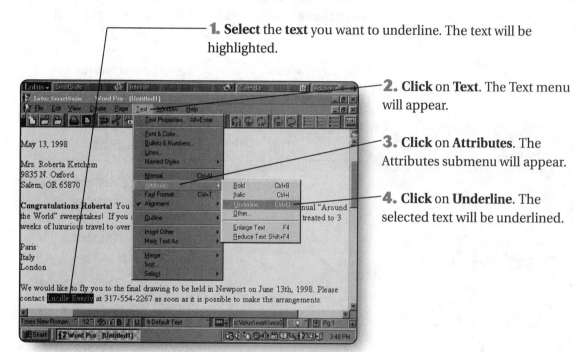

2. Click on **Text**. The Text menu will appear.

3. Click on **Attributes**. The Attributes submenu will appear.

4. Click on **Underline**. The selected text will be underlined.

Changing Text Attributes Using the Status Bar

You can change text attributes by using the status bar. The status bar has buttons to add attributes of bold, italic, and underline.

1. **Select** the **text** you want to format. The text will be highlighted.

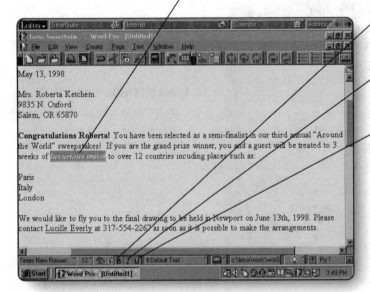

2. **Click** on the **Bold button**. The text will be bold.

3. **Click** on the **Italics button**. The text will be italicized.

4. **Click** on the **Underline button**. The text will be underlined.

TIP

Shortcut keys to format text include: Ctrl+B to bold, Ctrl+I to italicize, and Ctrl+U to underline.

5. **Repeat** any of **steps 2 through 4** to remove the attribute. The selected attribute will be removed.

WORKING WITH FONTS

Changing the font typeface of text is another way to make it stand out from the rest of your document.

Changing the Font Typeface Using the Text Menu

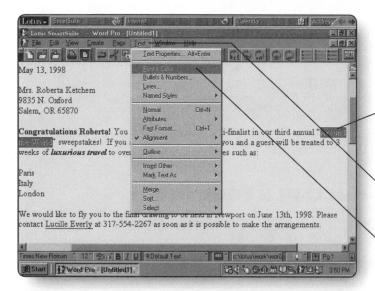

The font selections you have will vary depending upon any additional software you have installed on your computer.

1. Select the **text** you want to change. The text will be highlighted.

2. Click on **Text**. The Text menu will appear.

3. Click on **Font & Color**. The Properties for Text dialog box will open.

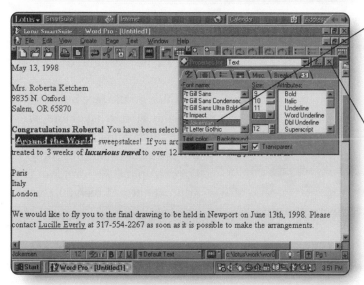

4. Click on a **font typeface name** from the Font name: list box. The font typeface change will be immediately applied to the selected text.

5. Click on the **Close button**. The dialog box will close.

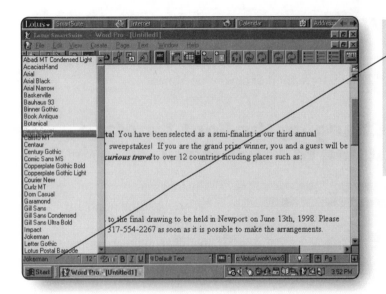

TIP

You can also change the font typeface by first selecting the text to be modified, clicking on the typeface list box on the status bar, and selecting the font you want to use.

Selecting a Font Size

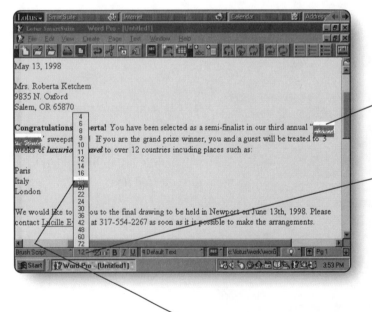

You may want to make portions of your text larger or smaller than the rest of the text in your document.

1. **Select** the **text** whose font size you want to change. The text will be highlighted.

2. **Click** on the **Size button** in the status bar. A list of font sizes will appear. The larger the number, the larger the font size. For example, a 72 point font is approximately 1 inch tall on the printed page.

3. **Click** on a **new size**. The font size change will be applied to the text.

SELECTING PARAGRAPH ALIGNMENT AND INDENTION OPTIONS

You may want to align certain paragraphs in your documents so that they are, for example, centered on a page. Headings and titles are frequently centered. You also may need to indent paragraphs so that they stand out from other text.

Setting Paragraph Alignment

Four types of alignment are available: left, center, right, and full justified.

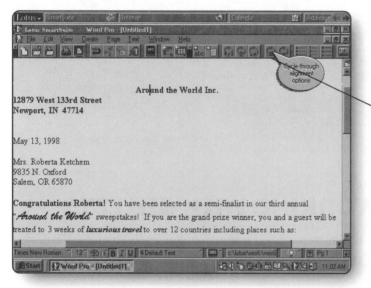

1. **Position** the **insertion point** within the paragraph to align. The insertion point will blink at the selected location.

2. **Click** on the **Cycle through alignment options button**. The paragraph changes its alignment with each click.

3. **Continue clicking** on the **Cycle through alignment options button** until you have the desired alignment. The paragraph will set to that alignment setting.

TIP

Shortcut keys to align text include: Ctrl+L to left align, Ctrl+R to right align, Ctrl+E to center align, and Ctrl+J to full justify.

Indenting a Paragraph

Sometimes you want to move an entire paragraph over to emphasize the information in it. This is known as indenting. By default, indents are set for every 1/4-inch.

1. **Position** the **insertion point** within the paragraph to indent.

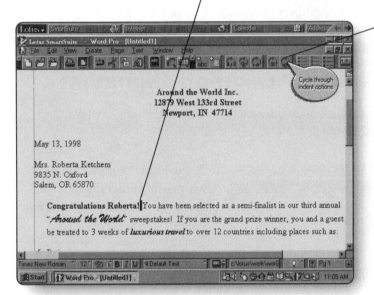

2. **Click** on the **Cycle through indent options button**. The paragraph will be indented 1/4-inch.

> **TIP**
>
> You can indent the paragraph multiple times by clicking repeatedly on the Cycle through indent options button. Each click will indent the paragraph another 1/4-inch.

WORKING WITH BULLETS

Word Pro supports a variety of bullet styles and makes it easy to create a bulleted paragraph.

Creating a Bulleted Paragraph

Often indenting a paragraph or group of paragraphs is not enough to draw attention to it. You might want to add a symbol in front of it. This is known as a bullet. A paragraph or list with bullets in front calls additional attention to the items.

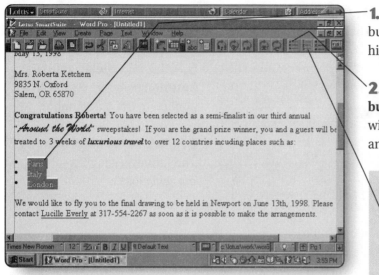

1. Select the **paragraphs** to bullet. The paragraphs will be highlighted.

2. Click on the **Insert default bullet button**. The paragraph will be immediately bulleted and indented.

Selecting a Bullet Style

Choose from a collection of bullet styles ranging from small black filled circles to check marks to funny little iconic symbols.

1. Select the **paragraphs** to modify the bullet. The paragraphs will be highlighted.

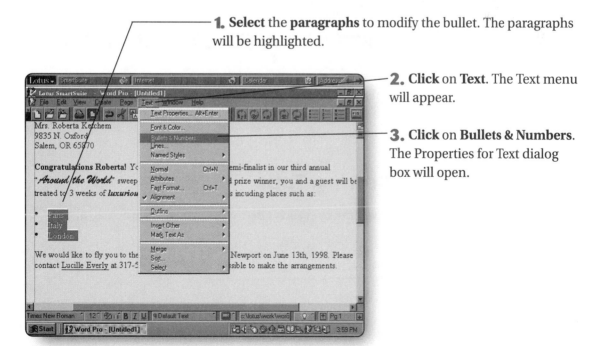

2. Click on **Text**. The Text menu will appear.

3. Click on **Bullets & Numbers**. The Properties for Text dialog box will open.

4. **Click** on the **Bullet & Number tab** if that tab is not in front. The Bullet & Number tab will come to the front.

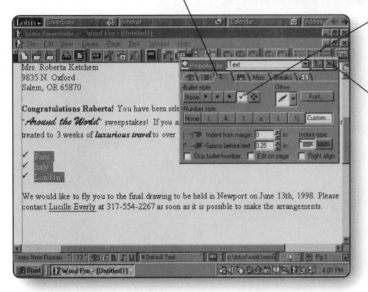

5. **Click** on a **bullet style button**. The bullet style will be applied to the paragraph.

6. **Click** on the **Close button**. The Properties for Text dialog box will close.

SETTING AND DELETING TABS

Often you need to create columns of text in your document. This can be easily accomplished by using tabs. By default, tabs are set at every 1/2-inch. Setting and deleting tabs can be done using the ruler.

Setting Tabs

Save time by setting tabs before you type the actual tabbed text.

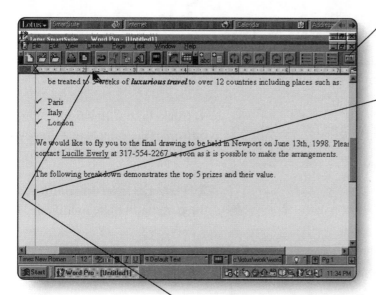

1. **Click** on the **Show/hide ruler button,** if the ruler is not already displayed. The ruler will display.

2. **Click** on the **insertion point** in the paragraph to be modified.

3. **Move** the **mouse pointer** to the ruler. The mouse pointer will become an arrow.

4. **Click** the **point of the arrow** on the **ruler** where you want to create a new tab. The tab will be set at that point.

Tabs are indicated on the ruler as small arrows.

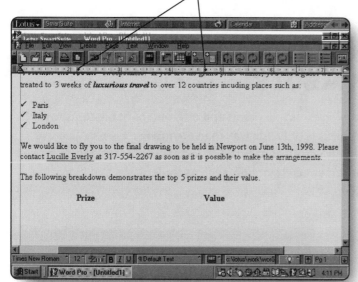

NOTE

Custom tabs override the default tabs to the left of the custom tab.

Deleting a Tab

Make sure your insertion point is in the paragraph that contains the tab that you want to delete.

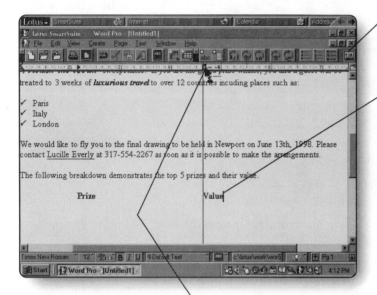

1. **Click** on the **Show/hide ruler button**, if the ruler is not already displayed. The ruler will display.

2. **Place** the **insertion point** in the paragraph to be modified.

3. **Drag** the **unwanted tab** anywhere off the ruler. The tab will be removed.

INSERTING SPECIAL SYMBOLS

Adding bullets to a paragraph or group of paragraphs to add emphasis is only one way to use symbols. You can also use symbols within your text. For instance, on occasion, you need to insert special symbols such as trademarks and copyright marks.

1. Click in the **area** where you want to place the symbol. A blinking insertion point will appear at the location you selected.

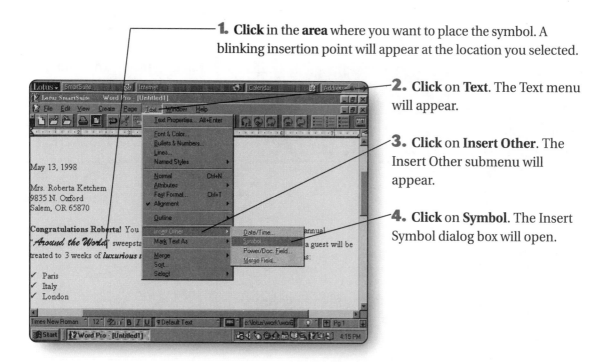

2. Click on **Text**. The Text menu will appear.

3. Click on **Insert Other**. The Insert Other submenu will appear.

4. Click on **Symbol**. The Insert Symbol dialog box will open.

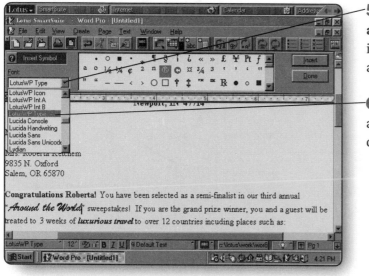

5. Click on the **Font down arrow**. A list of the fonts installed on your system will appear.

6. Select a **font**. The symbols associated with that font will be displayed.

7. **Click** on a **symbol**. The symbol will be selected.

8. **Click** on **Insert**. The symbol will be inserted into your document.

9. **Click** on **Done**. The Insert Symbol dialog box will close.

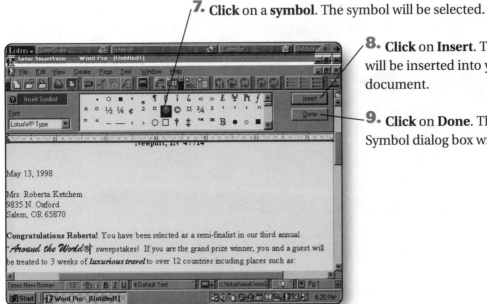

5 Working with Page Layout

One size doesn't always fit all in the world of word processing documents. You may need to adjust the size of the text area of a document. Headers and footers are often used to repeat key information on each page of a document, such as a company's name or the page number. These types of page layout features give your document a professional look. In this chapter, you'll learn how to:

- ✦ Set margins
- ✦ Change page size
- ✦ Change page orientation
- ✦ Add a page border
- ✦ Add a header or footer

SETTING MARGINS

The size of the text area is controlled by the size of the page margins. You can set left, right, top, and bottom margins. By controlling the margins, you control the amount of text area available.

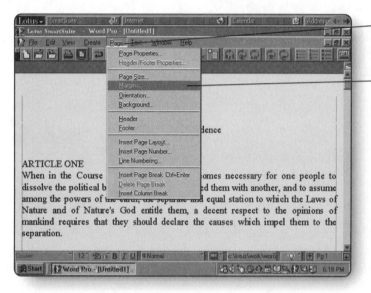

1. **Click** on **Page**. The Page menu will appear.

2. **Click** on **Margins**. The Properties for Page layout dialog box will open.

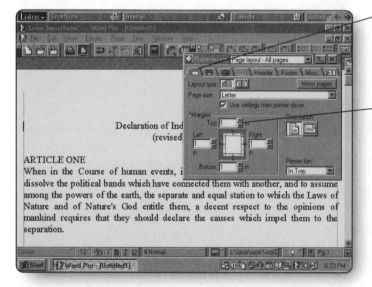

3. **Click** on the **Size and Margin tab,** if necessary. The Size and Margin tab will come to the front.

4. **Click** on the **up/down arrows** for each margin in the Top:, Left:, Right:, and Bottom: list boxes. The value in these boxes is measured in inches.

5. **Click** on the **Close button**. The Properties for Page Layout dialog box will close.

CHANGING PAGE SIZE

Word Pro lets you select from several page size options. The page size options used by Word Pro are based on the page size settings of your printer.

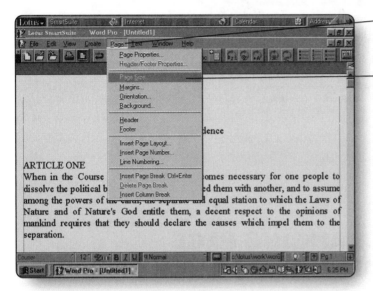

1. **Click** on **Page**. The Page menu will appear.

2. **Click** on **Page Size**. The Properties for Page layout dialog box will open.

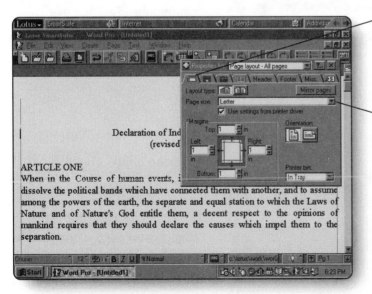

3. **Click** on the **Size and Margin tab,** if necessary. The Size and Margin tab will come to the front.

4. **Click** on the **down arrow** at the right of the Page size: list box. The list of available page size options will appear.

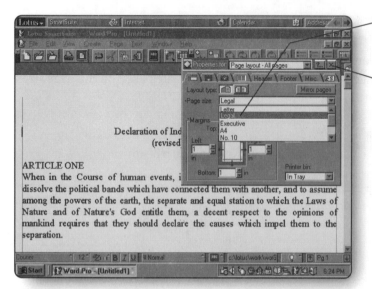

5. **Click** on a **page size**. The page size will be selected.

6. **Click** on the **Close button**. The Properties for Page layout dialog box will close.

CHANGING PAGE ORIENTATION

Word Pro lets you print a document using either a portrait or landscape orientation. Portrait orientation will print the document in a vertical layout, whereas landscape orientation will print horizontally across the page.

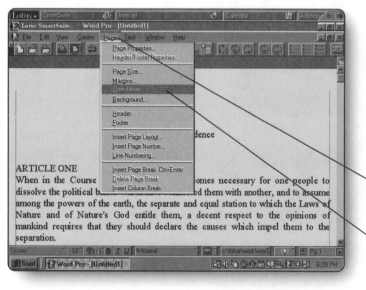

1. **Click** on **Page**. The Page menu will appear.

2. **Click** on **Orientation**. The Properties for Page layout dialog box will open.

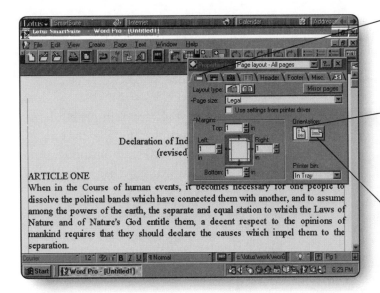

3. Click on the **Size and Margin tab,** if necessary. The Size and Margin tab will come to the front.

4a. Click on the **Portrait button**. The document's orientation will be portrait.

OR

4b. Click on the **Landscape button**. The document's orientation will be landscape.

5. Click on the **Close button.** The Properties for Page layout dialog box will close.

ADDING PAGE BORDERS

Decorate your page with a border. Word Pro offers a variety of borders that you can use.

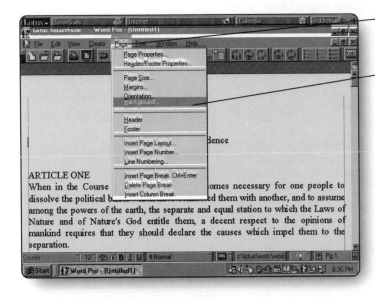

1. Click on **Page**. The Page menu will appear.

2. Click on **Background**. The Properties for Page layout dialog box will open.

3. **Click** on the **Color**, **Pattern**, and **Line Style tab**, if necessary. The Color, Pattern, and Line Style tab will appear.

4. **Choose** from the following **options**:

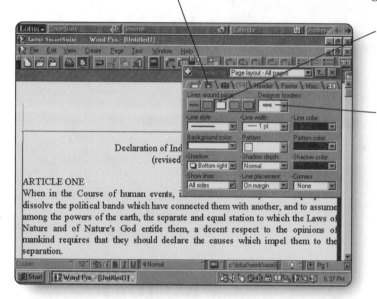

◆ If you want a simple border around your page, click on one of the buttons under the Lines around page: section.

◆ If you want a more detailed border, click on the down arrow under the Designer borders: list box and make a selection.

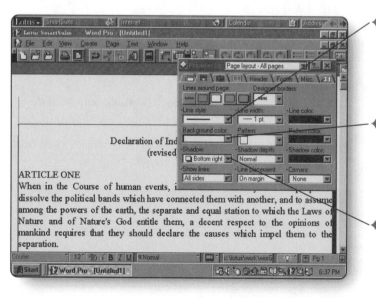

◆ To change the line style used by the border, click on the down arrow at the right of the Line style: list box and make a selection.

◆ If you want to pick another background color, click on the down arrow at the right of the Background color: list box and make a selection.

◆ To add a shadow to the border, click on the down arrow at the right of the Shadow: list box and make a selection.

✦ Select where to put the line by clicking on the check beside the Show lines: list box.

✦ If you want to change the line width used by the border, click on the down arrow beside the Line width: list box and make a selection.

✦ To change the border's pattern, click on the down arrow next to the Pattern: list box and make a selection.

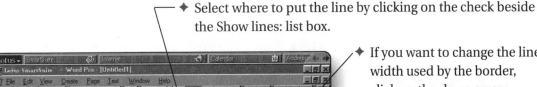

✦ If the border you are creating has a shadow, you can select the shadow depth by clicking on the down arrow next to Shadow depth: list box and make a selection.

✦ To control the line placement, click on the down arrow beside the Line placement: list box and make a selection.

✦ You can pick a line color by clicking on the down arrow beside the Line color: list box and make a selection.

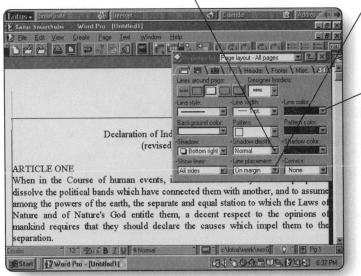

✦ To change the pattern color of the border, click on the down arrow beside the Pattern color: list box and make a selection.

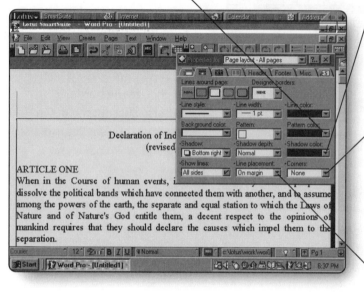

✦ If the border you are creating has a shadow, you can select a shadow color by clicking on the down arrow next to the Shadow color: list box and making a selection.

✦ You can select the type of corners your border will have by clicking on the down arrow beside the Corners: list box and making a selection.

TIP

Click on Line placement and choose Page Edge if you want the border to also surround your header or footer.

5. **Click** on the **Close button**. The Properties for Page layout dialog box will close.

ADDING A HEADER OR FOOTER

Two areas in a document are reserved for repeating text. When this text is at the top of a page, it is called a header. When this text is at the bottom of a page, it is called a footer.

Creating a Header or Footer

Examples of text you may want to place in a header or footer are the date the document was created, the document name, your company's name, or the current page number.

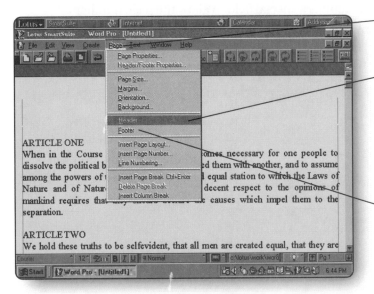

1. **Click** on **Page**. The Page menu will open.

2a. **Click** on **Header**. The Header/Footer bar will appear and the insertion point will be located in the header area of the document.

OR

2b. **Click** on **Footer**. The Header/Footer bar will appear and the insertion point will be located in the footer area of the document.

3. **Type** some **text**. The text will be added to the header or footer.

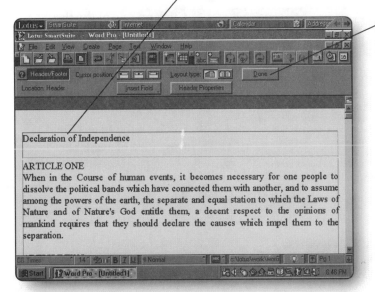

4. **Click** on **Done**. The Header/Footer bar will close.

Inserting a Page Number in a Footer

When creating a footer, do not just type a number for the page number. Doing so will not increment the page numbers. Word Pro requires a special field to allow the page number to increment.

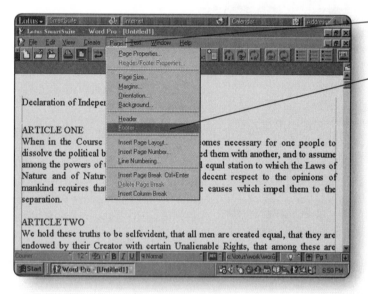

1. **Click** on **Page**. The Page menu will open.

2. **Click** on **Footer**. The Header/Footer bar will appear and the insertion point will be located in the footer area of the document.

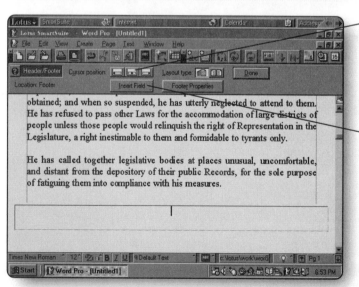

3. **Click** on one of the three **Cursor position: buttons**; left, center, or right. The insertion point will move to the left, center, or right edge of the page.

4. **Click** on the **Insert Field button**. A list of available choices will appear.

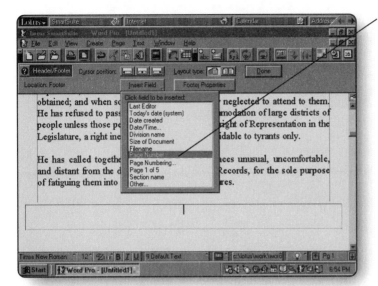

5. Click on **Page Number** or any other desired style. The current page number will be inserted into the footer.

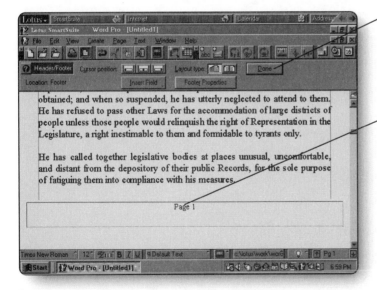

6. Click on **Done**. The Header/Footer bar will close.

TIP

If you want the page number to be preceded by text, such as the word "Page", type the text in front of the page numbering field.

6 Working with Tables

Prior to tables, a typist had to spend a lot of time pressing the Tab key to line up text in columns. Tables have greatly simplified this process. Tables have columns and rows, making it easy to enter columnar text. In this chapter, you'll learn how to:

✦ Create a table

✦ Modify a table size

✦ Format a table

✦ Create a repeated heading for a table

CREATING A TABLE

Word Pro has made creating a table extremely easy through its
Create table grid button.

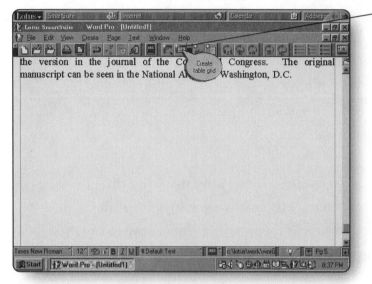

1. Click on the **Create table grid
SmartIcon**. The table grid will
display.

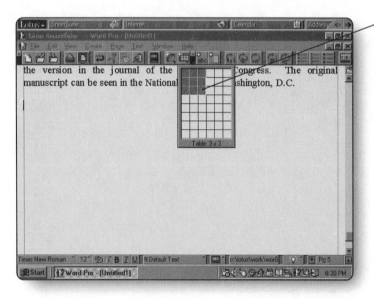

2. Click on the **cell**
representing the last cell of the
table you want to create. The
table will be created in your
document and the SmartIcons
will change to reflect table
options.

ENTERING TEXT INTO A TABLE

Text typed in a table cell is restricted by the boundaries of each table cell. The Tab key is used to move from one cell to the next, whereas the Shift+Tab key moves the insertion point backwards to the previous cell. You can also use your arrow keys to move from cell to cell.

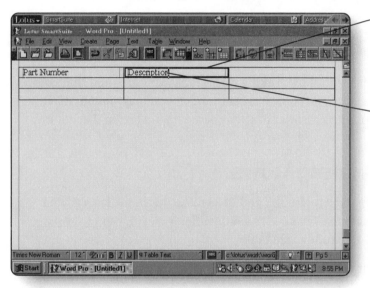

1. Click on the **cell** where you want to enter data. The border around the cell will be highlighted.

2. Type some **text**. The text will appear in the cell.

3. Press the **Tab** key. The insertion point will move to the next cell.

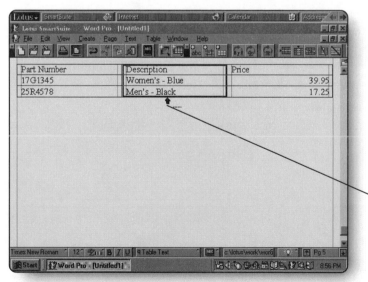

SELECTING TABLE CELLS

To modify a table, you'll need to select the cells you want to change.

✦ To select a single cell, click on a cell.

✦ To select an entire column, position the mouse at the top or bottom of a column until it turns into a small yellow arrow, then click.

+ To select an entire row, position the mouse at the right or left of a row until it turns into a small yellow arrow, then click.

+ To select a block of cells, click on the beginning cell, hold down the mouse button and drag across the additional cells. Then release the mouse button.

+ To select the entire table, right-click anywhere on top of the table, choose Select, then choose Entire Table.

MODIFYING TABLE SIZE

After you start working with a table, you may find that you need to add rows and columns. Or you may want to make a column narrower or wider based on the text in that column.

Adding Rows

To add a row at the end of a table, click in the last cell and press the Tab key. It's a little different if you want to add a row in the middle of a table.

1. **Click** on the **row** above where you want the new row to appear. A cell in that row will be selected.

2. **Click** on the **Insert row in table SmartIcon**. The new row will be inserted after the selected row.

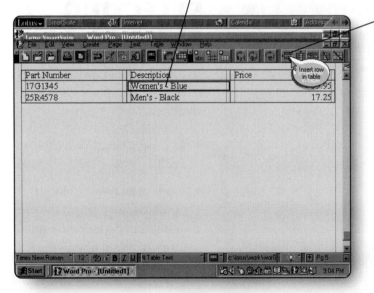

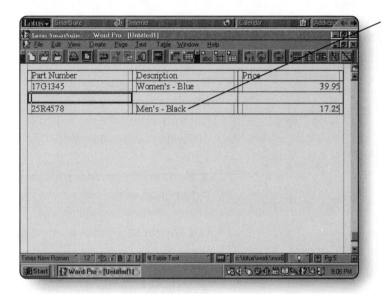

All rows below the new row move down.

Adding Columns

Adding additional columns to your table is only a mouse click away!

1. **Click** on the **column** to the left of where you want the new column to appear. A cell in that column will be selected.

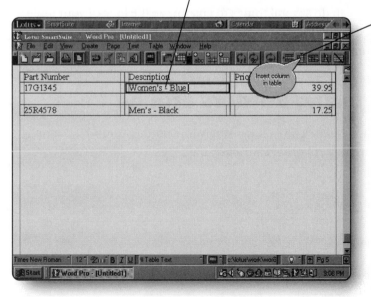

2. **Click** on the **Insert column in table SmartIcon**. The new column will be inserted to the right of the selected column.

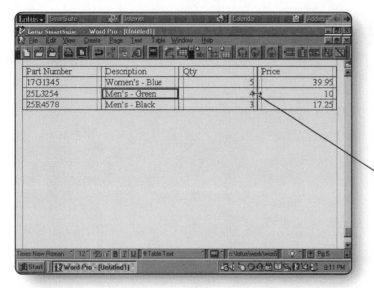

Changing Column Width

By default, all columns are equally spaced and a table expands across the entire width of the document margins.

1. Position the **pointer** over the right border of the column to resize. The pointer will change to a horizontal double-headed arrow.

2. Drag the **border** until the column is the correct size. The column will be resized.

FORMATTING A TABLE

You can do several things to customize the look of your table. These include adding a border around cells and selecting a number format.

Placing Borders around Cells

Each cell in a table has a single line border around it. Many varieties of borders are available.

1. Select the **cells** to be modified. The selected cells will be highlighted.

2. Click on **Table**. The Table menu will appear.

3. Click on **Lines & Fill Color**. The Properties for Table Cell dialog box will open.

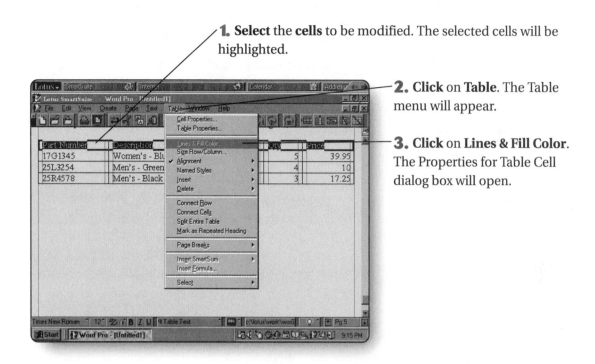

4. Click on the **Color, Pattern & Line Style tab**, if necessary. The tab will come to the front.

5. Click on a **button** under Lines around cells. The selected border will be applied.

NOTE

Optionally, you can select different styles, thicknesses, and colors for the lines.

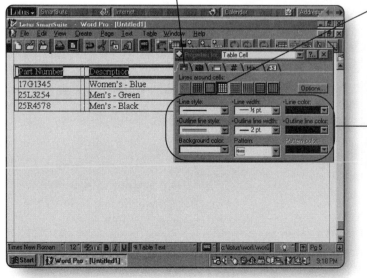

6. Click on the **Close button**. The Properties for Table Cell dialog box will close.

Setting Number Formats for Cells

Make your numbers appear like currency, percentages, or other numerical formats.

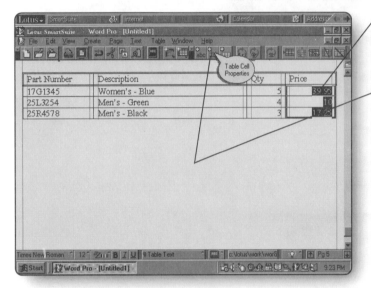

1. **Select** the **cells** to be formatted. The cells will be highlighted.

2. **Click** on the **Table Cell Properties SmartIcon**. The Properties for Table Cell dialog box will open.

3. **Click** on the **Number format tab**. The Number format tab will appear.

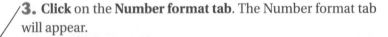

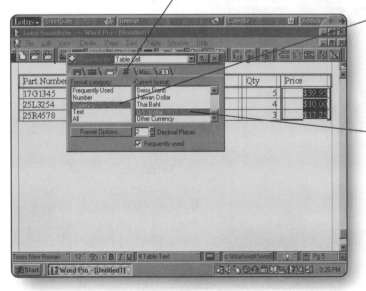

4. **Click** on a **category** in the Format category: section. Options from the format category will be displayed in the Current format: section.

5. **Click** on the **format** that you want to use in the Current format: section. The number format will be applied to the selected column.

6. **Click** on the **Close button**. The Properties for Table Cell dialog box will close.

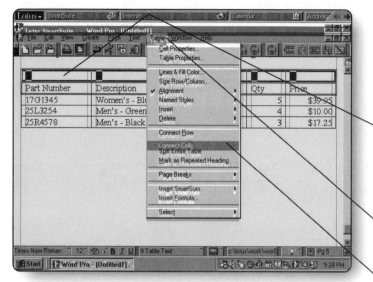

Connecting Cells

You may want to connect cells when creating a heading for your table.

1. **Press** and **hold** the **mouse button** and **drag** across the cells you want to connect. The cells will be selected.

2. **Click** on **Table**. The Table menu will appear.

3. **Click** on **Connect Cells**. The cells will connect.

Creating a Repeated Heading

If you have a table that spans more than one page, you may want to mark a heading as a repeated heading. This tells Word Pro to place the marked heading at the top of each page of the table.

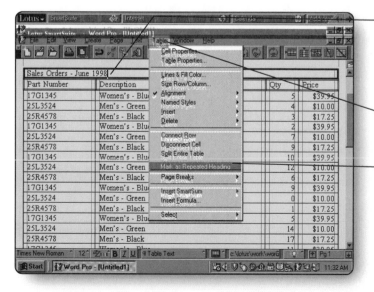

1. **Click** on a **cell** in the row that you want to mark as a repeated heading. The cell will be selected.

2. **Click** on **Table**. The Table menu will appear.

3. **Click** on **Mark as Repeated Heading**. The heading will automatically repeat on each page of the table.

7 Creating Reports

Reports are second only to letters in popularity and use. Whether you are a student, consultant, or other professional, you will have many uses for reports. Students are often called upon to do reports as part of their class work; professionals often need to do reports for a variety of reasons ranging from cost and project justifications to recommendations and strategic directions. In this chapter, you'll learn how to:

✦ Add footnotes

✦ Create and update a table of contents

ADDING FOOTNOTES

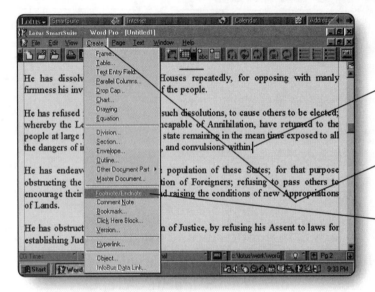

Footnotes comment on and provide reference information for the text in your document.

1. **Click** on the **location** for the footnote. The insertion point will be moved to that location.

2. **Click** on **Create**. The Create menu will appear.

3. **Click** on **Footnote/Endnote**. The Footnotes dialog box will open.

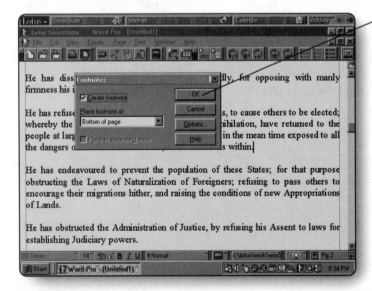

4. **Click** on **OK**. The footnote will be added to the document and the Footnotes dialog box will close. The insertion point will be placed in the footnote area of the document.

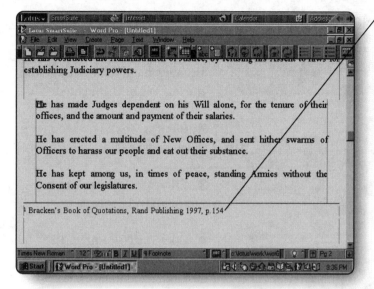

5. **Type** the **text** of the footnote. The text will be entered for this footnote.

6. **Press** the **Esc key**. You will return to the main text of the document.

CREATING A TABLE OF CONTENTS

Because reports are typically documents that contain several pages, it is useful to include a table of contents. Word Pro makes it easy to mark text for your table of contents and to generate the table of contents.

Marking the TOC Headings

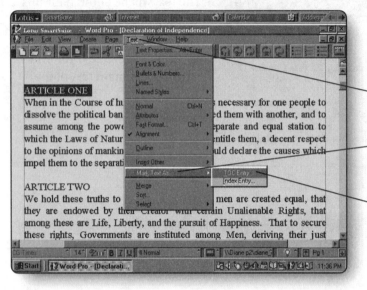

1. **Highlight** some **text** to be included in the Table of Contents. The text will be highlighted.

2. Click on **Text**. The text menu will appear.

3. Click on **Mark Text As**. A submenu will appear.

4. Click on **TOC Entry**. The Mark Text bar will appear at the top of the document.

5. Click on the **up/down arrows** next to the TOC level: area to set the level for the selected heading. The level will be set.

6. Click on **Mark**. This sets the level.

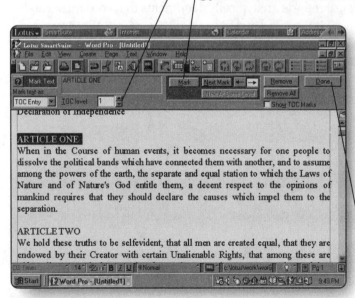

7. Select the **next text** to be included in the Table of Contents. The text will be highlighted.

8. Click on the **up/down arrows** in the TOC level: area to set the level for the selected heading. The level will be set.

9. Repeat steps 7 and 8 for each heading.

10. Click on **Done**. The Mark Text bar will close.

Generating the Table of Contents

Next, you'll need to tell Word Pro the location and options you want for your Table of Contents.

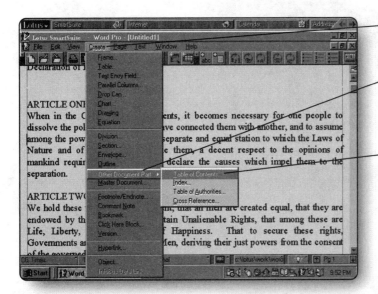

1. **Click** on **Create**. The Create menu will appear.

2. **Click** on **Other Document Part**. The Other Document Part submenu will appear.

3. **Click** on **Table of Contents**. The Table of Contents Assistant will open.

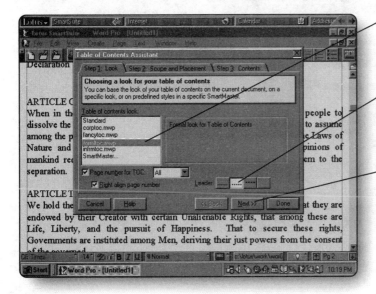

4. **Click** on an **option** from the Table of contents look: text box. The option will be highlighted.

5. **Click** on a **leader style** for the page number in the Leader: style area. The option will be selected.

6. **Click** on **Next** to continue to step 2.

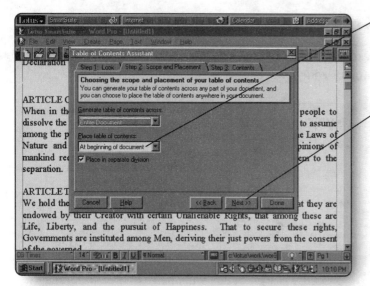

7. **Choose** the **location** of the Table of Contents. The default location is to place it at the beginning of the document.

8. **Click** on **Next** to continue to step 3.

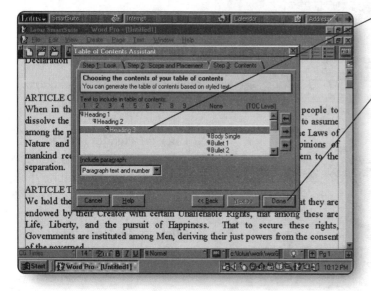

9. **Click** on the **highest level** you want in your TOC. The level will be highlighted.

10. **Click** on **Done**. The table of contents will be automatically generated.

Updating Your Table of Contents

If you make changes by adding to or deleting from the items to be included in the table of contents, you will need to update the table of contents.

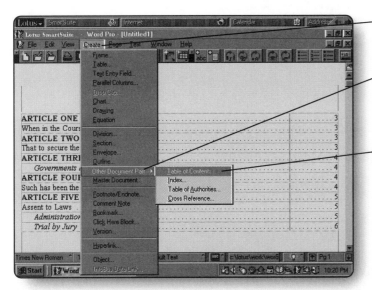

1. **Click** on **Create**. The Create menu will appear.

2. **Click** on **Other Document Part**. The Other Document Part submenu will appear.

3. **Click** on **Table of Contents**. The Update or create Table of Contents dialog box will open.

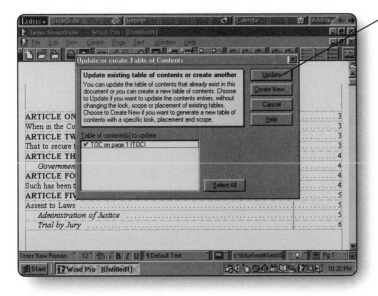

4. **Click** on **Update**. The table of contents will be automatically updated.

8 Improving Your Writing

Word Pro's goal is to make document creation as easy as possible. To reach this goal, several features have been included in Word Pro to improve your writing. You probably misspell a word now and then or you may have a grammar error in your document. Word Pro can catch many of these problems for you. If you can't think of the exact word you want to use, Word Pro's thesaurus can help you out. These and other features can be used to improve your writing style. In this chapter, you'll learn how to:

✦ Use Find & Replace Text

✦ Work with SmartCorrect

✦ Check your spelling

✦ Use the thesaurus feature

✦ Check your grammar

USING FIND & REPLACE TEXT

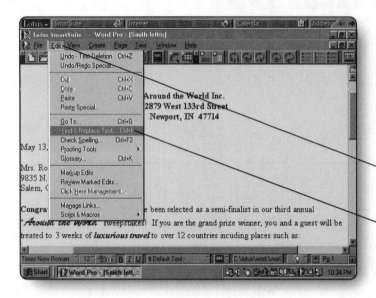

Use the Find & Replace Text feature to search for words or phrases in a document and optionally replace those items with something else. You can replace some or all occurrences of the text with other text.

1. Click on **Edit**. The Edit menu will appear.

2. Click on **Find & Replace Text**. The Find & Replace bar will appear at the top of your document.

3. Type the **text** that you want to find in the Find: text box. The text will appear in the box.

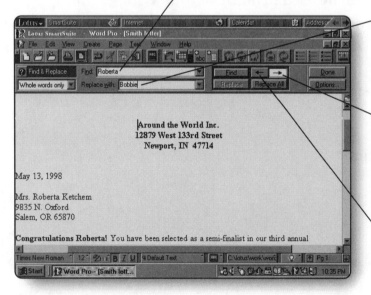

4. Type the **text** in the Replace with: text box that will replace the Find text in step 3. The text will appear in the box.

5a. Click on the **right arrow** to search forward from your insertion point in the document. The arrow will be selected.

OR

5b. Click on the **left arrow** to search backward from your insertion point in the document. The arrow will be selected.

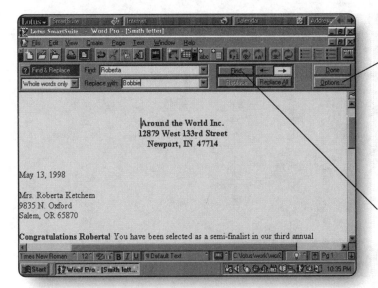

6. **Click** on **Find**. The first location of the Find text will be highlighted.

7. **Click** on **Replace** if you want to replace the found text. The replacement text will be placed in the document.

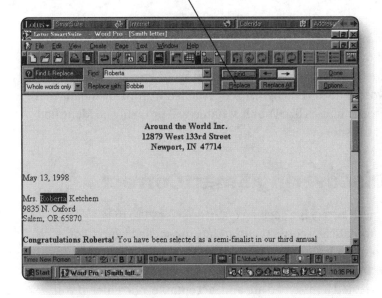

8. **Repeat steps 6** and **7** for each occurrence of the text you are searching for. When the search is completed, a dialog box will appear advising you the search is finished.

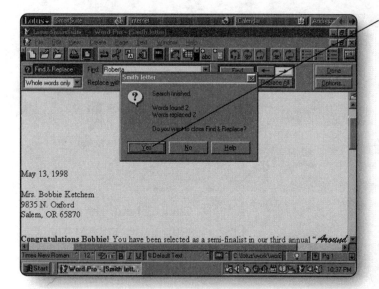

9. **Click** on **Yes**. The Find & Replace bar will close.

CORRECTING YOUR SPELLING

Word Pro has several spelling features. One feature corrects some of your misspelled words automatically for you. Another allows you to locate and correct all misspelled words after you are finished typing. Be aware that Word Pro considers any word it doesn't recognize a misspelled word. This means that proper names like your last name will probably be identified as misspelled.

Discovering SmartCorrect

SmartCorrect is a spelling feature of Word Pro that automatically corrects commonly misspelled words. For example, if you typed **teh**, SmartCorrect would automatically change it to **the**. Other examples of words that would be corrected if mistyped are **and**, **acceptable**, and **chief**. If you have a particular word you frequently misspell, add it to SmartCorrect.

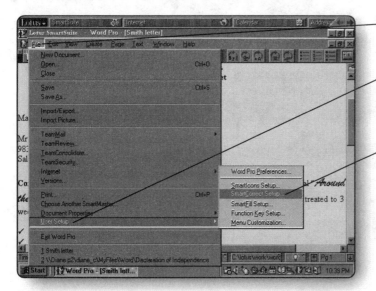

1. Click on **File**. The File menu will appear.

2. Click on **User Setup**. The User Setup submenu will be displayed.

3. Click on **SmartCorrect Setup**. The SmartCorrect dialog box will open.

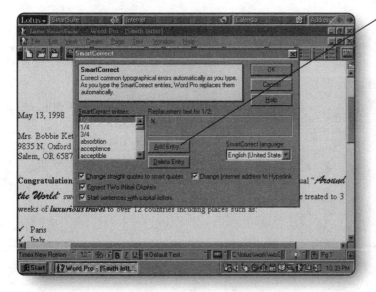

4. Click on **Add Entry**. The Add SmartCorrect Entry dialog box will open.

5. **Type** the **incorrect text** in the SmartCorrect entry: text box. The text you type will be displayed.

6. **Type** the **correct text** in the Replacement text text box. The text you type will be displayed.

7. **Click** on **OK**. The entry will be added to SmartCorrect.

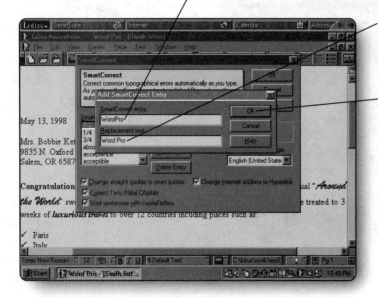

8. **Click** on **OK**. The SmartCorrect dialog box will close. SmartCorrect will automatically place the correction whenever you type the incorrect entry.

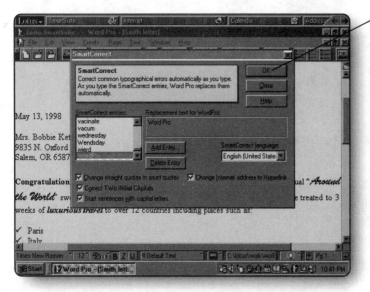

Using the Word Pro Spell Check

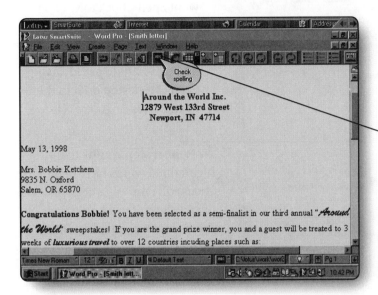

If you don't want to correct your spelling as you go, you can check your spelling when you are finished typing by using the Check Spelling feature.

1. **Click** on the **Check spelling SmartIcon**. The Spell Check bar will appear.

Any misspelled words will be highlighted. The word that Spell Check is currently working with will be highlighted in a different color.

2. **Choose** from these **options**:

✦ To replace this single occurrence of this word, click on the correct spelling from the Spell Check word list and click on Replace. The word will be corrected in your document.

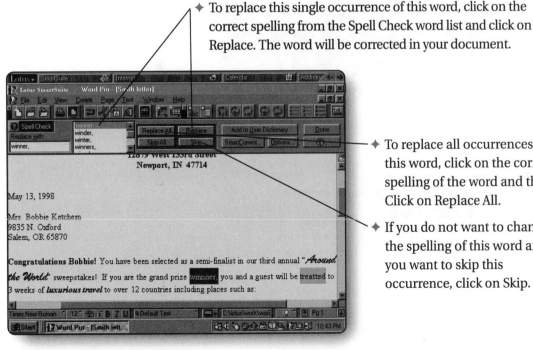

✦ To replace all occurrences of this word, click on the correct spelling of the word and then Click on Replace All.

✦ If you do not want to change the spelling of this word and you want to skip this occurrence, click on Skip.

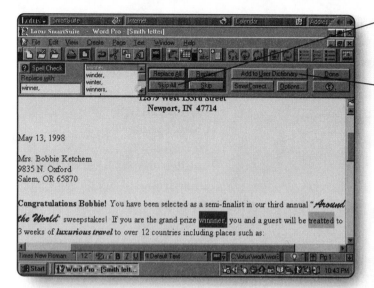

◆ Click on Skip All if you do not want Spell Check to stop on any occurrences of this word.

◆ If the word is correctly spelled and you want to avoid having Spell Check stop on it in the future, click on Add to User Dictionary.

3. **Repeat step 2** until all the highlighted words have been checked. A message box will display letting you know that there are no more misspelled words.

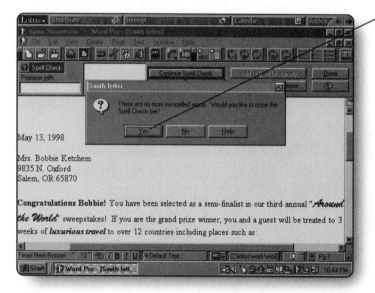

4. **Click** on **Yes**. The Spell Check bar will close.

USING THE THESAURUS

Word Pro's thesaurus gives you an easy way to find just the right words to use in your document.

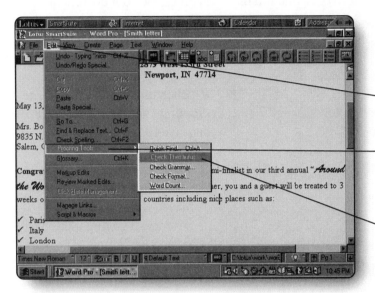

1. **Click** in the **word** you want to replace. A flashing insertion point will appear in the word.

2. **Click** on **Edit**. The Edit menu will appear.

3. **Click** on **Proofing Tools**. The Proofing Tools submenu will appear.

4. **Click** on **Check Thesaurus**. The Thesaurus dialog box will open.

5. **Click** on a **meaning** in the Meanings for: list box. A list of synonyms for that meaning will be displayed.

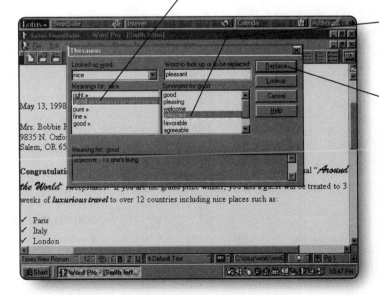

6. **Click** on a **word** from the Synonyms list box. The word will be highlighted.

7. **Click** on **Replace**. The word will be immediately replaced in the document.

8. **Click** on the **Close button**. The Thesaurus dialog box will close.

CHECKING YOUR GRAMMAR

Word Pro can point out many types of grammatical errors and offer possible corrections. Be careful—a grammar check can still skip a lot of errors. You must still proofread your document.

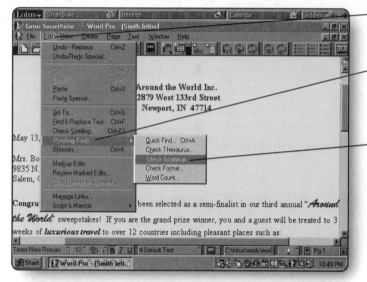

1. Click on **Edit**. The Edit menu will appear.

2. Click on **Proofing Tools**. The Proofing Tools submenu will be displayed.

3. Click on **Check Grammar**. The Grammar Check bar will be displayed with the first occurrence of grammar in question highlighted.

An explanation of the error is displayed along with a possible alternative. At this point you have up to three alternatives:

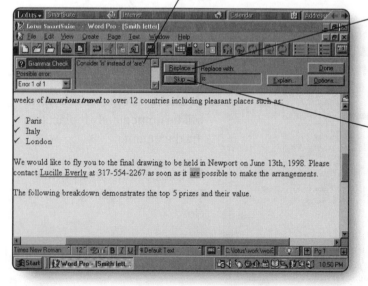

4a. Click on **Replace**. The error will be replaced with Word Pro's suggestion. This option may not be available for all errors.

OR

4b. Click on **Skip**. The error will be ignored and the next error displayed.

OR

4c. Click in the **document** and **manually correct** the error. The error will be corrected.

NOTE

After you have manually corrected the error, the Replace button will turn into a Continue button. Click on Continue to resume the grammar check.

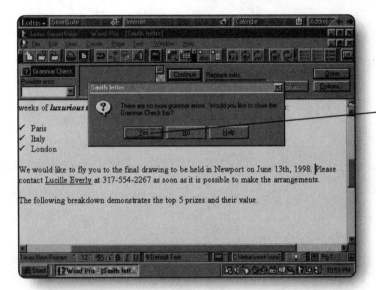

When the grammar check is completed, a dialog box will appear advising that there are no more grammar errors.

5. **Click** on **Yes**. A Readability Statistics dialog box will appear stating general statistics about the document.

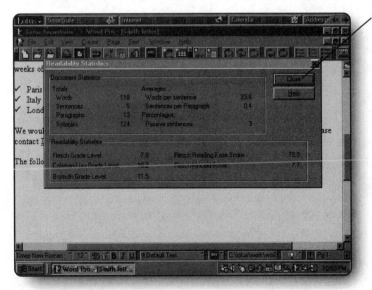

6. **Click** on the **Close button**. The Readability Statistics dialog box will close.

9 Completing Your Document

One of the most important things you learn to do with any application is save your work. Who wants to spend hours on a document only to lose it because it wasn't saved? Saving a document also allows you to exit from Word Pro and return to your document later so that you can work on it further. You'll also need to know how to print your work. Using Word Pro, you can create a variety of printed documents, including letters, memos, faxes, and newsletters. In this chapter, you'll learn how to:

✦ Save a document

✦ Print a document

✦ Close and open a document

✦ Exit Word Pro

SAVING A DOCUMENT

You should save your work often. Saving your document not only retains your work, but also files it electronically for you so that you can find it and use it again at a later time.

Saving a Document the First Time

When you first create a document, it has no name. If you want to use that document later, it must have a name so Word Pro can find it.

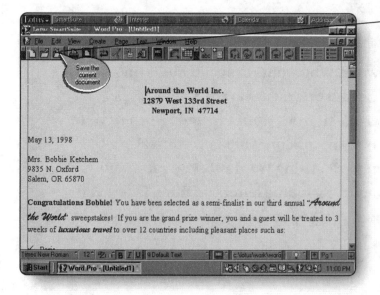

1. **Click** on the **Save the current document button**. The Save As dialog box will open.

2. **Type** a **name** for your file in the File name: text box. The file name will be displayed.

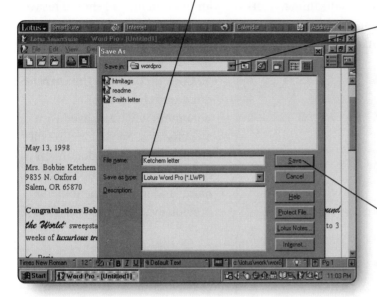

The Save in: drop-down box lists the folder where the file will be saved. The default folder that appears is wordpro. If you don't want to save to this folder or you want to save your document to another disk, you can select another one. Click on the down arrow to browse.

3. **Click** on **Save**. Your document will be saved and the name you specified will appear in the title bar.

Resaving a Document

As you continue to work on your document, you should resave your document every ten minutes or so. This will ensure that you do not lose any changes you have made.

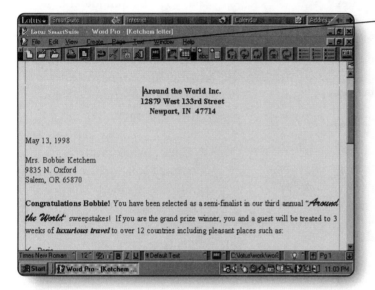

1. Click on the **Save the current document button**. The document will be resaved with any changes. No dialog box will appear because the document is being resaved with the same name and in the same folder as previously specified.

TIP

If you want to save the document with a different name or in a different folder, click on File, then choose Save As. The Save As dialog box will prompt you for the new name or folder.

PRINTING A DOCUMENT

Word Pro is a graphical word processing program, meaning that text and other elements, such as graphics, appear on the screen the same way they will look when they print out.

Viewing a Document Full Screen

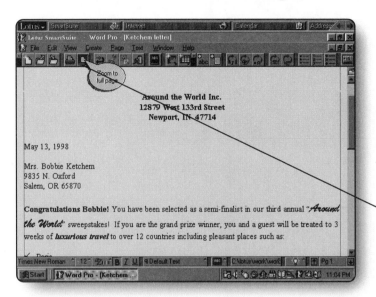

Before you print your document, you should view it full screen. Viewing a Document full screen allows you to size the document so that an entire page is visible. That way, you can get an idea of how document layout settings such as margins will look on the printed document.

1. Click on the **Zoom to full page button**. The document will be sized so that an entire page is visible on the screen.

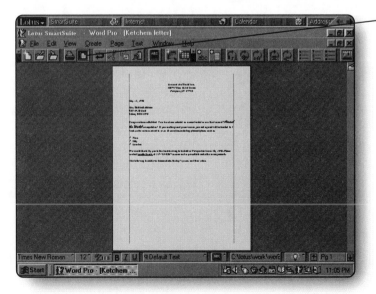

2. Click on the **Zoom to full page button** again. The document will be returned to 100% magnification.

Printing with the Print Button

Typically, the end result of entering a document into Word Pro is to get text onto paper. Word Pro gives you a quick and easy way to get that result.

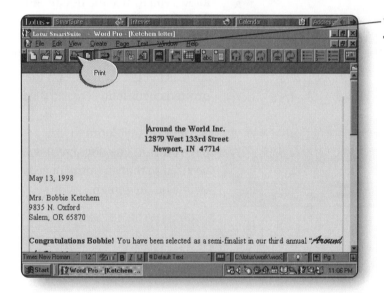

1. Click on the **Print button**. The Print dialog box will open.

Many options are available from the Print dialog box:

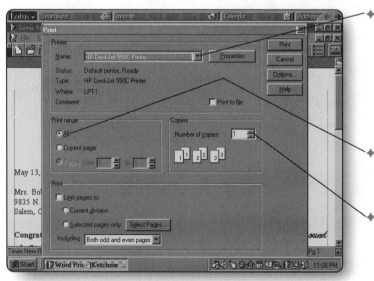

✦ If you are connected to more than one printer, you can choose the name of the printer to use for this print job. Click on the down arrow in the Name: list box and make a selection.

✦ Choose which pages of your document to print in the Print range box.

✦ Choose the number of copies to be printed by clicking on the up/down arrows in the Number of copies: list box.

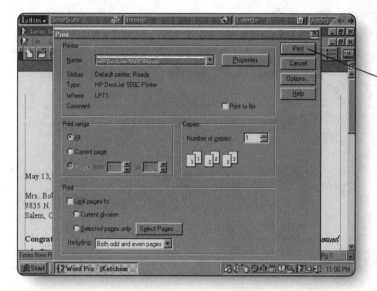

2. Click on any desired **option.** The option will be activated.

3. Click on **Print** after you have made your selections. The document will be sent to the printer.

CLOSING A DOCUMENT

When you are finished working on a document, you should close it. *Closing* is the equivalent of putting it away for later use. When you close a document, you are only putting the document away—not the program. Word Pro is still active and ready to work for you.

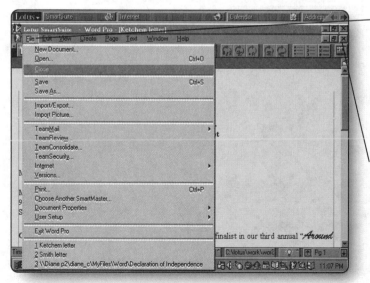

1. Click on **File**. The File menu will appear.

2. Click on **Close**. The document will be put away.

OR

3. Click on the **Close button**. The document will be put away. By choosing this step, you skip steps 1 and 2.

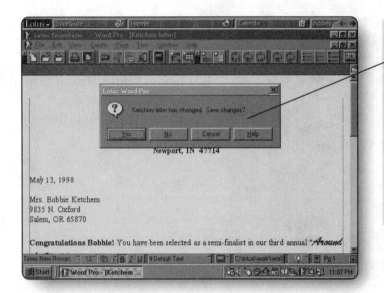

If you have made changes to a document and have not saved those changes, Word Pro will prompt you with a dialog box. Choose Yes to save the changes before closing the file or No to close the file without saving the changes.

OPENING A DOCUMENT

When you open a file, you are putting a copy of that file up into the computer's memory and your screen so you can continue to work on it. After you make any changes, be sure to save the file again.

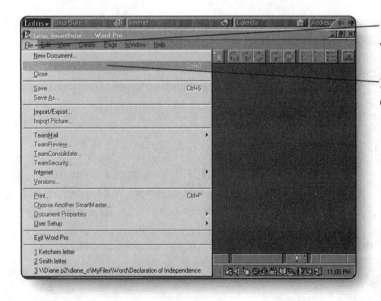

1. Click on **File**. The File menu will appear.

2. Click on **Open**. The Open dialog box will open.

3. Click on the **file name** you wish to open. The file name will be highlighted and will appear in the File name: text box.

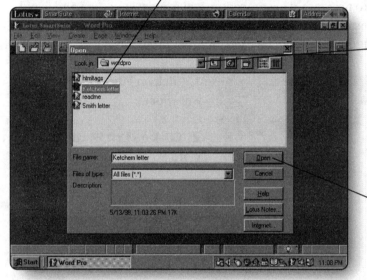

If your file is located in a different folder than the one displayed in the Look in: list box, click on the down arrow to navigate to the proper folder.

4. Click on **Open**. The file will be placed on your screen, ready for you to edit.

EXITING WORDPRO

When you are finished working with Word Pro, exit the Word Pro program. This procedure will protect your data and avoid possible program damage. It also frees up valuable computer memory that can be used for other programs.

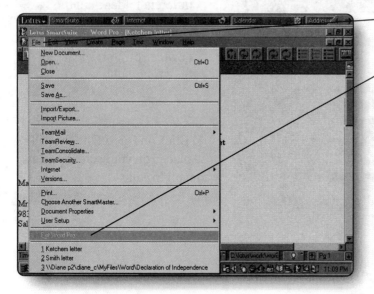

1. Click on **File**. The File menu will appear.

2. Click on **Exit Word Pro**. The Word Pro program will be closed.

OR

3. Click on the application's **Close box**. The Word Pro program will be closed.

NOTE

If any documents are open that haven't been saved, Word Pro will ask you whether you want to save changes to those files.

PART II REVIEW QUESTIONS

1. **What does a dynamic date do?** *See "Inserting the Date and Time" in Chapter 3*

2. **What is the shortcut key to center align text?** *See "Setting Paragraph Alignment" in Chapter 4*

3. **How would you insert the copyright symbol into your document?** *See "Inserting Special Symbols" in Chapter 4*

4. **What areas in a document are reserved for repeating text?** *See "Adding a Header or Footer" in Chapter 5*

5. **Where do you change a document layout from portrait to landscape?** *See "Changing Page Orientation" in Chapter 5*

6. **What can you do if you have a table that spans more than one page?** *See "Creating a Repeated Heading" in Chapter 6*

7. **Where is Word Pro's default location for a Table of Contents?** *See "Generating the Table of Contents" in Chapter 7*

8. **What is SmartCorrect?** *See "Discovering SmartCorrect" in Chapter 8*

9. **What feature gives you an easy way to find just the right words to use?** *See "Using the Thesaurus" in Chapter 8*

10. **What happens when you try to exit Word Pro with an unsaved document?** *See "Exiting Word Pro" in Chapter 9*

PART III
Using 1-2-3

$27,540.0(
$31,212.7!
$18,400.0(
$11,235.5(
$88,388.2!

0.00 $12,000.0(

10 Creating a Simple Workbook

1-2-3 has been one of the world's most popular spreadsheet programs for many years. It can do calculations, create charts, drawings, maps, and even sort data for you! But, like any other software program, you must start at the beginning. In this chapter, you'll learn how to:

✦ Start 1-2-3

✦ Explore and move around in the 1-2-3 screen

✦ Enter labels, values, and totals

✦ Undo mistakes

✦ Insert rows and columns in a worksheet

✦ Delete rows and columns

STARTING 1-2-3

When you start 1-2-3, it gives you the option to create a new workbook. You can also create a new workbook by using the File menu.

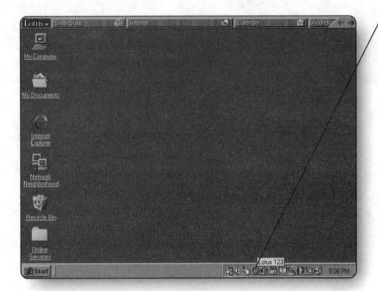

1. **Click** on the **1-2-3 icon** from the SuiteStart icon palette. The Welcome to 1-2-3 dialog box will appear.

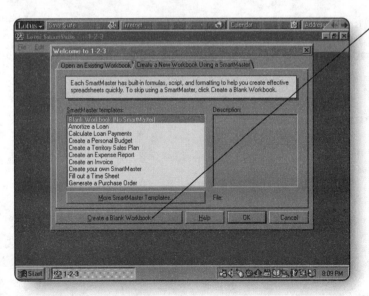

2. **Click** on **Create a Blank Workbook**. A blank workbook will appear on your screen.

EXPLORING THE 1-2-3 SCREEN

Many items you see when you open a new 1-2-3 worksheet are standard to any Windows 95 program. However, the following list illustrates a few elements that are specific to the 1-2-3 program. These include:

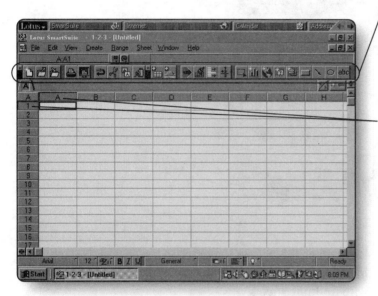

✦ **SmartIcon Toolbar.** A toolbar with a series of commonly used 1-2-3 features. You can customize the SmartIcon toolbar.

✦ **Row and Column Headings.** Each worksheet has 256 columns and 65,536 rows.

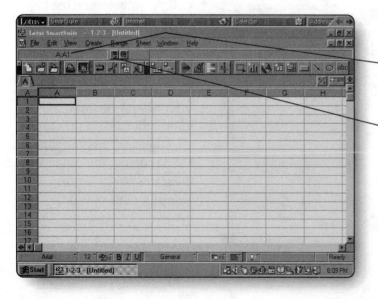

✦ **Edit Line.** This line consists of several parts:

 ✦ The Selection Indicator shows the address or name of the current selection.

 ✦ The Range Navigator lets you go to and select a named range.

✦ The @Function Selector lets you insert an @function in a cell.

✦ The Contents box displays the entry you are typing or editing, or the contents of the current cell.

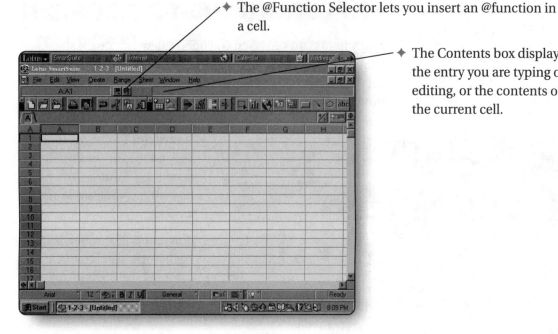

✦ **Worksheet Tab.** Shows the name of the current worksheet in a workbook. 1-2-3 allows you to create a 3-D workbook with multiple sheets.

✦ **Cell.** An intersection of a column and row. Sometimes called a *cell address*. It is indicated by a heavy border around the selected cell.

✦ **Status Bar.** Gives you information about the current selection and tells you what 1-2-3 is doing. You can use the status bar to perform many functions with the mouse.

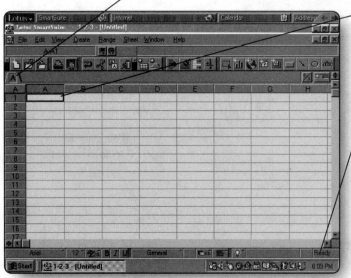

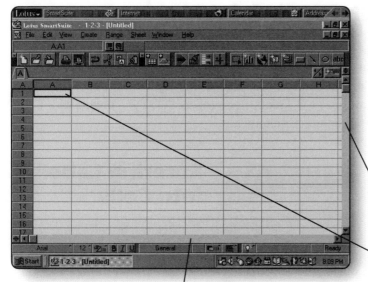

MOVING AROUND THE 1-2-3 SCREEN

You can use your mouse or keyboard to quickly move around in a worksheet.

1. **Click** on the **vertical scroll bar** until the row you are looking for is visible.

2. **Click** on the **desired cell**. It will become the current cell.

3. **Click** on the **horizontal scroll bar** until the column you are looking for is visible.

4. **Click** on the **desired cell**. It will become the current cell.

The following table describes keyboard methods for moving around in your worksheet:

KEYSTROKE	RESULT
Arrow keys	Move one cell at a time up, down, left, or right
Tab	Moves one screen right
Shift+Tab	Moves one screen left
Page Down	Moves one screen down
Page Up	Moves one screen up
Home	Moves to cell A1
F5	Displays the GoTo dialog box, which enables you to specify a cell address
End, then Home	Moves to the cell in the rightmost column and lowest row that has information in it.

ENTERING DATA

Spreadsheet data is made up of three components: labels, values, and formulas. Labels are traditionally descriptive pieces of information, such as names, months, or types of products. 1-2-3 identifies a cell as a label if it begins with a letter or a prefix character.

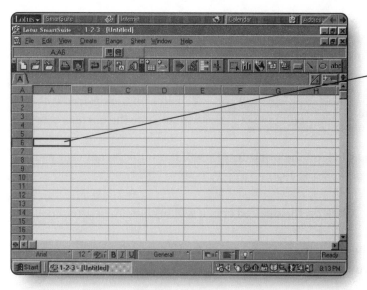

Entering Labels into Cells

1. Click on the **cell** where you want to place the label. A border will appear around the selected cell.

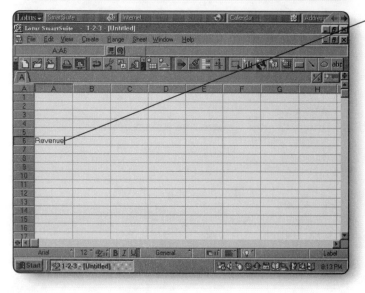

2. Type some **text**. A blinking insertion point will appear.

3. Press the **Enter key** to accept the label. The text will be entered into the cell and will align along the left edge of the cell.

4. Press an **arrow key**. The next cell is selected.

TIP

If you make a mistake and you have not yet pressed Enter, press the Backspace key to delete characters and type a correction, or press the Escape key to cancel the typing.

NOTE

Optionally, you could press an arrow key instead of the Enter key. This will not only accept the cell you were typing in, but move to the next cell at the same time.

Entering Values into Cells

Values are the raw numbers you track in a worksheet. There is no need to enter commas or dollar signs. You'll let 1-2-3 do all the work for you later.

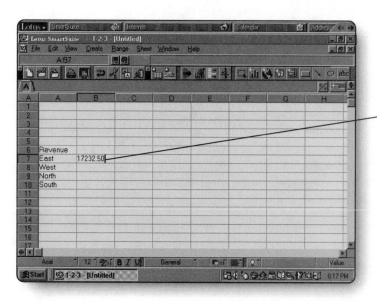

1. Click on the **cell** where you want to place the value. A border will appear around the selected cell.

2. Type the numerical **value**. A blinking insertion point will appear.

3. **Press Enter** to accept the value. The number will be entered into the cell.

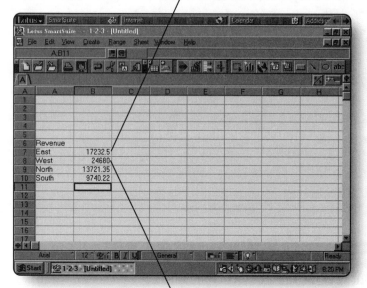

4. **Press** an **arrow key**. The next cell will be selected.

Entering Totals

1-2-3 will automatically total a column of values for you.

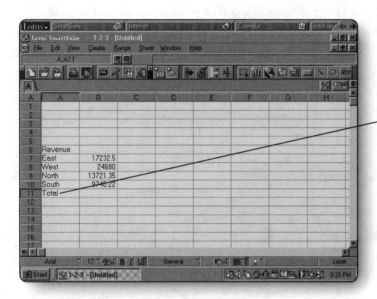

1. Click on the **cell to the left** of where you want the total to appear. The selected cell will have a border surrounding it.

2. Type the word **Total** or **Totals**. It doesn't matter if it is typed in capital letters or not.

3. Press Enter. The sum of the values will be in the next cell to the right.

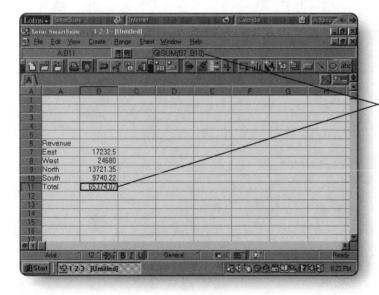

Look at the difference between what is displayed in the cell (the answer) and what is displayed in the Contents box (the formula).

EDITING DATA

You can edit your data in a variety of ways. You may need to change the contents of a cell or you may want to move the data to another part of the worksheet.

Replacing the Contents of a Cell

You can make changes to the contents of a cell in two ways. One is by typing over the contents of a cell.

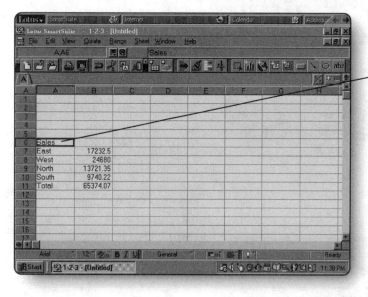

1. **Click** on a **cell**. The cell will be selected.

2. **Type** some new **text**. The text will appear in the cell.

3. **Press** the **Enter key**. The text will be entered in the selected cell.

Editing the Contents of a Cell

The other method used to make changes to the contents of a cell is the Edit feature.

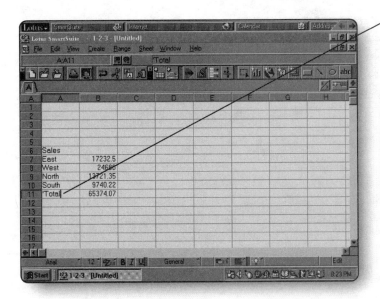

1. Double-click on the **cell** to be edited. The insertion point will blink within the cell.

2. Position the **insertion point** within the cell by using the Right and Left Arrow keys. The insertion point will be relocated within the current cell.

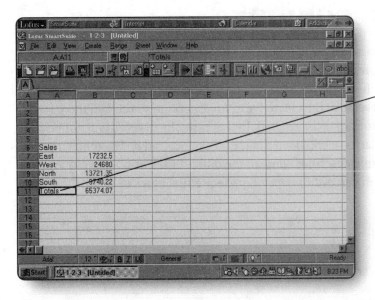

3. Type the **changes**. The changes will appear in the current cell.

4. Press the **Enter key**. The changes will be entered into the current cell.

Undoing Mistakes

If you make a mistake while working in a spreadsheet, stop! 1-2-3 will reverse the last step you took.

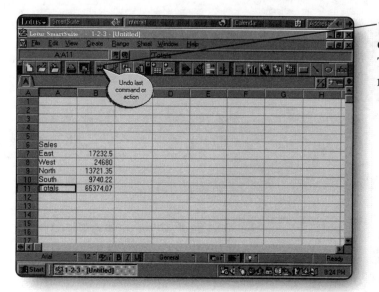

1. **Click** on the **Undo last command or action button**. The last step you took will be reversed.

LEARNING SELECTION TECHNIQUES

To move, copy, delete, or change the formatting of data in the spreadsheet, the cells to be modified must first be selected. When cells are selected, they appear black onscreen—just the reverse of unselected text. An exception to this is if there is a block of cells selected. In this case, the first cell will not be black—it will have a black border around it. The following table describes some of the different selection techniques. You can even select a non-sequential block of cells.

TIP

Make sure the mouse pointer is a white arrow before attempting to select cells.

To Select	Do This
A row	Click on the row number on the left side of the screen.
A cell	Click on the desired cell.
A column	Click on the column letter at the top of the screen.

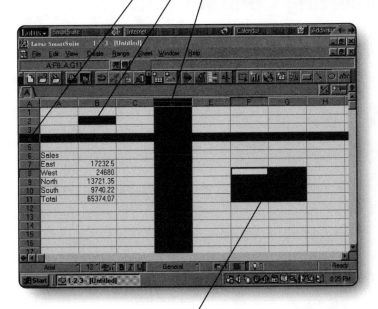

TIP

To deselect a block of cells, click the mouse in any other cell or press the Esc key.

To Select	Do This
A sequential block of cells	Click on the first cell and drag to highlight the rest of the cells.
A non-sequential block of cells	Press and hold the Ctrl key while clicking on any subsequent cells.

CHANGING THE SIZE OF THE SPREADSHEET

Inserting a row or column moves existing data to make room for blank rows or columns. Each worksheet always has 256 columns and 65,536 rows.

Inserting Columns and Rows

Occasionally you need a column or a row in the middle of information you have already entered. This is done using the Range menu.

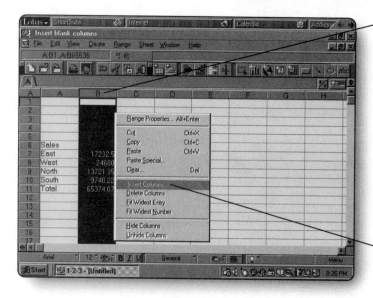

1. Click on the **Column Heading letter** or the **Row Heading number** where you want to insert the new column or row. The entire column or row will be selected.

2. Click the **right mouse button** anywhere on the highlighted area. A shortcut menu will appear.

3. Click on **Insert Columns** or **Insert Rows**. A new column or row will be inserted.

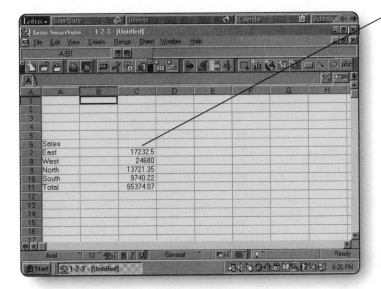

Existing columns move to the right and existing rows move down.

Deleting Columns and Rows

Use caution when deleting a row or column. Deleting a row will delete it across all 256 columns; deleting a column will delete it down all 65,536 rows.

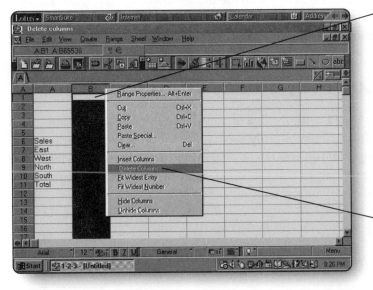

1. Select the **Column Heading letter** or **Row Heading number** of the column or row you want to delete. The Column or Row will be highlighted.

2. Click the **right mouse button** anywhere on the highlighted area. A shortcut menu will appear.

3. Choose **Delete Columns** or **Delete Rows**. The highlighted column or row will be deleted.

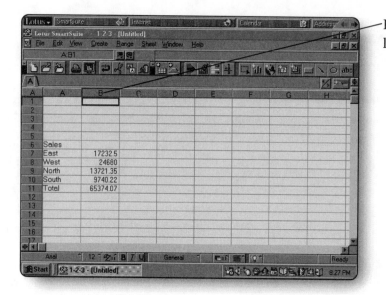

Remaining columns move to the left; remaining rows move up.

MOVING DATA AROUND

If you're not happy with the placement of data, you don't have to delete it and retype it. 1-2-3 makes it easy for you to move it around.

Copying and Pasting Cells

Windows comes with a feature called the *Clipboard*. The Clipboard temporarily holds information. It is extremely helpful if you want to duplicate information from one place to another. To copy information from one location to another, 1-2-3 will use the features called *copy* and *paste*.

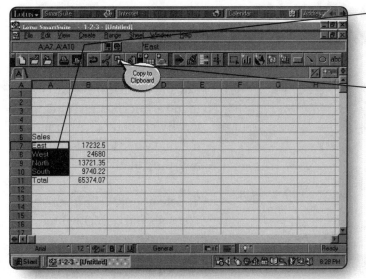

1. **Select** some **cells** to be duplicated. The cells will be highlighted.

2. **Click** on the **Copy to Clipboard SmartIcon**. The text will be duplicated to the Clipboard.

TIP

If you want to move the information from one cell to another, click on the Cut to Clipboard button instead.

Look at the instructions in the title bar of your window. This is 1-2-3's way of telling you that the information has been copied and that it is waiting for instructions as to where to paste it.

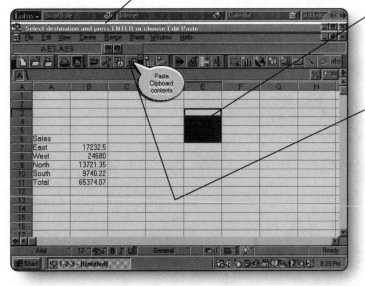

3. **Click** on the beginning **cell** where you want to place the duplicated information. The cell will be highlighted.

4. **Click** on the **Paste Clipboard contents SmartIcon**. The information will be copied to the new location.

TIP

If you pasted the cells to the wrong area, click on the Undo button to reverse the step.

Using Drag-and-Drop to Move Cells

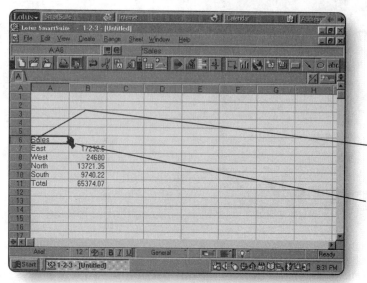

As mentioned, you can use the Cut and Paste features of 1-2-3 to move information from one location to another. Another method you can use is the drag-and-drop method.

1. Select some **cells** to move. The cells will be highlighted.

2. Position the **mouse pointer** around one of the outside edges of the selection. The mouse pointer will change to become a small hand.

3. Press and **hold** the **mouse button** and **drag** the hand to a new location. A small dashed box will follow the hand. The dashed box represents the moved cells.

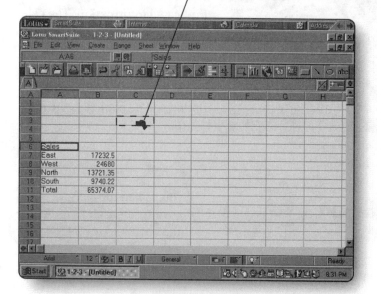

4. Release the **mouse button**. The cells will be moved.

TIP

If you make a mistake and move the cells to the wrong location, click on the Undo button to reverse the movement.

USING SPEEDFILL

1-2-3 has a great built-in timesaver called SpeedFill. If you give 1-2-3 the beginning Month, Day, Quarter, or numbers, it can fill in the rest of the pattern for you. For example, if you type January, 1-2-3 fills in February, March, April, and so on.

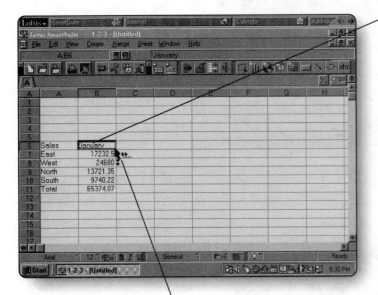

1. **Type** the **beginning Month, Day, Quarter, or number** in the beginning cell. The text will be displayed in the cell.

TIP

If you want the program to SpeedFill a non-sequential pattern for you, you must advise it of the pattern. For example, if you want the pattern 5, 10, 15, 20, and so on, you must start by entering the value 5 in one cell and 10 in the next cell. You then must highlight both cells before you begin the next step.

2. **Position** the **mouse pointer** on the lower-right corner of the beginning cell. The mouse pointer will become an arrow with four small green arrowheads around it.

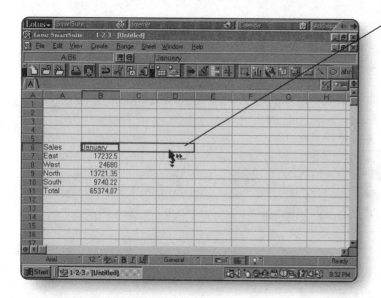

3. **Press** and **hold** the **mouse button** and **drag** to select the next cells to be filled in. The cells will be highlighted.

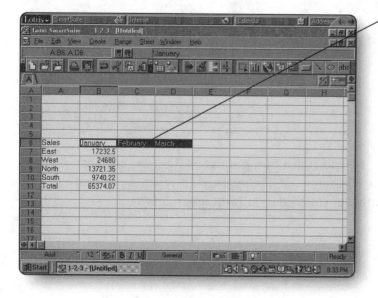

4. **Release** the **mouse button**. The pattern will be repeated.

11 Working with @Functions and Formulas

Formulas in a 1-2-3 spreadsheet will do the calculations for you. For example, by referencing cell addresses in a formula, if the data changes, so will the formula answer. In this chapter, you'll learn how to:

✦ Create simple and compound formulas

✦ Copy formulas

✦ Create an absolute reference

✦ Use @Functions

CREATING FORMULAS

All 1-2-3 formulas must begin with the plus (+) sign, regardless of whether the formula consists of adding, subtracting, multiplying, or dividing.

Creating A Simple Formula

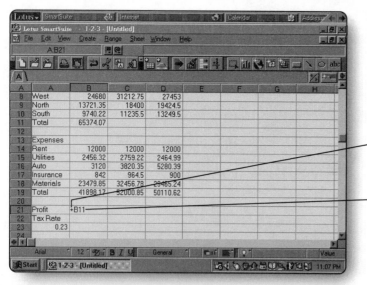

An example of a simple formula might be +B11×B19.

1. **Click** on the **cell** in which you want to place the formula answer. The cell will be selected.

2. **Type** a **plus sign** (+) to begin the formula.

3. **Type** the **cell address** of the first cell to be included in the formula. This is called the cell *reference*.

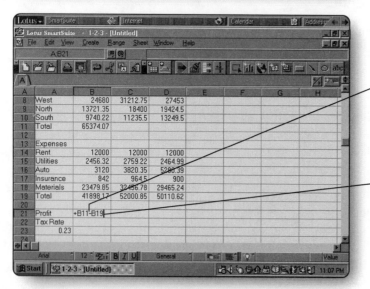

A formula needs an *operator* to suggest the next action to be performed.

4. **Type** the **operator**: plus (+), minus (–), multiply (*), or divide (/). The operator will display in the formula.

5. **Type** the **reference** to the second cell of the formula.

6. **Press** the **Enter key**. The result of the calculation will appear in the cell.

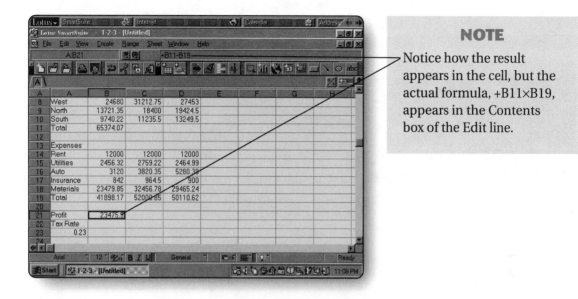

Creating a Compound Formula

You use compound formulas when you need more than one operator. An example of a compound formula might be +B11×B19*A23.

1. **Click** on the **cell** in which you want to place the formula answer. The cell will be selected.

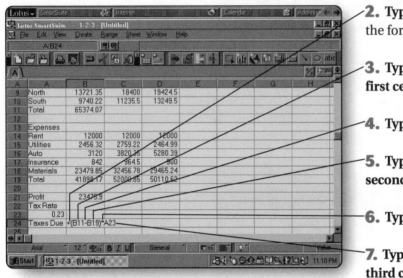

2. **Type** a **plus sign** (+) to begin the formula.

3. **Type** the **reference to the first cell** of the formula.

4. **Type** the **operator**.

5. **Type** the **reference to the second cell** of the formula.

6. **Type** the **next operator**.

7. **Type** the **reference to the third cell** of the formula.

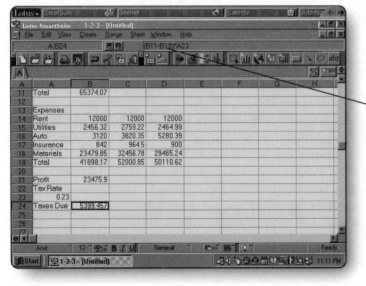

8. **Repeat steps 6** and **7** until the formula is complete, adding the parentheses wherever necessary.

9. **Press** the **Enter key** to accept the formula. The calculation answer will be displayed in the cell and the formula will be displayed in the edit bar.

Try changing one of the values you originally typed in the spreadsheet and watch the answer to the formula change.

COPYING FORMULAS

If you're going to copy a formula to a surrounding cell, you can use the SpeedFill method. If the cells are not sequential, you can use copy and paste. Both SpeedFill and copy and paste were discussed in Chapter 10, "Creating a Simple Workbook."

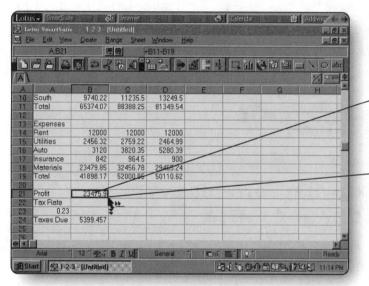

Copying Formulas Using SpeedFill

1. **Click** on the **cell** that has the formula. The cell will be selected.

2. **Position** the **mouse pointer** on the lower-right corner of the beginning cell. The mouse pointer will become an arrow with four small green arrowheads around it.

3. **Press** and **hold** the **mouse button** and **drag** to select the next cells to be filled in. The cells will be selected.

4. **Release** the **mouse button**. The formula will be copied.

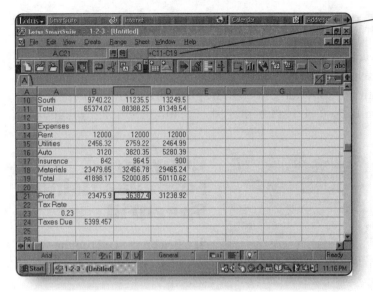

When 1-2-3 copies a formula, the references change as the formula is copied. If the original formula was +B11×B19 and you copied it to the next cell to the right, the formula will read C11×C19. The next cell to the right will be D11×D19, and so on.

Copying Formulas with Copy and Paste

1. **Select** the **cell** with the formula you want to duplicate. The cell will be selected.

2. **Click** on the **Copy to Clipboard button**. The formula will be copied to the Clipboard.

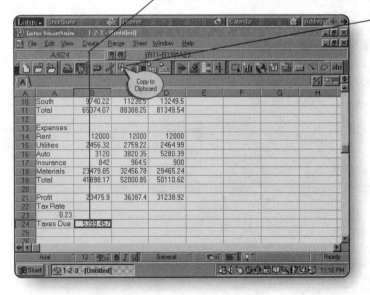

3. Highlight the **cells** in which you want to place the duplicated formula. The cells will be selected.

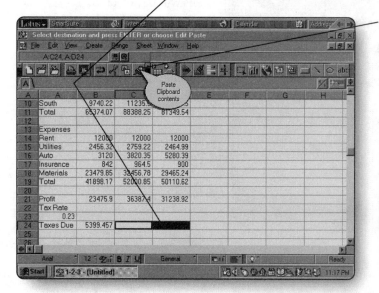

4. Click on the **Paste Clipboard contents button**. The information will be copied to the new location.

NOTE

If you are following the examples in the book, don't be alarmed at the answers you see from the last exercise. You will understand the results shortly.

CREATING AN ABSOLUTE REFERENCE IN A FORMULA

Occasionally when you copy a formula, you do not want one of the cell references to change. That's when you need to create an absolute reference. The secret key to remember is the dollar sign ($).

It's called an *absolute reference* because when you copy it, it absolutely and positively remains that cell reference and never changes. An example of a formula with an absolute reference might be +B21*B23. The reference to cell B23 will not change when copied.

For this exercise, you will delete the original formulas and start again.

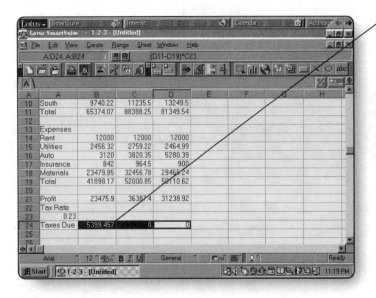

1. **Highlight** the **cells** in which the original formulas exist. The cells will be selected.

2. **Press** the **Delete key**. The information in these cells will be deleted.

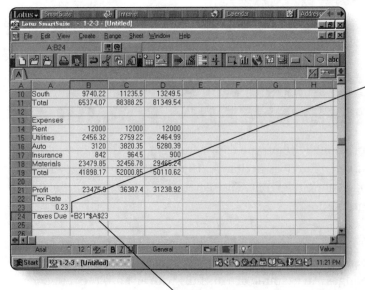

3. **Click** on the **cell** in which you want to place the formula answer. The cell will be selected.

4. **Type** a **plus sign** (+) to begin the formula.

5. **Type** the **reference to the first cell** of the formula, adding dollar signs ($) in front of both the column reference and the row reference if this reference is to be an absolute reference.

6. **Type** the **operator**.

7. **Type** the **reference to the second cell** of the formula, adding dollar signs ($) in front of both the column reference and the row reference if this reference is to be an absolute reference.

8. **Press** the **Enter key** to complete the formula.

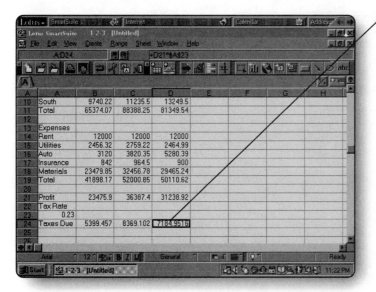

9. **Copy** the **formula** to the adjacent cells using one of the methods in steps 1 through 4 of the preceding section.

USING @FUNCTIONS

Sometimes, formulas can be quite complex and time-consuming to build. 1-2-3 has more than 200 different @functions to assist you with your calculations. All 1-2-3 functions begin with the @ symbol and have the basis (arguments) for the formula in parentheses.

Using @SUM

The @SUM function totals a range of values. The syntax for this function is @SUM(*range of values to total*). An example might be @SUM(B7..D7).

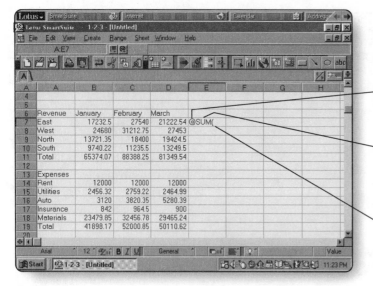

1. Click on the **cell** in which you want to place the sum of values. The cell will be selected.

2. Type the **@** symbol. The symbol will display in the cell.

3. Type the function name **SUM.** The characters will display in the cell.

4. Type the **open parentheses** symbol. The symbol will display in the cell.

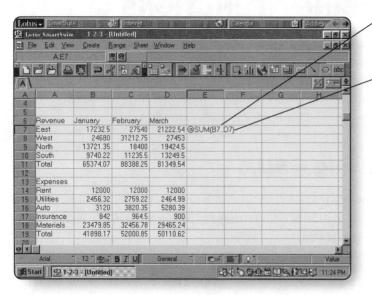

5. Type the **range** to be totaled. The range will display in the cell.

6. Type the **close parentheses** symbol. The symbol will display in the cell.

7. Press the **Enter key**. The result will be displayed in the selected cell.

Using @AVG

The @AVG function finds an average of a range of values. The syntax for this function is @AVG(*range of values to average*). An example might be @AVG(B7..D7).

1. **Click** on the **cell** in which you want to place the average. The cell will be selected.

2. **Type** the @ symbol. The symbol will display in the cell.

3. **Type** the function name **AVG**. The characters will display in the cell.

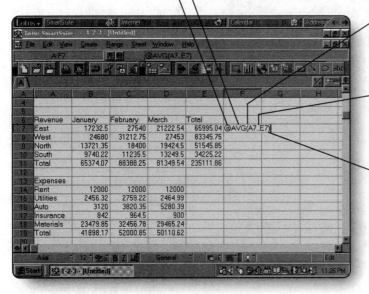

4. **Type** the **open parentheses** symbol. The symbol will display in the cell.

5. **Type** or **highlight** the **range** to be averaged. The range will display in the cell.

6. **Type** the **close parentheses** symbol. The symbol will display in the cell.

7. **Press** the **Enter key**. 1-2-3 will average the values in the selected range.

TIP

Instead of typing the range as noted in step 4, you can highlight the range with the mouse. 1-2-3 will fill in the cell references for you.

NOTE

Other similar @functions are the @MAX, @MIN, and @COUNT functions. The @MAX function finds the largest value in a range of cells. The @MIN function finds the smallest value in a range of cells. The @COUNT function counts the non-blank cells in a range of cells. Examples might include @MAX(B7..B15) or @COUNT(B7..B15).

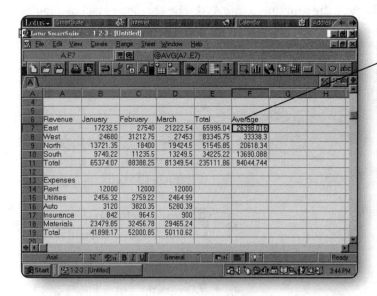

TIP

A really fast way to average a row or column of cells is to just type the word **Average** in the cell above or to the left of where you want the average to appear. When you press the Enter key, the average value will be displayed. However, you need to use caution with this method. In this example, typing the word **Average** created formulas that also included column A (with a value of zero) and column E (the totals column) as part of the average. The resulting answer is not correct. In such a situation, you'll want to type the @function manually.

12 Formatting Worksheets

The days of the dull spreadsheet are gone. Liven up your spreadsheet by changing the appearance of your worksheet. In this chapter, you'll learn how to:

- ✦ Work with range properties

- ✦ Set number formatting

- ✦ Adjust column width

- ✦ Change alignment

- ✦ Add borders to cells

- ✦ Change page properties

- ✦ Create a header or footer

CHANGING FONTS

The default font in a 1-2-3 spreadsheet is Arial, but it can easily be changed.

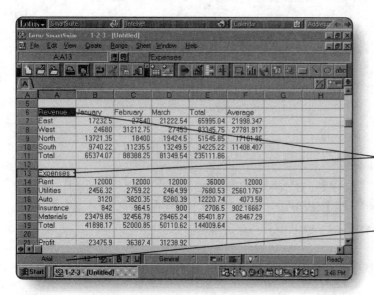

Selecting a Font Typeface

Your font choices will vary depending on the software installed on your computer.

1. Select some **cells** to change the typeface. The cells will be highlighted.

2. Click on the **Font Selector button** on the status bar. A list of available fonts will appear.

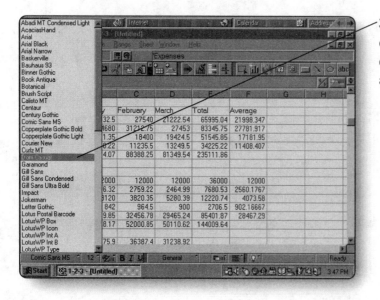

3. Click on the **font** of your choice. The selection list will close and the new font will be applied to the selected cells.

Selecting a Font Size

The default font size in a 1-2-3 spreadsheet is 12 points. A 12-point font is approximately one-sixth of an inch tall. A 72-point font is approximately one inch tall.

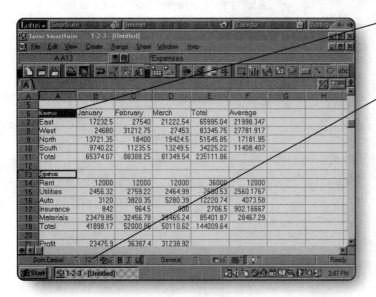

1. **Select** some **cells** to change the font size. The cells will be highlighted.

2. **Click** on the **Size Selector button** on the status bar. A list of available font sizes will appear.

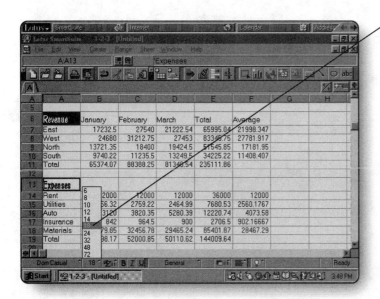

3. **Click** on the **size** of your choice. The selection list will close and the new font size will be applied to the selected cells.

Selecting a Font Style

Font styles include attributes like **bold**, *italics,* and underlining.

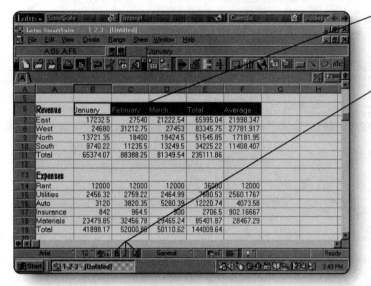

1. **Select** some **cells** to change the style. The cells will be highlighted.

2. **Click** on the **Bold button**, **Italics button**, or **Underline button** on the status bar. The attributes will be applied to the text in the cell.

TIP

The Bold, Italics, and Underline buttons are like toggle switches. Click on them a second time to turn off the attribute.

NOTE

Underlining is not the same as a cell border. Cell borders are discussed later in this chapter.

Working with Range Properties

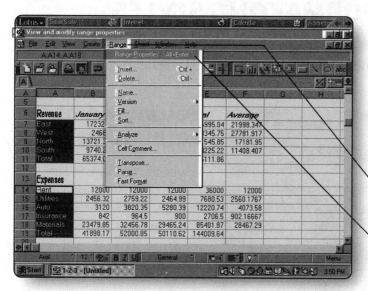

All of the attributes discussed in this chapter so far can be applied in one step by using the Range Properties feature.

1. Select some **cells** to change the appearance. The cells will be highlighted.

2. Click on the **Range** menu. The Range menu will open.

3. Click on **Range Properties**. The Range Properties dialog box will open.

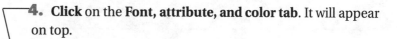

4. Click on the **Font, attribute, and color tab**. It will appear on top.

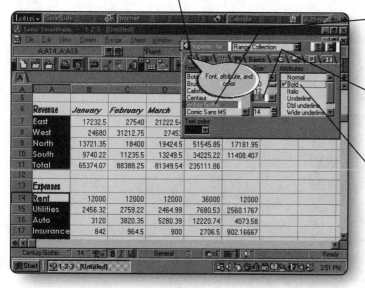

5. Click on a **font** in the Font Names: list box. The font name will be selected.

6. Click on a **font size** in the Size: list box. The font size will be selected.

7. Click on a **font attribute** in the Attributes: list box. The attributes will be selected.

8. Click on the **Close button**. The Range Properties dialog box will close.

USING OTHER FORMATTING STYLES

Other types of formatting can include the appearance of numbers and alignment of text in a cell.

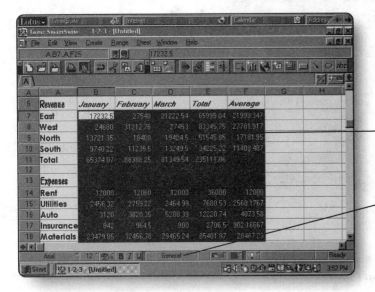

Setting Number Formatting

Values can be displayed as US dollars or other foreign currency.

1. Select some **cells** to be formatted. The cells will be highlighted.

2. Click on the **Number Format button** on the status bar. A list of choices will appear.

3. Click on the **number style** of your choice. The list of choices will close.

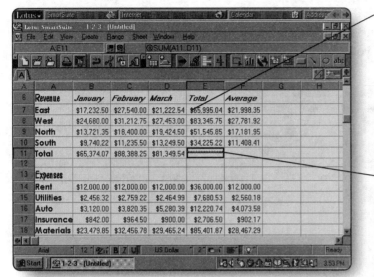

The new number format will be applied to the selected cells. Notice the dollar signs and two decimal points. These cells had the US Dollar number style applied to them.

NOTE

Don't be alarmed if some of the cells display a series of asterisks (*****) instead of your values. This is due to the column width being too small, which you will change in the next section.

Adjusting Column Width

The default width of a column is nine characters, but each individual column can be from one to 240 characters wide.

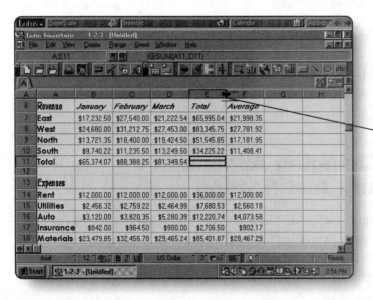

A line located at the right edge of each column heading divides the columns. You will use this line to change the column width.

1. Position the **mouse pointer** on the right column line for the column you want to change. The mouse pointer will become a gray bar with two green arrows.

2. **Press** and **hold** the **mouse button** and **drag** the column line. If you drag it to the right, the column width will increase; if you drag it to the left, the column width will decrease.

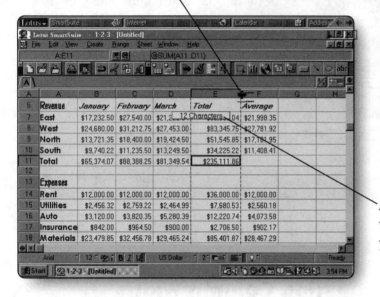

TIP

Instead of dragging the column line left or right, you can double-click on it. 1-2-3 will adjust the column width to fit the data in that particular column.

As you are changing the column width, a box appears to advise you of the width.

3. **Release** the **mouse button**. The column width will be changed.

TIP

If you select several columns before changing the width, all selected columns will be changed at one time.

Changing Alignment and Justification

Labels are left-aligned and values are right-aligned by default; however, you can change the alignment of either one to be left, right, centered, or full justified. Also by default, both are vertically aligned to the bottom of the cell.

Wrapping text in cells is useful when text is too long to fit in one cell. Text also can be centered across a group of columns.

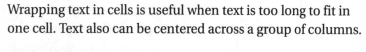
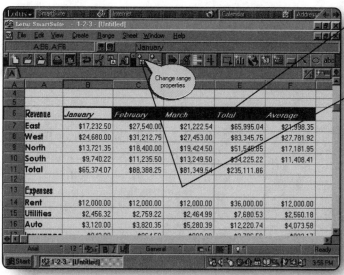

1. **Select** the **cells** to be formatted. The cells will be highlighted.

2. **Click** on the **Change range properties button**. The Range Properties dialog box will appear.

3. **Click** on the **Alignment tab**. It will come to the top of the stack.

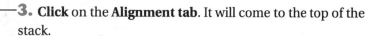
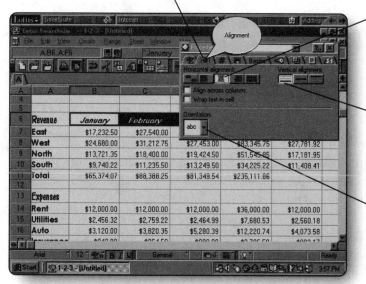

4. **Click** on the desired **button** for Horizontal alignment. The horizontal alignment of the text in the cell will change.

5. **Click** on the desired **button** for Vertical alignment. The vertical alignment of the text in the cell will change.

6. **Click** on the **down arrow** next to the Orientation box. A list of available orientations will appear.

7. Click on the **desired choice** for orientation. The orientation selection will be displayed.

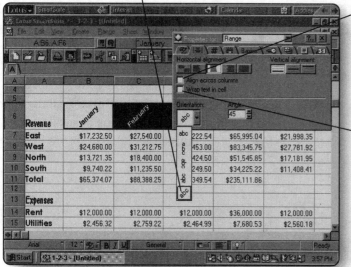

8a. Click on the **Align across columns check box,** if desired. A check will appear in the selection box.

OR

8b. Click on the **Wrap Text in cell check box**, if desired. A check will appear in the selection box.

> **TIP**
>
> The Wrap Text in cell feature treats each cell like a miniature word processor, with text wrapping around in the cell.

9. Click on the **Close button** of the Range Properties dialog box. The dialog box will close and the alignment choices will be applied to the selected cells.

Adding Borders

You can add borders, lines, and designer frames to cells to emphasize important data. Borders are different from the grid lines that separate cells in the sheet. You can change the style and color of borders.

A designer frame is a special kind of border that can include drop shadows and beveled edges.

1. Select the **cells** you want to have borders or lines. The cells will be highlighted.

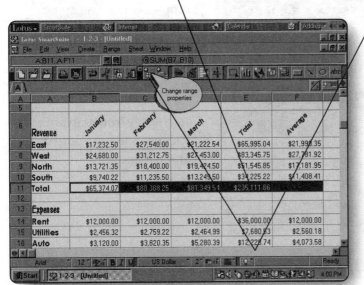

2. Click on the **Change range properties button**. The Range Properties dialog box will appear.

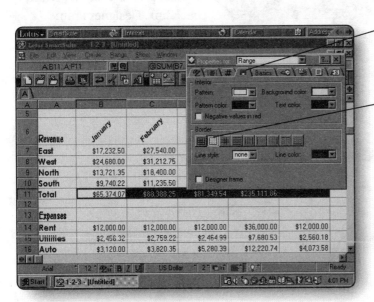

3. Click on the **Color, Pattern, and Line Style tab**. The tab will come to the top of the stack.

4. Click on a **Border button** of your choice. The border button you selected will appear to be pressed.

There are nine styles of borders you can apply to your spreadsheet.

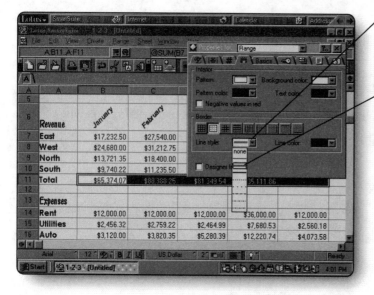

5. **Click** on the **down arrow** next to the Line Style: list box. A drop-down list will appear.

6. **Click** on a **line style**. Your selection will display in the Line Style: box.

Choices vary from thin lines to thick lines and from dotted lines to dashed lines.

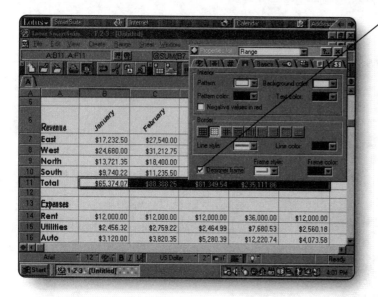

7. **Click** on the **Designer frame check box**. Designer Frame options will appear.

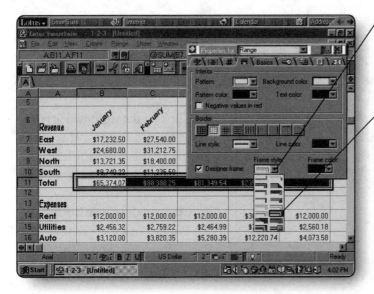

8. Click on the **down arrow** under the Frame style: list box. A selection of designer frame styles will appear.

9. Click on a **Designer frame Style**. There are 16 designer frame styles from which to choose.

10. Click on the **Close button** of the Range Properties dialog box. The dialog box will close and the selected cells will have a border around them.

FORMATTING THE ENTIRE PAGE

As your spreadsheets grow larger and larger, you need better ways to print and display them.

Changing Margins

The default margin setting is one-half inch on each side of the paper.

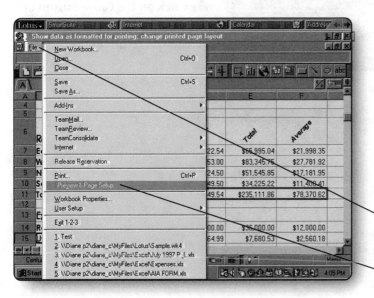

1. Click on **File**. The File menu will open.

2. Click on **Preview & Page Setup**. The screen will change dramatically. The Properties for the Preview & Page Setup dialog box will appear and the spreadsheet will display on half of the screen. The other half of the screen is Print Preview. Print Preview is discussed in Chapter 13, "Completing Your Workbook."

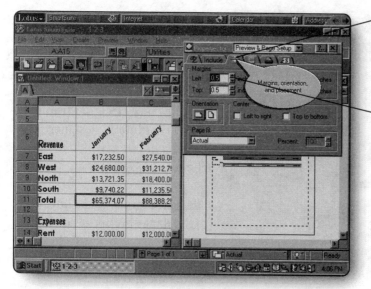

3. Click on the **Margins, orientation, and placement tab**. The tab will come to the front of the stack.

4. Click on the **up/down arrows** of the Margin options. This will increase or decrease the left, right, top, or bottom margin.

5. Click on the **Close button** of the Properties for Preview & Page Setup dialog box. The dialog box will close.

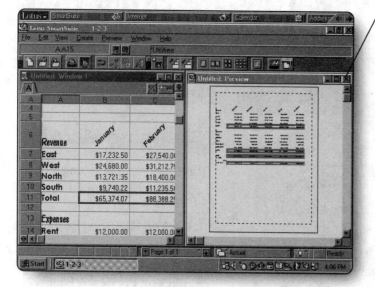

6. Click on the **Close button** of the Print Preview window. The screen will return to normal.

Changing Page Orientation

Orientation determines which direction a document prints. *Portrait orientation* prints with the short edge of the paper along the top; *landscape orientation* prints with the long edge of the paper across the top. The default choice for 1-2-3 is portrait orientation.

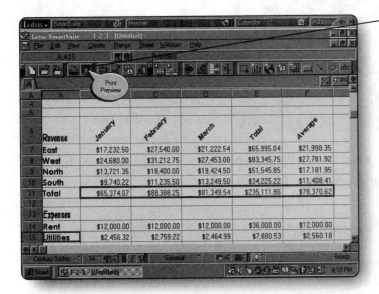

1. **Click** on the **Print Preview button**. The screen will divide and the Properties for Preview & Page Setup dialog box will appear.

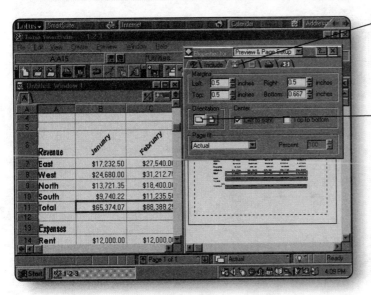

2. **Click** on the **Margins, orientation, and placement tab**. The tab will come to the front of the stack.

3. **Click** on the **Landscape button** in the Orientation area. The document orientation will change to landscape. Landscape is the first of the two choices. The second is Portrait Orientation.

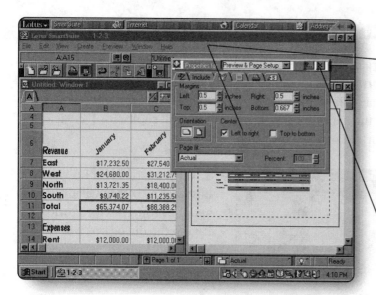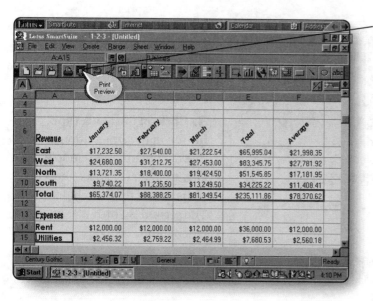

You also can choose to center the spreadsheet on the paper either horizontally or vertically by clicking on one or both of the choices in the Center area of this dialog box.

4. **Click** on the **Close button** of the Properties for Preview & Page Setup dialog box. The dialog box will close.

5. **Click** on the **Close button** of the Print Preview window. The screen will return to normal.

Creating a Header or Footer

Headers appear at the top of every printed page in your spreadsheet and footers appear at the bottom of every printed page.

1. **Click** on the **Print Preview button**. The screen will divide and the Properties for the Preview & Page Setup dialog box will appear.

2. Click on the **Headers and footers tab**. The tab will come to the front of the stack. Text for the header or footer can appear aligned with the left margin, in the center, or with the right margin of the paper. You can enter up to 240 characters for each part of a header or footer.

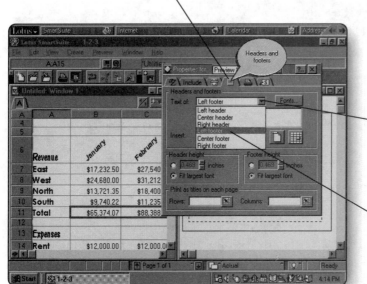

3. Click on the **down arrow** at the right of the Text of: list box. A list of placement locations will appear.

4. Click on the **area** of the header or footer that you want to work with. Your selection will be displayed in the Text of: list box.

5. Type any **desired text** in each text box. The text will be displayed in the text boxes.

6. Optionally, **Click** on any of the six **buttons** in the Insert area. 1-2-3 inserts a code symbol for each button. The following table explains these buttons from left to right.

1-2-3 Code	Actually Prints
@ (at sign)	The date of printing
+ (plus sign)	The time of printing
# (pound sign)	Consecutive page numbers
% (percent sign)	The total number of pages
^ (caret)	The file name
\ (backslash)	The contents of a cell by a cell address

TIP

If you see overlapping text in a header or footer, this means you have typed too much text in one of the header or footer boxes. To fix this, delete some of the text or enter the text in a different location.

NOTE

You can combine the date, time, page number, and file name with other header and footer text you type. For example, you can type **Page** and then enter # (pound sign), or click on the page number icon to print Page 1, Page 2, Page 3, and so on.

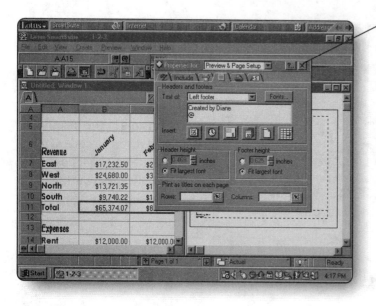

7. Click on the **Close button** of the Properties for Preview & Page Setup dialog box. The dialog box will close.

8. Click on the **Close button** of the Print Preview window. The screen will return to normal.

Making a Page Fit

You can reduce or enlarge the size of printed work to fit on a single page. Letting 1-2-3 scale the document up or down eliminates the need for you to guess about the fonts and column widths necessary to make the spreadsheet print on one page.

1. **Click** on the **Print Preview button**. The screen will divide and the Properties for Preview & Page Setup dialog box will appear.

2. **Click** on the **Margins, orientation, and placement tab**. The tab will come to the front of the stack.

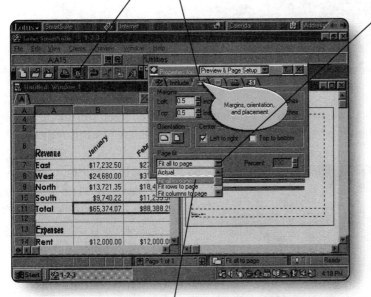

3. **Click** on the **down arrow** next to the Page Fit box. A list of choices will appear.

◆ **Actual**. Prints the selection in the size it appears on screen.

◆ **Fit all to page**. Fits all the data on a single printed page.

◆ **Fit rows to page**. Shrinks all the rows of data to fit on a single printed page.

◆ **Fit columns to page**. Shrinks all the columns of data to fit on a single printed page.

◆ **Custom**. Shrinks or enlarges the printed data by a percentage you enter. You can enter a percentage from 15 to 1000. For example, enter 75 to shrink the selection to 75 percent of its original size.

4. **Click** on the desired **Page fit choice**. The option will be selected.

When 1-2-3 shrinks or scales a spreadsheet, it does it proportionally so the overall appearance of the spreadsheet is the same as it was originally.

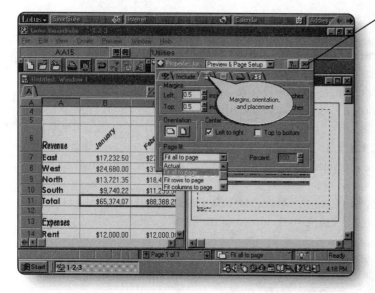

5. **Click** on the **Close button** of the Properties for Preview & Page Setup dialog box. The dialog box will close.

6. **Click** on the **Close button** of the Print Preview window. The screen will return to normal.

Selecting a Paper Size

The default paper size is 8 1/2" x 11". You can choose from a variety of sizes, depending on the type of printer you use.

1. **Click** on the **Print Preview button**. The screen will divide and the Properties for Preview & Page Setup dialog box will appear.

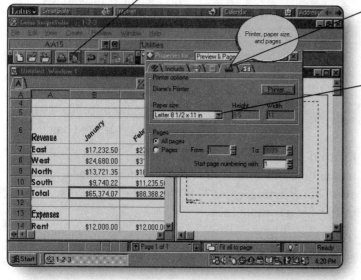

2. **Click** on the **Printer, paper size, and pages tab**. The tab will come to the front of the stack.

3. **Click** on the **desired paper size** from the Paper Size drop-down list. The selection will display in the Paper Size box.

4. **Click** on the **Close button** of the Properties for Preview & Page Setup dialog box. The dialog box will close.

5. **Click** on the **Close button** of the Print Preview window. The screen will return to normal.

13 Completing your Workbook

Now that you have created your workbook with all its text, values, and formulas, you'll want to prepare it for final output. You'll want to proof it for errors as well as specify what area you want to print. In this chapter, you'll learn how to:

✦ Check your spelling

✦ Save and close a workbook

✦ Open and print a workbook

✦ Hide and unhide rows and columns

✦ Specify print titles

✦ Use Print Preview

CHECKING YOUR SPELLING

The spell check feature of 1-2-3 checks for misspellings, repeated words, or words with numbers.

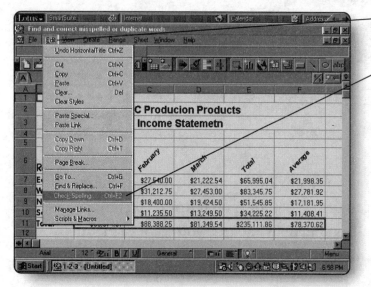

1. **Click** on **Edit**. The Edit menu will open.

2. **Click** on **Check Spelling**. The Check Spelling dialog box will appear.

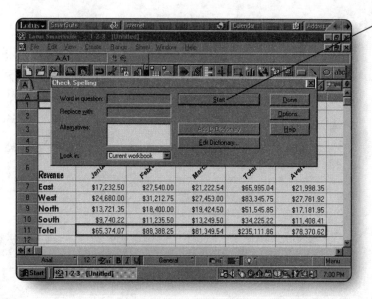

3. **Click** on **Start**. 1-2-3 will find the first error and offer you replacement suggestions.

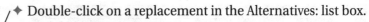

4. Choose one of the following **options**:

✦ Double-click on a replacement in the Alternatives: list box.

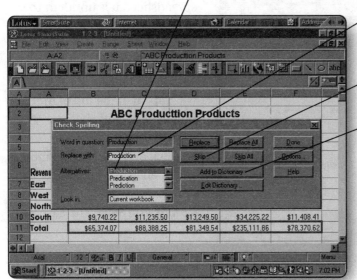

✦ Type your own replacement word in the Replace with: text box, and then click on Replace.

✦ Click on Skip to ignore the error.

✦ Add this error to your personal dictionary so 1-2-3 will not see it as an error in the future.

1-2-3 will then proceed to the next error.

5. Continue through the **spell check** until no more errors are found. When the spell check is complete, a message box will appear.

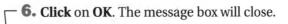

6. Click on **OK**. The message box will close.

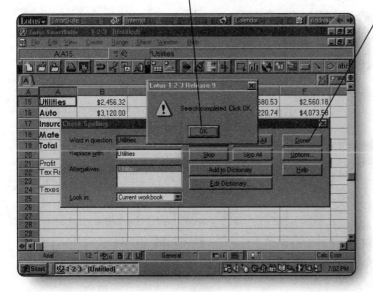

7. Click on **Done**. The Check Spelling dialog box will close.

SAVING A WORKBOOK

As you create a spreadsheet in 1-2-3, it is stored temporarily in the computer's memory. That memory gets erased at various times, such as when you turn the computer off. To prevent losing your work, you need to save it.

Saving a Workbook the First Time

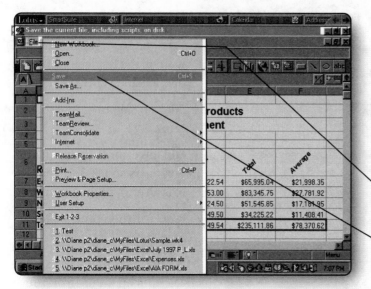

When you first create a spreadsheet, it is untitled. To save the spreadsheet for use again at a later date, you must give it a name. When you have saved a spreadsheet, the name will appear at the top of the screen, in the title bar.

1. **Click** on **File**. The File menu will open.

2. **Click** on **Save**. The Save As dialog box will appear.

3. **Enter** a descriptive **name** for the file in the File name: text box. The name will be displayed in the text box.

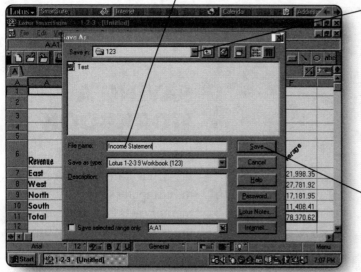

The Save in: drop-down list box lists the folder where the file will be saved. The default folder that appears is wordpro. If you don't want to save to this folder or you want to save your workbook to another disk, you can select another one. Click on the down arrow to browse.

4. **Click** on **Save**. The file will be saved and the file name appears at the top of the screen.

Resaving a Workbook

As you continue to work on your workbook, you should resave your document every ten minutes or so. This will ensure that you do not lose any changes you have made.

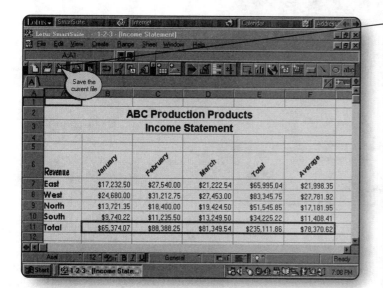

1. **Click** on the **Save the current file SmartIcon**. The workbook will be resaved with any changes. It will be resaved with the same name and in the same folder as previously specified.

TIP

If you want to save the workbook with a different name or in a different folder, click on File, then choose Save As. The Save As dialog box will prompt you for the new name or folder.

CLOSING A WORKBOOK

When you finish working on a spreadsheet, you should close it. *Closing* is the equivalent of putting it away for later use. When you close a spreadsheet, you put the spreadsheet away—not the program. 1-2-3 is still active and ready to work for you.

1. **Click** on **File**. The File menu will open.

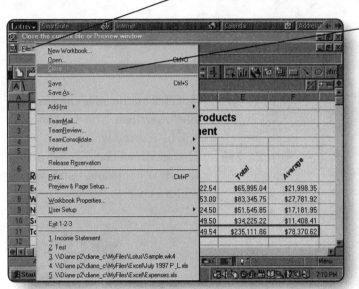

2. **Click** on **Close**. The document will close; however, the 1-2-3 program still will be active.

OPENING A SAVED WORKBOOK

To edit a spreadsheet you have already closed, you must open that document again. If you want to open a spreadsheet when you begin the 1-2-3 program, the screen will look different if you are already in a spreadsheet and want to open another one.

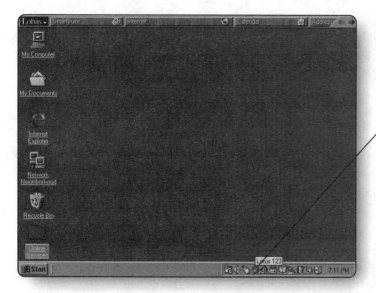

Opening a File from the Windows Desktop

1. **Start 1-2-3**. The Welcome to 1-2-3 dialog box will appear.

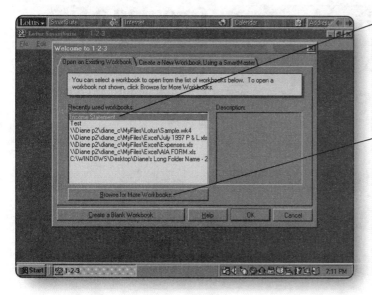

2a. **Double-click** on the **file name** in the Recently used workbooks list. The file will open.

OR

2b. **Click** on **Browse for More Workbooks** if the file you want is not in the Recently Used Workbooks list. The Open dialog box will appear.

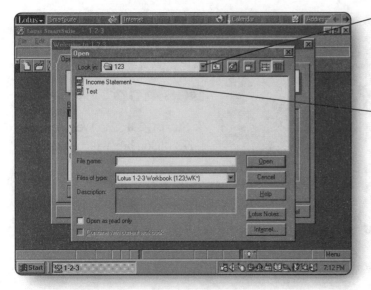

3. **Open** the **folder**, if necessary, containing the spreadsheet you want to open. A list of file names will display.

4. **Double-click** on the desired **file name**. The file will become active in the 1-2-3 window.

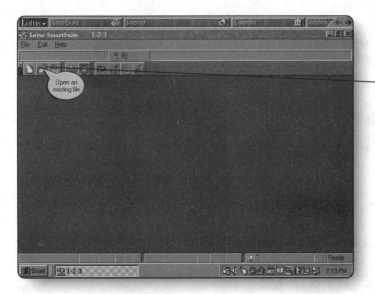

Opening a File from 1-2-3

1. **Click** on the **Open an existing file SmartIcon**. The Open dialog box will appear.

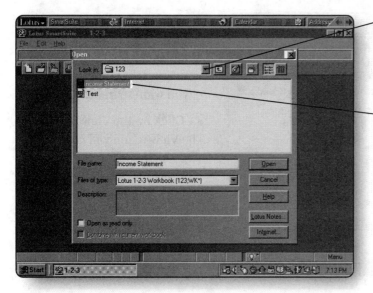

2. **Open** the **folder** containing the spreadsheet you want to open. A list of file names will display.

3. **Double-click** on the desired **file name**. The file will become active in the 1-2-3 window.

FREEZING WORKSHEET TITLES

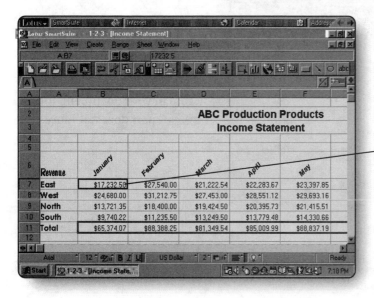

You can freeze columns, rows, or both so that column and row titles remain in view as you scroll through the sheet instead of scrolling off the screen with the rest of the spreadsheet.

1. **Click** on the desired **cell**:

✦ To freeze columns, position the mouse pointer one cell to the right of the columns you want to freeze.

✦ To freeze rows, position the cell pointer one cell below the rows you want to freeze.

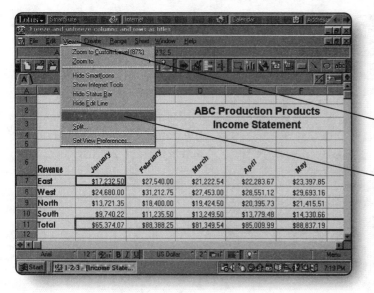

✦ To freeze both columns and rows, position the cell pointer in the cell below the rows and to the right of the columns you want to freeze.

2. **Click** on the **View menu**. The View menu will open.

3. **Click** on **Titles**. The Titles dialog box will appear.

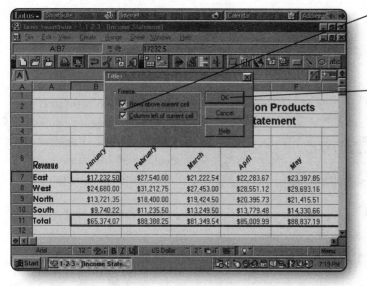

4. **Click** on **one** or **both** of the **check boxes**. A check will appear in the check boxes.

5. **Click** on **OK**. The dialog box will close.

As you scroll downward or across in your document, the "frozen" part does not move.

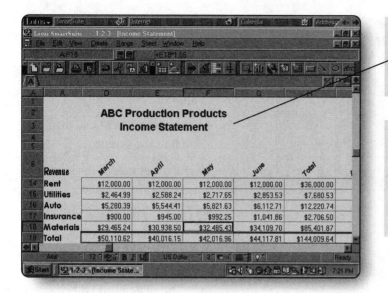

NOTE

No gridlines appear in the frozen title area.

TIP

Repeat steps 2 through 5 and deselect the check boxes in step 4 to "unfreeze" the windows.

PRINTING A WORKBOOK

After you have created your spreadsheet, you probably will want a hard copy for your records or to send to someone else.

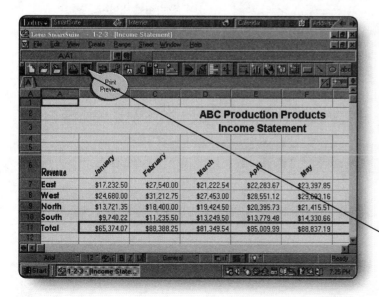

Using Dynamic Print Preview

Printing is a slow, expensive process and it uses valuable resources. Print Preview allows you to check the overall document prior to printing. It's a "bird's-eye view" of your spreadsheet.

1. Click on the **Print Preview SmartIcon**. Several things will

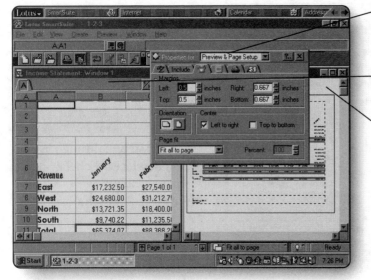

happen:

✦ The Properties for Preview & Page Setup dialog box will appear.

✦ The spreadsheet will display on half the screen.

✦ The other half of the screen will be Print Preview.

2. Click on the **Close button** for the Properties for Preview & Page Setup dialog box if you don't need to make any changes to it. The dialog box will close.

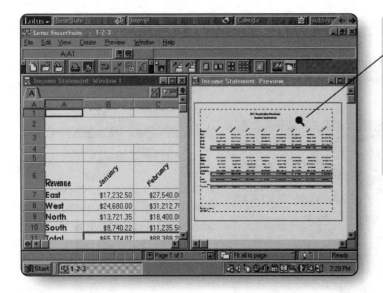

TIP

Don't strain your eyes trying to read the text in the Preview windows. You are looking at the overall perspective here, not necessarily the individual cells.

TIP

If you do need to see the cells up close, click on the Preview window. The spreadsheet zooms in so you can read it. Click again and it zooms even more! Click a third time and you return to the full page view mode. This is a *dynamic* view, which means that as you change the spreadsheet, you immediately see the changes in the Preview window.

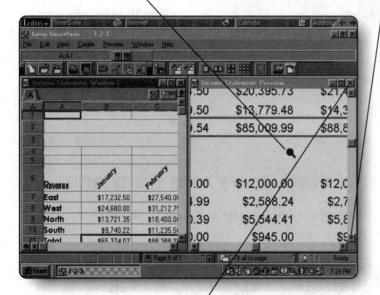

3. **Click** on the **down arrow** of the scroll bar. You will see subsequent pages of the spreadsheet, if any. The current page number is reflected at the bottom of the screen.

4. **Click** on the **Close button** of the Print Preview window. The screen will return to normal.

Hiding Rows and Columns

You can hide rows or columns in your spreadsheet so that they do not display on the screen or print. For example, you may have a column listing service dates for sales people that impact their commission. You probably do not want to have that available on a sales report, but it is needed to calculate their commission. Hiding the column will allow it to continue with calculations but not display on the screen or printed copy.

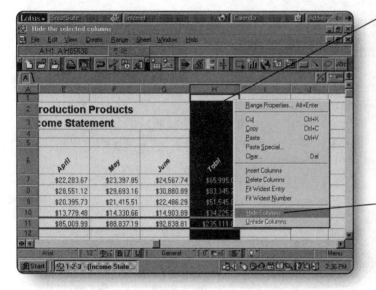

1. **Select** the **row or column** you want to hide (if you want to hide more than one row or column, select them first). The row or column will be highlighted.

2. **Click** the **right mouse button**. A shortcut menu will appear.

3. **Click** on **Hide Columns** or **Hide Rows**. The column or row will be hidden and will not print.

Unhiding Rows and Columns

OK, now you've hidden rows or columns. The question is, how do you get them back?

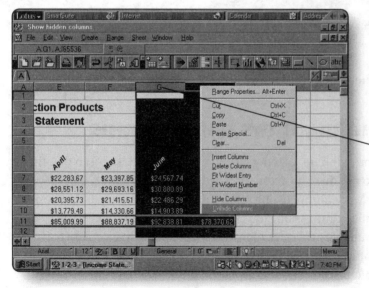

1a. **Click** on the **row** above the hidden rows and **drag** the mouse pointer to the next row below the hidden row. The two rows will be highlighted.

OR

1b. **Click** on the **column** before the hidden columns and **drag** the mouse pointer to the column after the hidden columns. The two columns will be highlighted.

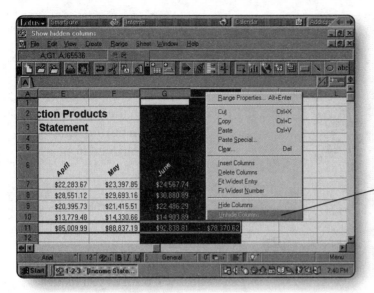

2. Right-click on the **selected area**. A pop-up menu will appear.

3a. Click on **Unhide Rows**. The rows will redisplay onscreen.

OR

3b. Click on **Unhide Columns.** The columns will redisplay onscreen.

Printing a Range

By default, 1-2-3 assumes you want to print the entire spreadsheet. If this is not the case, you need to specify the area you want to print. That area is called a *print range*.

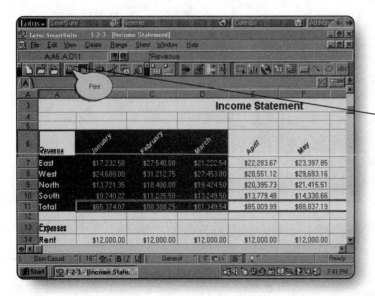

1. Select the **cells** you want to print if you do not intend to print the entire spreadsheet. The cells will be highlighted.

2. Click on the **Print SmartIcon**. The Print dialog box will appear.

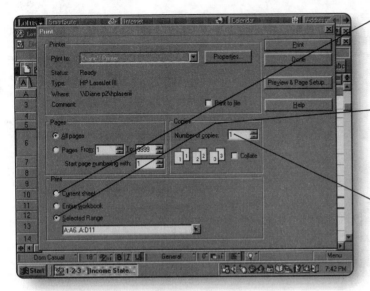

3a. **Click** on the **Current sheet option button**. The entire worksheet will print.

OR

3b. **Click** on the **Selected Range option button**. Only the area you highlighted in step 1 will print.

4. Specify the **number of copies** to print (up to 9,999).

5. Click on **Print**. The spreadsheet will print as you requested.

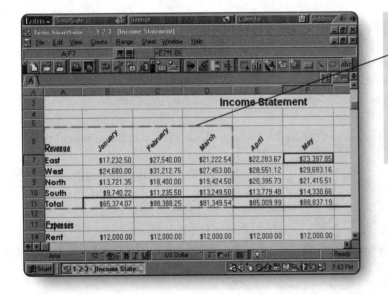

NOTE

If you specified a specific range to print, when you return to the normal spreadsheet view, you will see gray dashed lines around the specified area.

14 Creating Charts

A chart is an effective way to illustrate the data in your spreadsheet. It can make relationships among numbers easier to see because it turns numbers into shapes and the shapes can then be compared to one another. In this chapter, you'll learn how to:

✦ Create a chart

✦ Move and resize a chart

✦ Modify a chart

✦ Delete a chart

CREATING A CHART

Creating a chart is just a two-step process using 1-2-3. All you need to know is what you want to chart and where you want to put the chart.

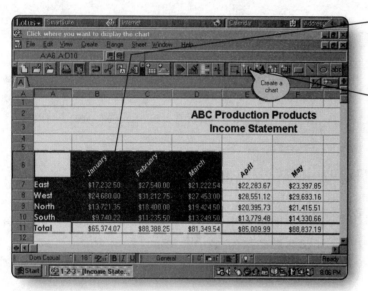

1. **Select** the **range** you what to chart. The range will be highlighted.

2. **Click** on the **Create a chart SmartIcon**. The pointer will change to look like a small bar chart.

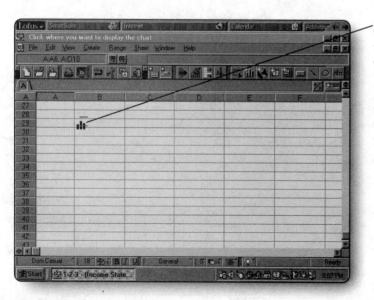

3. **Click** on the **worksheet** where you want the chart to go. The chart will be created. The chart is created with its upper-left corner positioned where you clicked on the worksheet. The type of chart created is a bar chart.

The data from the selected cells of the spreadsheet is plotted out into a chart. If the data in the spreadsheet changes, the chart will also change.

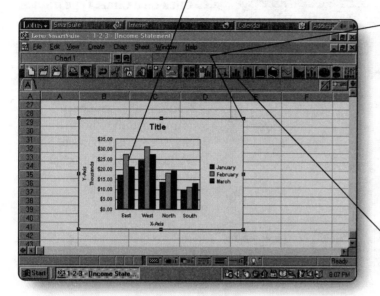

The chart is selected and "active" because it has eight small black *handles* around the outside edge of it.

NOTE

Don't worry if the box is too big or too small. You'll learn how to size a chart soon.

While a chart is active, the toolbar changes to reflect charting tools.

MODIFYING A CHART

With very little effort, you have a chart. As a matter of fact, creating a chart is so simple that it probably made you want to enhance the chart to improve its appearance. You can change the style of the chart, make it a 3-D chart, or add titles to the chart to further explain its use.

Changing a Chart Style

If you do not want a simple bar chart, you can change the chart type. Chart types that you can select include stacked bar, area, pie, and line as well as others.

1. Click on the **chart**. Handles will appear around the outside edges.

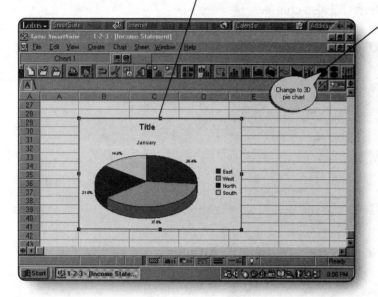

2. Click on a **Chart Type** from the SmartIcons toolbar. The chart style will change.

NOTE

Traditionally, bar charts compare item to item, pie charts compare parts of a whole item, and line charts show a trend over a period of time.

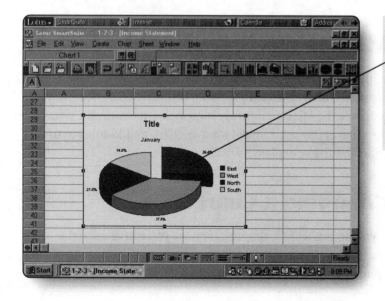

TIP

If you are working with a pie chart, click on a piece of the pie and drag it away from the rest of the pie to call attention to that piece.

Adding Chart Titles

If you do not preselect a title before you create the chart, Lotus 1-2-3 gives it one called "Title." You can change the generic title or not have a title at all.

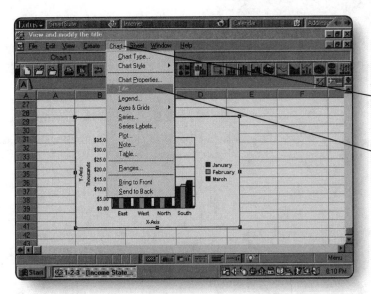

1. Click on the **chart**. Handles will appear around the outside edges.

2. Click on **Chart**. The Chart menu will open.

3. Click on **Title**. The Chart Title will be selected and the Properties for Title dialog box will appear.

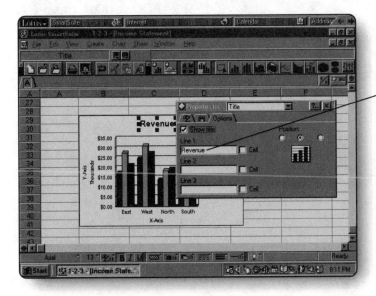

4. Double-click on the **Line 1** text box. This will be the first line of the title.

5. Type the **desired text** for the title. The text will display. The default font for the title is Arial. You can change the title font.

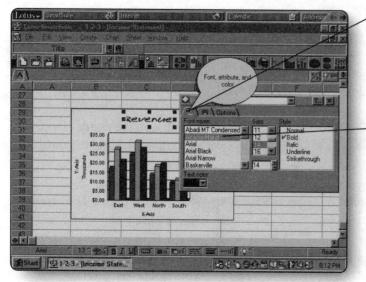

6. Click on the **Font, attribute, and color tab** of the Title Properties dialog box. The tab will come to the front of the stack.

7. Click on the desired **font name, style, size, or color** for the title. The chart title will change instantly.

8. Click on the **Close button**. The Properties dialog box will close.

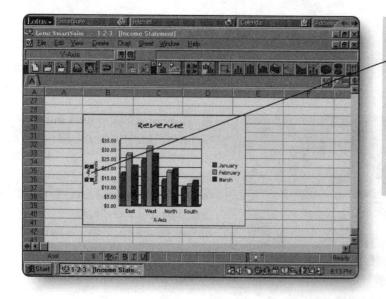

TIP

You may notice there are titles around the category (x axis) and value (y axis) sides of a bar chart. You can click on either of these titles and type a new one, or press the Delete key to delete them.

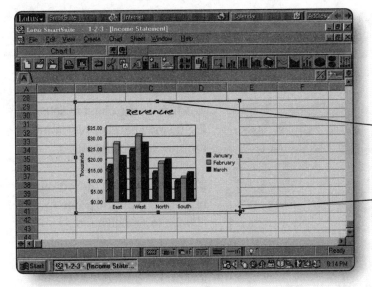

Resizing a Chart

If the chart is too small or too large, you can resize it to fit your needs.

1. **Click** on the **chart** to select it. Eight small handles will appear around the outside edges.

2. **Position** the **mouse pointer** over one of the handles. The mouse pointer turns into a cross with four arrow heads.

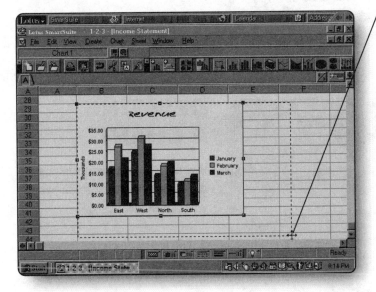

3. **Drag** the **handle** until the chart is the desired size. An outline of the chart will be displayed around the original chart.

4. **Release** the **mouse button**. The chart will be resized.

MOVING A CHART

If a chart is laying on top of your spreadsheet data, you will want to move it to a new location.

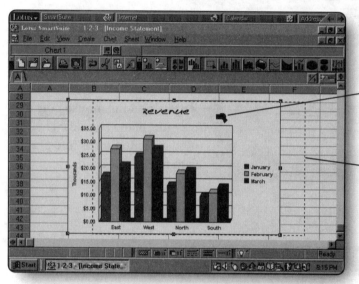

1. **Click** on the **chart** to select it. Eight small handles will appear around the outside edges.

2. **Press** and **hold** the **left mouse button**. The mouse pointer will change to a small hand.

3. **Drag** the **chart** to a new location. A dotted box will follow the mouse pointer as you move it.

4. **Release** the **mouse button**. The chart will be moved.

DELETING A CHART

If you no longer want the chart displayed in your spreadsheet, you can delete it.

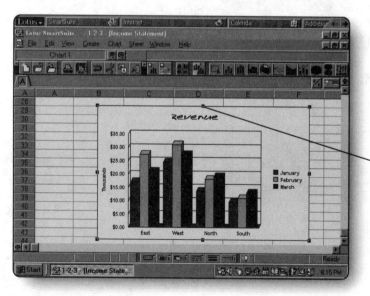

1. **Click** on the **chart**. Handles will appear around the outside edges.

2. **Press** the **Delete key**. The chart will disappear.

PRINTING A CHART

If you choose to print the entire spreadsheet, the chart will print along with it. However, you can specify to print only the chart.

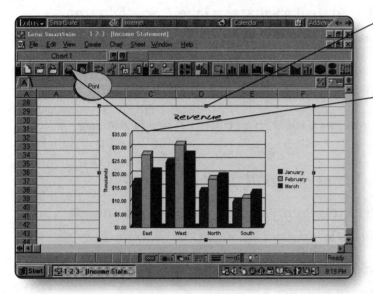

1. **Click** on the **chart**. Handles will appear around the outside edges.

2. **Click** on the **Print SmartIcon**. The Print dialog box will appear.

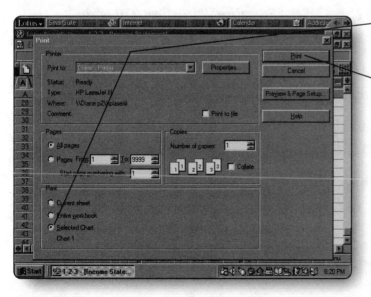

3. **Click** on **Selected Chart**. The option will be selected.

4. **Click** on **Print**. The chart will print.

PART III REVIEW QUESTIONS

1. What must you type first to treat a value as a label? *See "Entering Values into Cells" in Chapter 10*

2. What is one way to move the contents of a cell to a new location? *See "Moving Data Around" in Chapter 10*

3. What is the fastest way to get a total in a column? *See "Entering Totals" in Chapter 10*

4. What is SpeedFill? *See "Using SpeedFill" in Chapter 10*

5. How do the Rules of Priorities apply when creating a compound formula? *See "Creating a Compound Formula" in Chapter 11*

6. What does a $ mean in a cell reference? *See "Creating an Absolute Reference in a Formula" in Chapter 11*

7. What can you do so the column and row titles remain in view as you scroll through the sheet? *See "Freezing Worksheet Titles" in Chapter 13*

8. How can you prevent a column from printing? *See "Hiding Rows and Columns" in Chapter 13*

9. What happens to a chart if the spreadsheet data changes? *See "Creating a Chart" in Chapter 14*

10. How can you print a chart without the spreadsheet data? *See "Printing a Chart" in Chapter 14*

PART IV

Using Freelance

February

$27,540.0(

$31,212.7!

$18,400.0(

$11,235.5(

$88,388.2!

0.00 $12,000.0(

15 Creating a Simple Presentation

Freelance Graphics is a tool that aids you in creating presentation graphics. Using Freelance, you can create slides and speaker notes. Freelance provides you with SmartMasters to help you create attractive presentations. In this chapter, you'll learn how to:

✦ Use SmartMasters to create a professional-looking presentation

✦ Work with your presentation's slides to add text and graphics

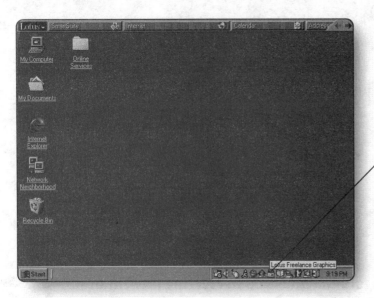

STARTING FREELANCE

The easiest method to start the Freelance program is to use the SuiteStart tools.

1. Click on the **Lotus Freelance Graphics button** from the SuiteStart tools. A Welcome to Lotus Freelance Graphics dialog box will open.

USING SMARTMASTERS

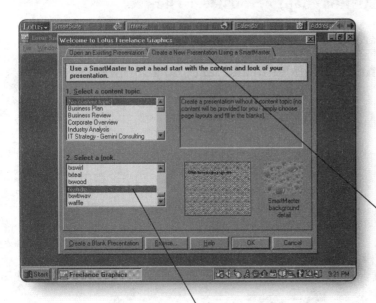

The fastest and easiest way to create a professional-looking presentation is to use one of Freelance's many SmartMasters. Freelance's SmartMasters have been designed by a professional graphic designer so that your presentations will look great with a minimum amount of effort.

1. If necessary, **Click** on the **Create a New Presentation Using a SmartMaster tab**. A list of content topics and looks will be displayed.

2. Click on a **look** from the Select a look list box. A preview of each one will be displayed.

3. Click on **OK**. The New Page dialog box will open.

Selecting a Page Layout

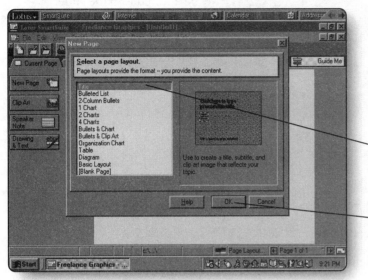

The page layouts will vary depending upon the type of information you want to put into this page. Each page in the presentation can have a different layout.

1. **Click** on the **layout** of the page you want to create first. A sample page will be displayed.

2. **Click** on **OK**. The first page (slide) of your presentation will be displayed.

Entering Text on a Slide

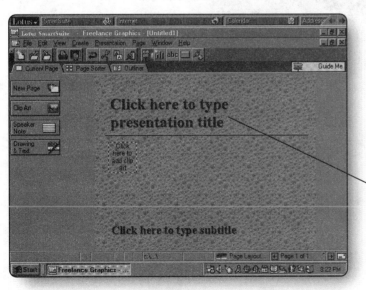

SmartMasters are set up so that their slides will give you clues on how to use them. On a slide, there will be different objects and instructions to click on. For example, each slide should have a title to describe the overall contents of the slide.

1. **Click** on the **object area** that begins with the phrase Click here to type. The text area will be changed to edit mode.

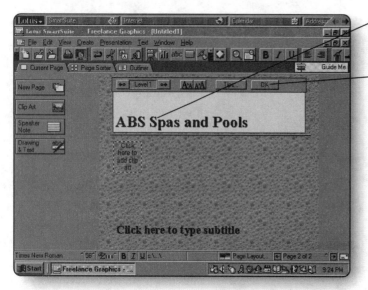

2. Type some **text**. The text will be entered into the slide.

3. Click on **OK**. The text object will no longer be in edit mode.

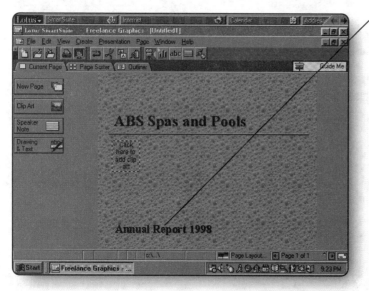

4. Repeat steps 1 through **3** until all text objects are complete.

ADDING CLIP ART TO A SLIDE

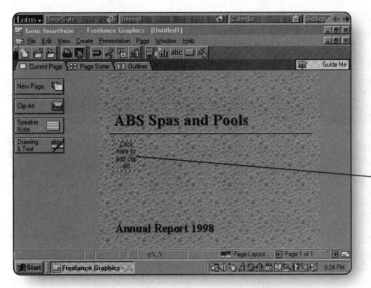

Some slides have objects designated for clip art. An example of this type of slide is a title slide.

1. **Click** on the **object area** as instructed to add clip art. The Add Clip Art or Diagram to the Page dialog box will open.

2. **Click** on the **down arrow** to the right of the Category: list box to select a category of clip art. The notebook at the bottom of the dialog box will display the clip art images associated with the selected category.

3. **Click** on the **arrow buttons** under the notebook. This will scroll through the images.

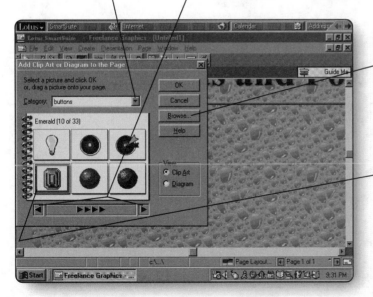

TIP

To add a company logo instead of clip art, click on the Browse button and then locate the logo file. Click on OK to insert the logo.

4. **Click** on the **clip art** picture you want. The selected image will have a small gray box surrounding it.

5. **Click** on **OK**. The clip art will be added to the slide.

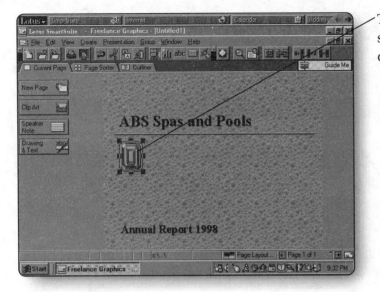

The clip art is automatically sized to fit within the clip art object.

ADDING SLIDES

You can add as many slides as you want to your presentation. Each slide has a page layout associated with it. The page layout determines the role of the slide in the presentation and the objects on the slide.

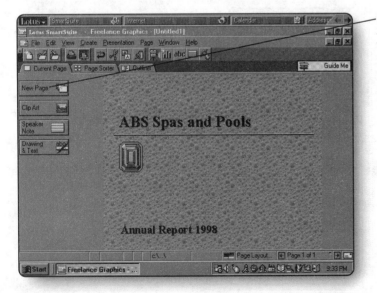

1. Click on **New Page**. The New Page dialog box will open.

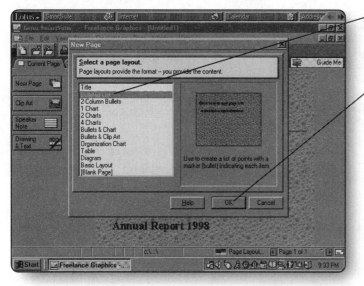

2. **Click** on the **layout** that you want for the new page. The layout will be highlighted.

3. **Click** on **OK**. The new slide will be displayed.

WORKING WITH BULLETED LISTS

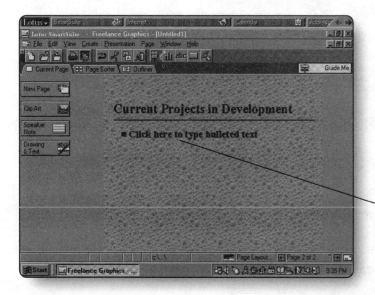

Working with bulleted lists is similar to working with text objects. The only difference is that when you press Enter, you add another bulleted item.

1. **Create** a **new slide page**. Choose one that includes the word "bullet" in the description.

2. **Click** on an **object area** as instructed to type bulleted text. The object will be changed to edit mode.

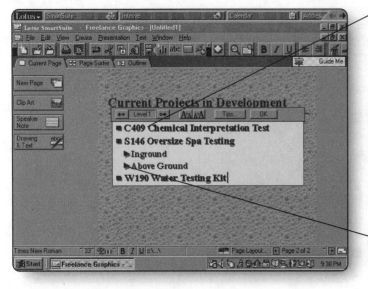

3. **Type** some **text** for the bulleted item. The text will be added to the bulleted list.

4. **Press** the **Enter key**. A new bulleted item will be added.

5a. **Type** some **text** for the next bulleted item. The text will be added to the list.

OR

5b. **Press** the **Tab key**. The next level in the bullet hierarchy will be added. **Type** some **text** for the item.

6. Repeat steps **3** and **4** until the bulleted list is complete.

7. **Click** on **OK**. The bullet list object will not be in edit mode.

To move backwards (return to the higher level in the bullet hierarchy) press Shift and the Tab key.

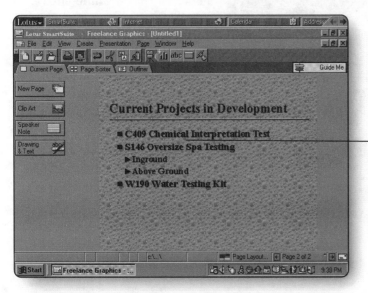

Moving a Bulleted Item

You can rearrange the order of the bulleted items.

1. **Double-click** on a **bullet list object**. The object will be changed to edit mode.

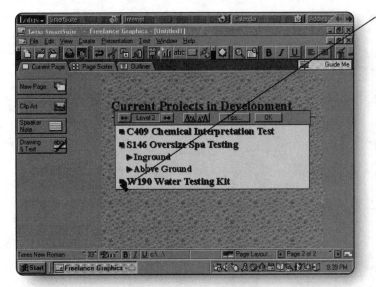

2. Position the **mouse pointer** over the bullet of the item to be moved. The mouse pointer turns into a hand.

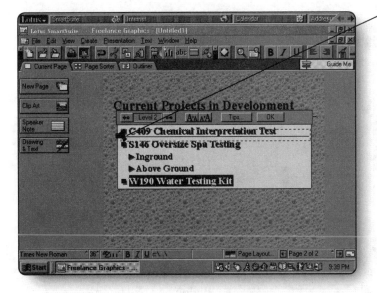

3. Click on and **drag** the **bulleted line item** above the new desired location. A dotted box represents the movement of the line.

4. Release the **mouse button**. The line item will be moved.

ADDING A CHART TO A SLIDE

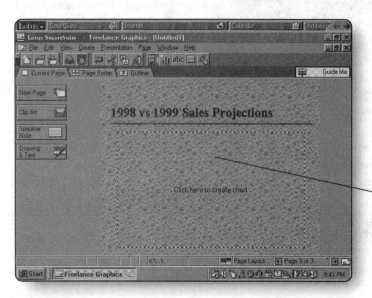

Charts are a great way to present data. Creating a chart in Freelance Graphics is similar to creating a chart in 1-2-3.

1. Create a **new slide page**. Select a page layout to add that has a chart object on it.

2. Click on the **object area** as instructed to create a chart. The Create Chart dialog box will open.

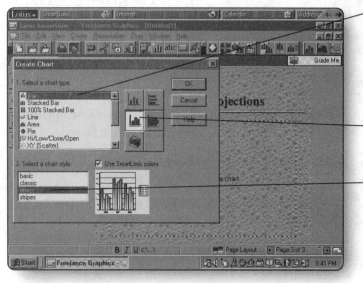

3. Click on a **chart type** from the Select a chart type: list box. The chart will be previewed in the lower-right corner of the dialog box.

4. Click on a **chart option**. The chart's layout will be changed.

5. Click on a **chart style** from the Select a chart style: list box. The chart's style will be changed.

6. Click on **OK**. The Edit Data dialog box will open.

7. Type the **data** for the chart. Typing the data here is similar to entering data in a 1-2-3 spreadsheet.

As you enter the data, the chart is created in the preview box.

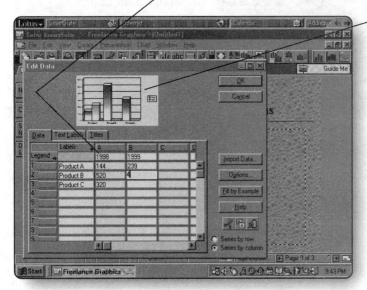

8. Click on the **Titles tab**. The tab will come to the front.

9. Type any desired **titles** or **notes** for the chart. The information will be added to the chart.

10. Click on **OK**. The chart is added to the slide.

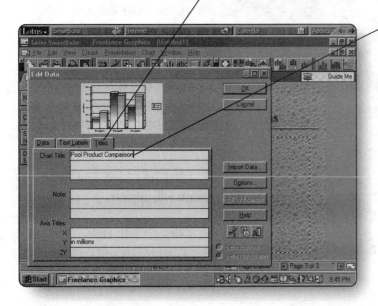

The chart automatically sizes on the slide to match the original size of the chart object.

Editing Chart Data

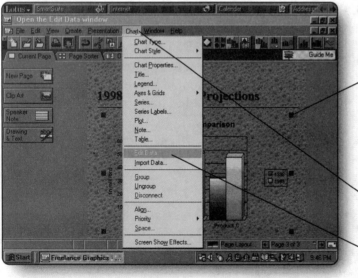

If you change the data for the chart, the chart will reflect the changes.

1. Click anywhere on the **chart**. The chart or a component of the chart will be selected. Handles appear around the selected object.

2. Click on **Chart**. The Chart menu will appear.

3. Click on **Edit Data**. The Edit Data dialog box will open.

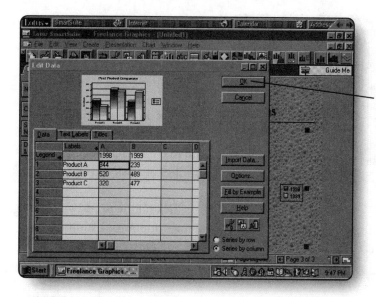

4. Make any necessary **changes** to the data. The Edit data dialog box will reflect the changes.

5. Click on **OK**. The Edit Data dialog box will close and the chart will be updated with the changes.

WORKING WITH TABLE SLIDES

A distinct way to present data is to create a table slide. Table slides look like a small spreadsheet on a page.

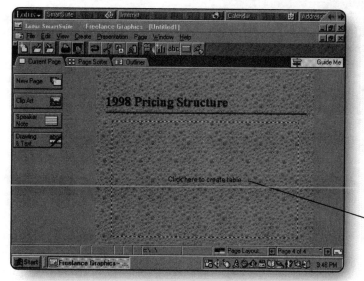

Creating a Table

One of the first things you'll need to know when working with tables is how many columns and rows you will need.

1. Create a **new slide page**. Select a page layout that has a table object on it.

2. Click on the **object area** as instructed to create a table. The Table Gallery dialog box will open.

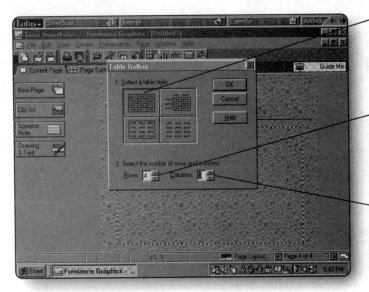

3. **Click** on a **table style** from the Select a table style: list box. This will set the style of the table you are creating.

4. **Click** on the **up/down arrows** under the Rows: list box and make a selection. The number of rows will be set.

5. **Click** on the **up/down arrows** under the Columns: list box and make a selection. The number of columns will be set.

6. **Click** on **OK**. The table will be created on the slide.

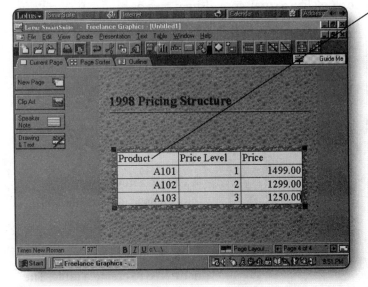

7. **Click** on the **first cell** in the table. The table will be changed to edit mode.

8. **Type** some **text**. The text will be added to the table.

9. **Press** the **Tab key**. The next cell in the table will be selected.

10. **Repeat steps 8 and 9** until all the necessary text is added to the table.

Changing the Font of Table Cells

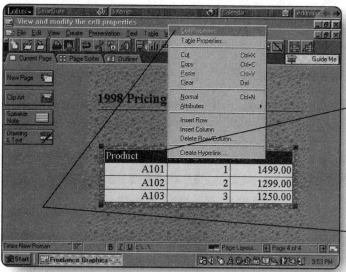

You can format a table so that the headings, for example, are a different font from the rest of the table.

1. **Click** on and **drag** across the **cells** to be modified. The cell or cells will be highlighted.

2. **Right-click** on the **cells**. A shortcut menu will appear.

3. **Click** on **Cell Properties**. The Properties for Selected Cell(s) dialog box will open.

4. **Click** on a **font** from the Font name: list box. The font will be applied to the selected cells.

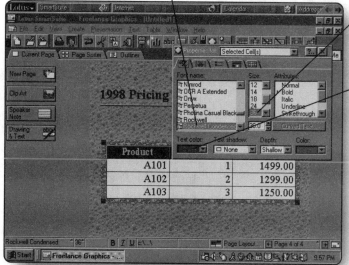

5. **Click** on a **size** from the Size: list box. The font size of the selected cells will change.

6. Optionally, **click** on a **text color** from the Text color: drop-down list. The text color of the selected cells will change.

TIP

To modify the alignment of cells, click on the alignment tab and select an alignment choice.

7. **Click** on the **Close button**. The dialog box will close.

8. **Click** anywhere **outside of the table**. The table will be deselected.

TIP
Press the Esc key to deselect any object in the presentation.

MOVING AROUND IN YOUR PRESENTATION

There are several ways to move from slide to slide in your presentation by using the status bar navigation buttons or by using the Page Sorter.

Using the Status Bar Navigation Buttons to Move to a Slide

The status bar at the bottom of the Freelance Graphics screen has buttons to quickly move you from slide to slide.

1. **Click** on the **previous slide button**. The previous slide in the presentation will appear.

2. **Click** on the **next slide button**. The next slide in the presentation will appear.

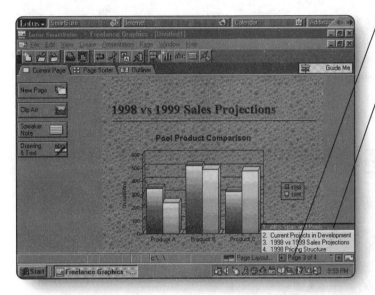

3. **Click** on the **page number button**. A menu listing the pages in the presentation will appear.

4. **Click** on a **slide**. The slide will appear.

Moving to a Slide Using Page Sorter

The Page Sorter is used for a variety of things including moving to a page in the presentation.

1. **Click** on the **Page Sorter tab**. The Page Sorter tab will appear.

2. **Double-click** on the **slide** that you want to use. The slide will appear.

DELETING SLIDES

If you do not want a slide to be a part of your presentation, delete it.

1. **Click** on the **Page Sorter tab**. The Page Sorter tab will appear.

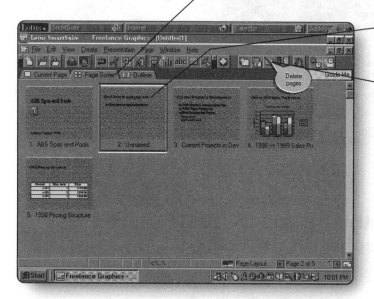

2. **Click** on the **slide** to be deleted. The slide will appear.

3. **Click** on the **Delete pages SmartIcon**. The Slide will be deleted from the presentation.

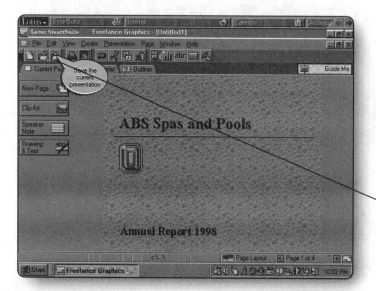

SAVING A PRESENTATION

When you first create a presentation, it has no name. If you want to use that document later, it must have a name so Freelance can find it.

1. **Click** on the **Save the current presentation button**. The Save As dialog box will open.

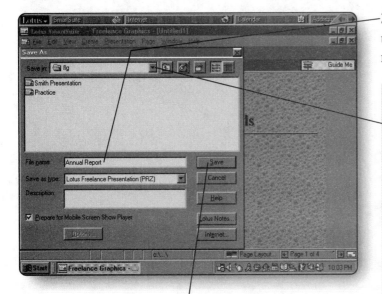

2. **Type** a **name** for your file in the File name: text box. The file name will be displayed.

NOTE

The Save in: drop-down list box lists the folder where the file will be saved. The default folder that appears is "flg". If you don't want to save to this folder or you want to save your document to another disk, you can select another one. Click on the down arrow to browse.

TIP

Type an optional description of the presentation in the Description: text box.

3. **Click** on **Save**. Your presentation will be saved and the name you specified will appear in the title bar.

16 Making Professional Slide Shows

After you create your presentation, you'll want to show it. You may need to print a copy of your presentation or show it on a monitor or both. Freelance provides you with tools to create a professional and visually interesting slide show. In this chapter, you'll learn how to:

✦ Add speaker notes to a presentation

✦ Print a presentation

✦ Create a slide show

WORKING WITH SPEAKER NOTES

A speaker note is a note that is associated with a presentation page. Use speaker notes as prompts while giving a presentation, to store supporting facts or data sources, or as messages to colleagues who might also deliver your presentation.

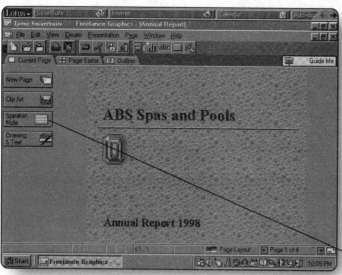

Adding a Speaker Note

You can create one speaker note for each presentation page. There is no limit to the amount of text you can put in a speaker note.

1. **Display** the **slide** to which you want to add the speaker note. The slide will become the current slide.

2. **Click** on **Speaker Note**. The Speaker Note dialog box will open.

3. **Type** the **text** of the speaker note. The text will appear in the text box.

> **TIP**
>
> Click on the left or right arrows to easily add notes to the next or previous slides.

4. **Click** on **OK**. The speaker note will be added to the slide.

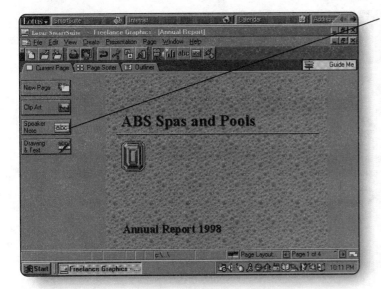

The speaker note button changes to indicate that there is text assigned. You see speaker note text only when you open the Speaker Note window or when you choose to print speaker notes with the presentation. A speaker note is not part of the presentation page.

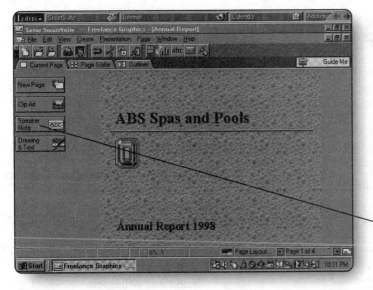

Editing a Speaker Note

Changing the text entered in a speaker note is easy.

1. Display the **slide** to which you want to edit the speaker note. The slide will become the current slide.

2. Click on **Speaker Note**. The Speaker Note dialog box will open with the current note text displayed.

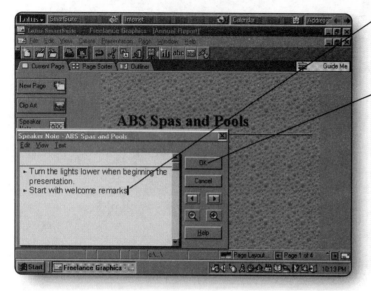

3. Type the **changes** to the speaker note. The change will be reflected in the text box.

4. Click on **OK**. The speaker note will be updated.

Deleting a Speaker Note

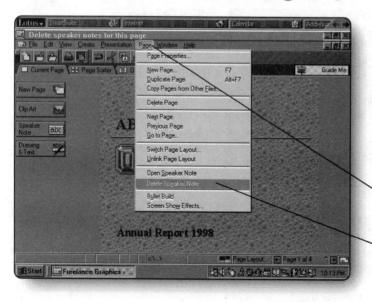

If you no longer want a speaker note associated with a slide, you can delete it.

1. Display the **slide** of which you want to delete the speaker note. The slide will become the current slide.

2. Click on **Page**. The Page menu will appear.

3. Click on **Delete Speaker Note**. The Delete Speaker Note dialog box will open.

4. **Choose one** of the following:

✦ If you want to delete the speaker note from this page only, click on Current page.

✦ If you want to delete all the speaker notes, click on All pages.

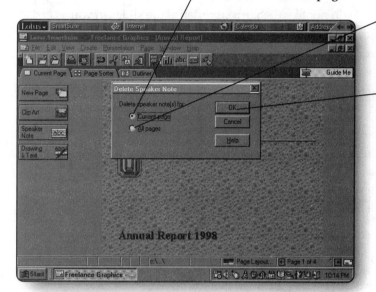

5. **Click** on **OK**. A warning message box will appear.

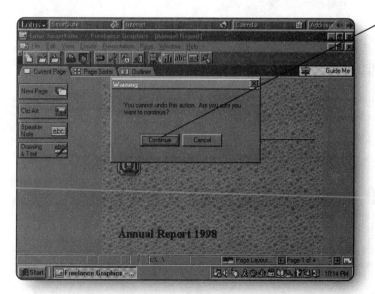

6. **Click** on **Continue**. The speaker note will be deleted.

REARRANGING SLIDES WITH THE PAGE SORTER

If you do not like the current order of the slides in your presentation, you can change it. This can be done easily using the Page Sorter.

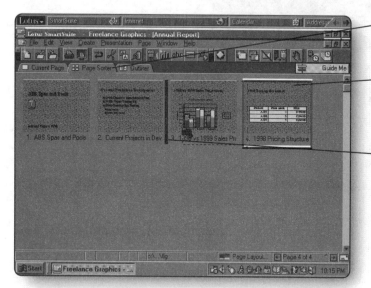

1. **Click** on the **Page Sorter tab**. The Page Sorter tab will appear.

2. **Click** on the **slide** you want to move. The slide will be selected.

3. **Drag** the **slide** to the new location. A bar will appear to identify the new location of the slide.

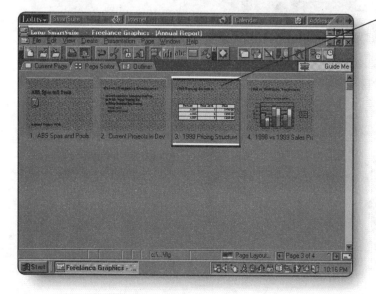

4. **Release** the **mouse button**. The slide will move to its new location.

PRINTING A PRESENTATION

Freelance provides four types of formats for your printed slide show: full page, handouts, speaker notes, and audience notes.

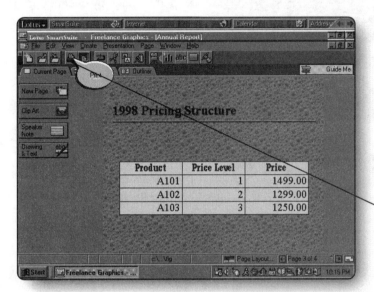

Audience handouts can be printed one, two, four, or six to a page. Speaker notes and audience notes can be printed one, two, or three to a page. Audience notes have the slide on one part of the page and a ruled area like notebook paper for the audience to take notes.

1. Click on the **Print SmartIcon**. The Print dialog box will open.

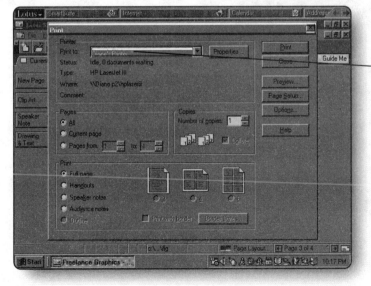

2. Choose from the following **options:**

♦ If you are connected to more than one printer, you can choose where to print to by clicking on the down arrow under the Print to: area and making a selection.

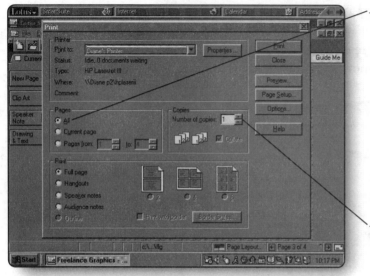

✦ Choose which pages to print in the Pages area. You can print all pages, just the current page, or you can print a specific page by clicking on the appropriate option button. To print a specific range of pages, click on the up/down arrows to select the beginning and ending pages of the range.

✦ Choose the number of copies to be printed by clicking on the up/down arrows in the Copies: list box.

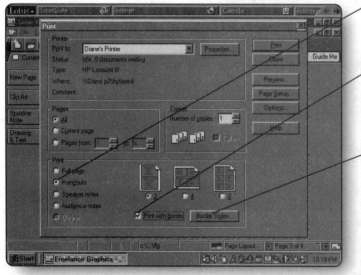

✦ In the Print box, select what to print and how many to print on a page.

✦ If you want a border around your handouts, speaker notes, or audience notes, check Print with border.

✦ Choose from different styles of borders by clicking on the Border Styles button and selecting a style and then clicking on OK.

3. Click on **Print**. The pages will be sent to the printer.

SHOWING THE PRESENTATION

Instead of discussing your presentation from printed handouts or overhead slides, you may want to present your slides on a computer monitor or television hooked up to your computer. This gives you more flexibility and impact than printed media.

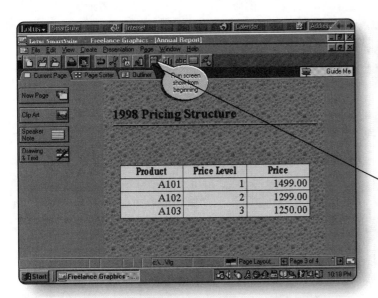

Running the Standard Slide Show

You can run your slide show at any time by just clicking on a button.

1. **Click** on the **Run screen show from beginning SmartIcon**. The slide show will appear.

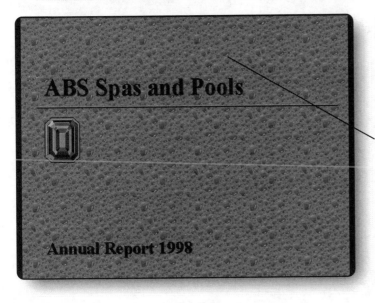

2. **Click** on the **slide**. The next slide in the presentation will appear.

3. **Repeat step 2** until the slide show is complete. When the slide show is complete, Freelance will return to the original view.

Setting a Trigger

When a slide is triggered, it closes so that the next slide can display. A slide can have a manual trigger, which means you have to click your mouse or press a key to move to the next slide or you can have an automatic trigger where the slide closes after a certain number of seconds.

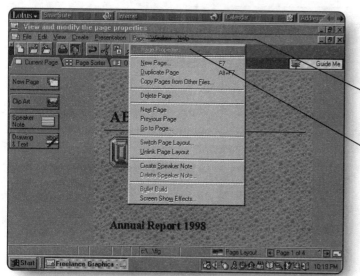

1. Display the **slide** for which you want to set a trigger. The slide will be selected.

2. Click on **Page**. The Page menu will appear.

3. Click on **Page Properties**. The Properties for Page dialog box will open.

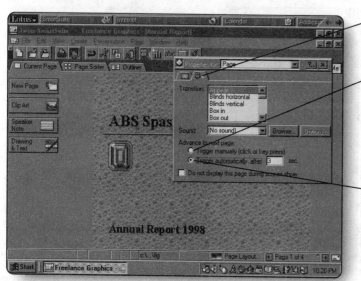

4. Click on the **Slide Show tab**. The Slide Show tab will appear.

5a. Click on the **Trigger manually option button**. A manual trigger will be set for this slide.

OR

5b. Click on the **Trigger automatically, after option button**. An automatic trigger will be set for this slide.

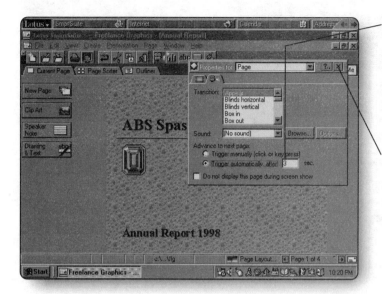

Three seconds has been preset for the amount of time for the automatic trigger. If you don't want the time to be three seconds, **type** a new **value** in the text box.

6. **Click** on the **Close button**. The Properties for Page dialog box will close.

Adding Transitions

Transitions can add visual excitement to your slide show by determining how one slide moves to the next.

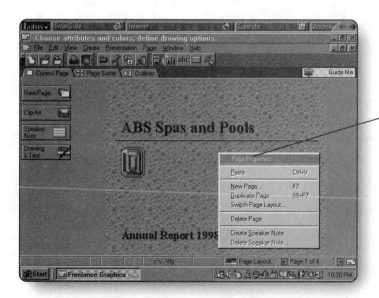

1. **Right-click** on the **slide** for which you want to set a transition. A shortcut menu will appear.

2. **Click** on **Page Properties**. The Properties for Page dialog box will open.

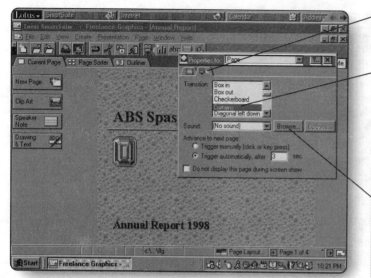

3. **Click** on the **Slide Show tab**. The Slide Show tab will appear.

4. **Click** on a **Transition** from the Transition: list box. The transition will be applied to the selected slide.

TIP

Optionally, click on Browse and select a sound to be played during the display of the current slide.

5. **Click** on the **Close button**. The Properties for Page dialog box will close.

View the screen show presentation and check out the special effects!

PART IV REVIEW QUESTIONS

1. Where did SmartMasters come from? *See "Using SmartMasters" in Chapter 15*

2. How many slides can be in a presentation? *See "Adding Slides" in Chapter 15*

3. Why might page layouts vary from slide to slide in a presentation? *See "Selecting a Page Layout" in Chapter 15*

4. When working with bulleted lists, what happens when you press Enter? *See "Working with Bulleted Lists" in Chapter 15*

5. How can you move from one slide to another when you are creating your pages? *See "Moving around in a Presentation" in Chapter 15*

6. How much text can be placed in a speaker note? *See "Adding a Speaker Note" in Chapter 16*

7. How do you provide your audience with printed copies of the slides with space for taking notes? *See "Printing a Presentation" in Chapter 16*

8. What view do you use to rearrange the slides in a slide show? *See "Rearranging Slides with the Page Sorter" in Chapter 16*

9. What is a slide show trigger? *See "Setting a Trigger" in Chapter 16*

10. In a slide show, what feature determines how one slide moves to the next? *See "Adding Transitions" in Chapter 16*

PART V
Using Organizer

$27,540.0
$31,212.7
$18,400.0
$11,235.5
$88,388.2

.00 $12,000.0

17 Discovering Organizer

The Organizer component of Lotus SmartSuite is a Personal Information Management (PIM) program. In this chapter, you'll learn how to:

✦ Identify the components of Organizer

✦ Save an Organizer file

✦ Set Organizer to open automatically

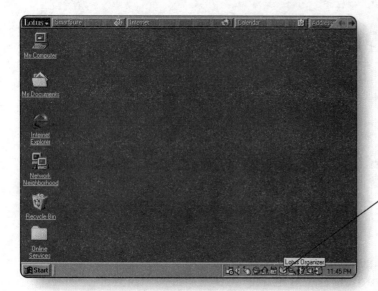

OPENING ORGANIZER

Opening Organizer is similar to other Lotus SmartSuite applications. You're only a mouse click away from getting organized!

1. Click on the **Organizer button** from the SuiteSmart tools. The Organizer program will launch with the Calendar displayed.

IDENTIFYING COMPONENTS OF ORGANIZER

Organizer is designed to replace the traditional paper-based appointment book, address book, and to do list. Not only is it the electronic equivalent of these three things, it also is a phone call manager, planner, notepad, and anniversary reminder. There are other features not covered in this book that include the ability to launch OAG FlightDisk (where you can book flights and car reservations), Web links to Zip2 maps, directions and yellow pages, and EasySync support for synchronization to hand-held organizers like the PalmPilot.

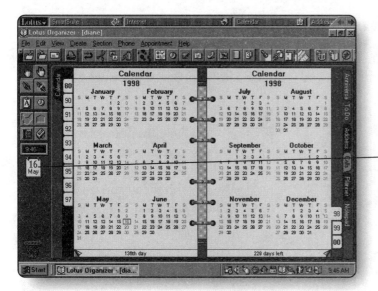

Browsing the Calendar

The first time Organizer launches, the yearly calendar will display.

1. **Click** on **today's calendar**. The current week calendar will be displayed.

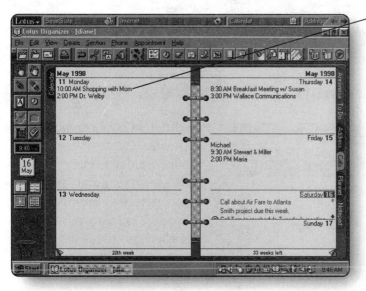

View your appointments for this week.

Browsing the To Do List

The To Do section helps you keep track of what you want to do and when you want to do it. Tasks can be prioritized.

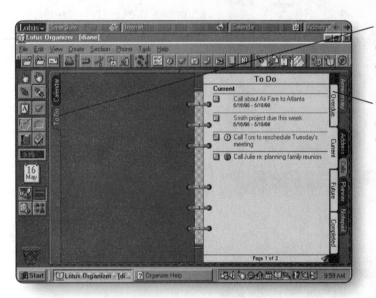

1. Click on the **To Do tab**. A list of your current tasks will be displayed.

Organizer categorizes the tasks as Overdue, Current, Future, or Completed.

Browsing the Address Book

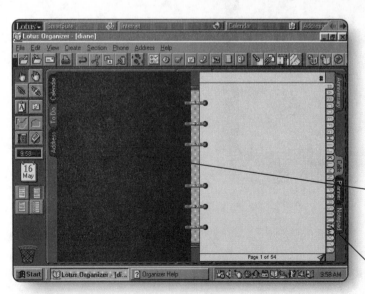

The Address Book component of Organizer stores names, business and personal addresses, phone and fax numbers, as well as e-mail addresses. You can even add miscellaneous notes about any Address Book entry.

1. Click on the **Address tab**. The index of the Address Book will be displayed.

2. Click on a **letter**. The entries for that letter will be displayed.

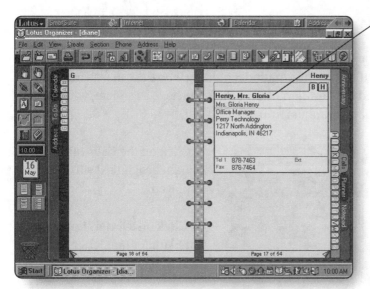

3. Double-click on an **entry**. The information about that entry will be displayed.

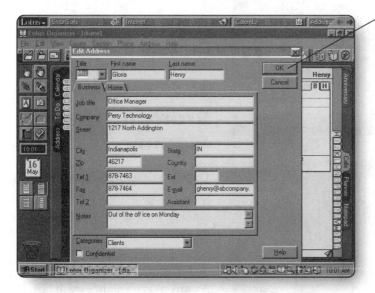

4. Click on **OK**. The entry information dialog box will close.

Browsing the Call List

The Calls section lets you keep track of your phone calls. You can record information including who the call was from or to and the duration of the call. If you have a modem, you can call phone numbers from the Call List.

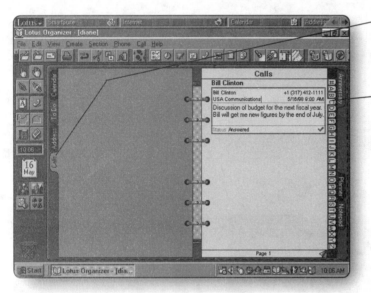

1. Click on the **Calls tab**. An alphabetical index will be displayed.

2. Click on a **letter**. Entries stored under that letter will be displayed.

Browsing the Planner

Organizer's Planner feature helps you schedule for events such as vacations, conferences, or training.

1. Click on the **Planner tab**. A current year planner will be displayed.

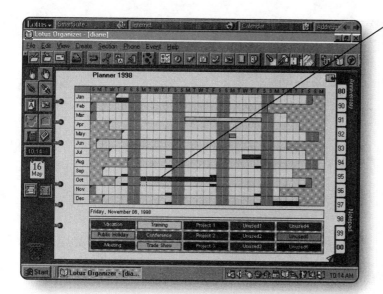

Immediately see your scheduled vacation.

Browsing the Notepad

The Organizer notepad is similar to a blank piece of paper. Store information such as directions or even store photographs or graphic images.

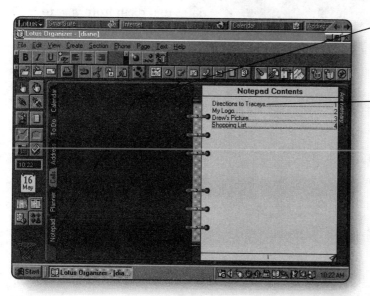

1. **Click** on the **Notepad tab**. An index of notepad entries will be displayed.

2. **Double-click** on any **entry**. The Notepad will open to the entry page.

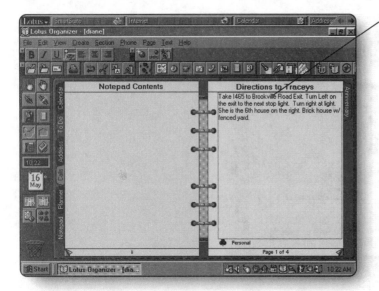

The details of the entry will be displayed.

Browsing the Anniversary Reminder

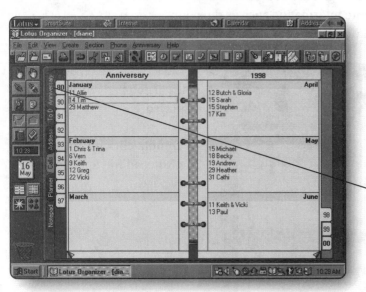

The Anniversary section helps you keep track of important dates that recur from year to year. Store birthdays, anniversaries, holidays, or other special events. You can even set an alarm to remind you that a date is approaching!

1. Click on the **Anniversary tab**. The yearly Anniversary page is displayed.

WORKING WITH YOUR ORGANIZER FILE

If you are the only or primary user of Organizer, you may want to set up Organizer to automatically open your Organizer file for you when you start Organizer.

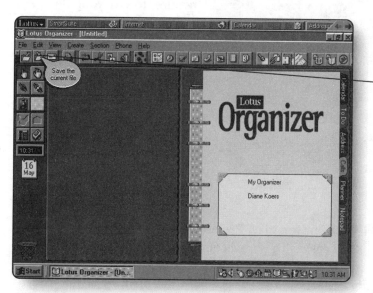

Saving Your Organizer File

1. **Click** on the **Save the current file SmartIcon**. The Save As dialog box will open.

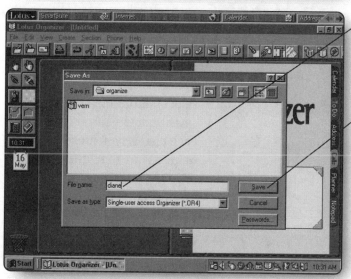

2. **Type** a **name** for the file in the File name: text box. The entered name will appear in the text box.

3. **Click** on **Save**. The file will be saved.

Letting Organizer Automatically Save Your File

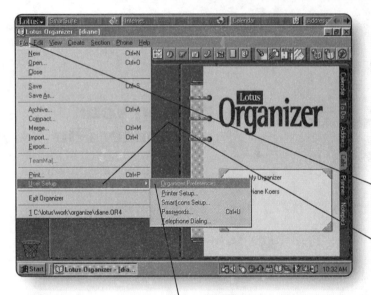

If you have made changes to your file and you exit Organizer, you will be prompted to save your file. You can set up Organizer to save your file automatically, either after every change or at a certain time interval.

1. **Click** on **File**. The File menu will appear.

2. **Click** on **User Setup**. The User Setup submenu will appear.

3. **Click** on **Organizer Preferences**. The Organizer Preferences dialog box will open.

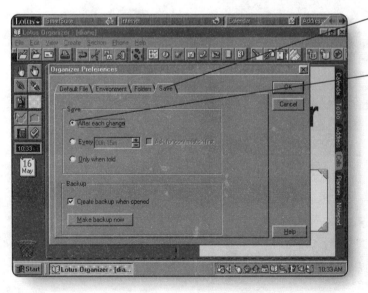

4. **Click** on the **Save tab**. The Save tab will appear.

5a. **Click** on the **After each change option button**. The option will be selected. If you select this option, Organizer saves your Organizer file after each change you make. This helps ensure that little or none of your data will be lost in the event of equipment failure or power loss.

OR

5b. **Click** on the **Every option button**. The option will be selected. If you don't want to save after every change, select this option. Organizer will save your work every 15 minutes. If you want to save more or less often than every 15 minutes, use the + and – button to select a new time interval.

6. **Click** on **OK**. The preference will be saved.

Setting Your Organizer File to Open Automatically

Using the Organizer Preferences dialog box, you want your Organizer file to open each time you start Organizer.

1. **Click** on **File**. The File menu will appear.

2. **Click** on **User Setup**. The User Setup submenu will appear.

3. **Click** on **Organizer Preferences**. The Organizer Preferences dialog box will open.

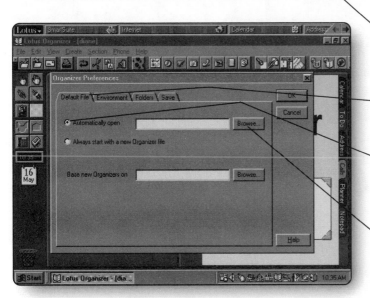

4. **Click** on the **Default File tab**. The Default File tab will appear.

5. **Click** on the **Automatically open option button**. The option will be selected.

6. **Click** on the **Browse button**. The Open dialog box will be displayed.

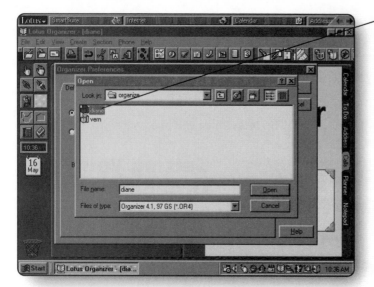

7. Double-click on the Organizer **file name** you want to automatically open. The Open dialog box will close and the file name and path will be displayed.

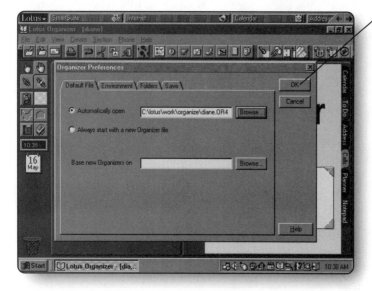

8. Click on **OK**. The preference will be saved. Each time you start Organizer, your file will automatically be displayed.

18 Working with the Calendar

The Calendar portion of Organizer is full-featured, yet remarkably easy to use. You can track appointments and meetings just as you would in its paper-based counterpart. In this chapter, you'll learn how to:

✦ Add an appointment

✦ Modify an appointment

✦ Print your appointments

✦ Change the Calendar view

ADDING AN APPOINTMENT

As far as Organizer is concerned, an appointment is anything that requires your time during a specific period. Items like meetings, calls to clients, or interviews are considered appointments.

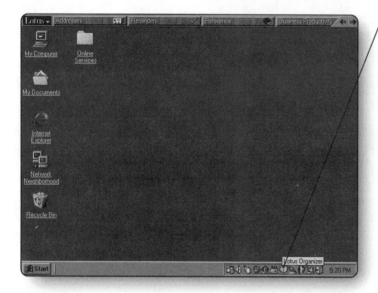

1. Click on the **Lotus Organizer button** on the SuiteStart bar. The Organizer program will launch.

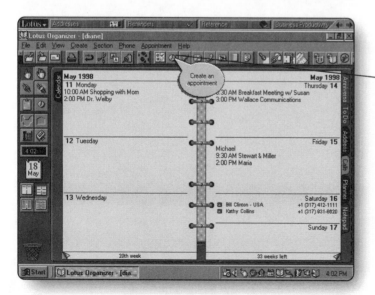

When Organizer begins, it displays a weekly calendar.

2. Click on the **Create an appointment SmartIcon**. The Create Appointment dialog box will appear.

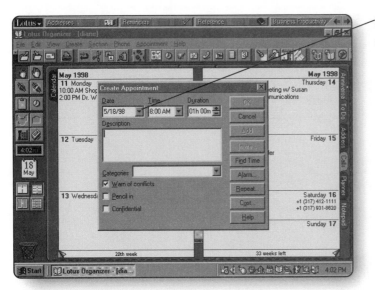

3. **Click** on the **Date down arrow**. A calendar will appear.

Today's date will appear in red.

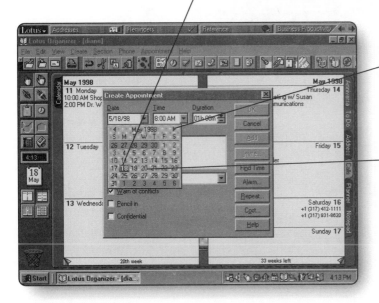

4. **Click** on the **date** of the appointment. The date will appear in the Date box.

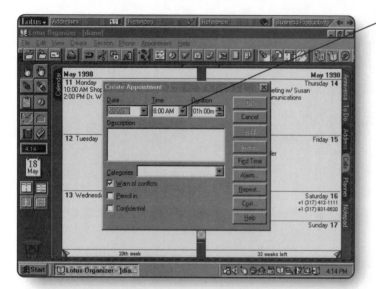

5. **Click** on the **Time down arrow**. A timeline will appear.

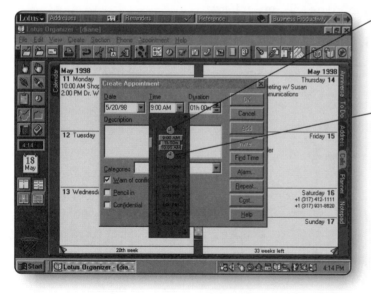

6. **Drag** the **top clock** onto the starting time of the appointment. This will set the beginning of the appointment.

7. **Drag** the **bottom clock** to the ending time of the appointment. This will set the ending of the appointment and will calculate the duration.

8. **Click** anywhere **outside of the timeline**. The timeline will close and the starting time will appear in the Time box.

9. Click on the **Description** text box. The insertion point will appear in the text box.

10. Type the **text** for the Description. The text will appear in the Description box.

11. Choose from the following **options**:

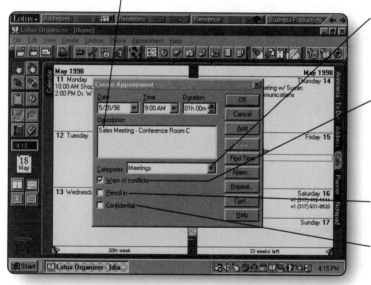

✦ If you want to assign a Categories entry to organize your entries, click on the down arrow.

✦ Warn of conflicts is preselected for you. If you do not want Organizer to warn you of conflicts, click on the check box to remove the check.

✦ To mark this appointment as tentative, check Pencil in.

✦ To make this a confidential appointment, check Confidential.

12. Click on **OK**. The appointment will be added.

CHANGING THE VIEW

When you click on the Calendar tab, a calendar of the current year appears. The Calendar can be viewed by the day, by the work week, by a calendar week, or by the month.

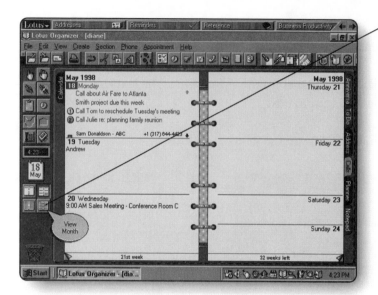

1. **Click** on a **View icon**. The view will change to reflect the selected icon.

2. **Click** on the **right turned pages**. View the next day/week/month.

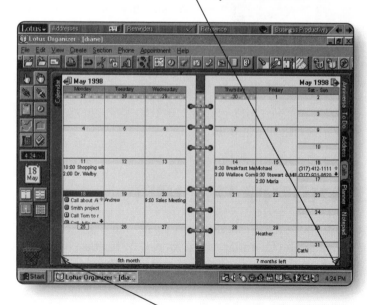

3. **Click** on the **left turned pages**. View the previous day/week/month.

MODIFYING AN APPOINTMENT

Appointments change. Often a meeting or interview is rescheduled, or you may need to change the description of an appointment.

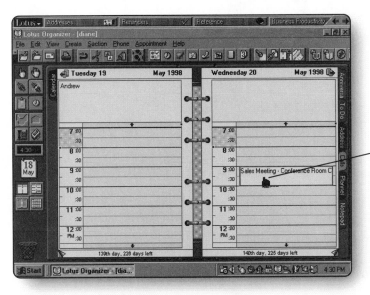

Editing an Appointment

Appointments can be edited from any of the views—daily, weekly, or monthly.

1. Double-click on the **appointment** you want to edit. The Edit Appointment dialog box will open.

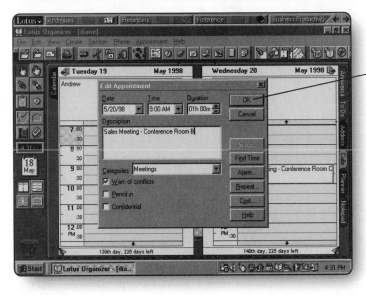

2. Make the necessary **changes** to the appointment.

3. Click on **OK**. The appointment will be updated.

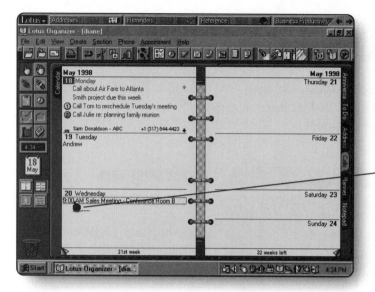

Moving an Appointment

Instead of editing an appointment to reschedule it, you can drag it to a new time slot.

1. Position the **pointer** over the time portion of the appointment. The pointer will change to a pointing finger.

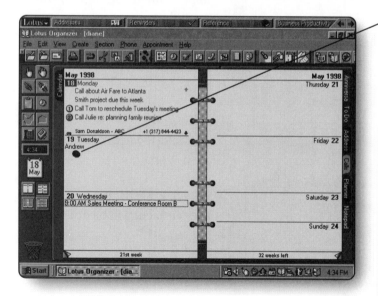

2. Click on and **drag** the **appointment** to its new time period. The pointer will change to a clock.

TIP

To move an appointment to a date not in the current week, right-click on the appointment, choose Cut, then click on the new date. Right-click and choose Paste. The appointment will be moved.

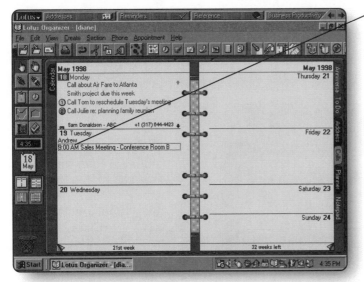

3. **Release** the **mouse button**. The appointment time will be changed.

Adding an Alarm to an Appointment

If you want Organizer to remind you of an appointment, you can set an alarm. At the assigned time before the appointment, an alarm will sound and a dialog box will appear.

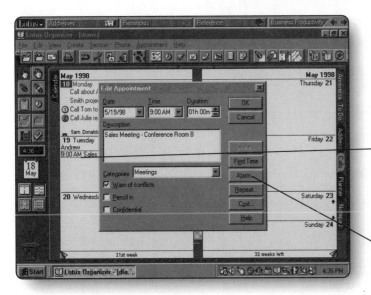

1. **Double-click** on the **appointment** you want to edit. The Edit Appointment dialog box will open.

2. **Click** on **Alarm.** The Alarm dialog box will appear.

3. Choose from the following **options**:

✦ To select whether the alarm occurs on, before, or after the start of the appointment, click on the appropriate option button.

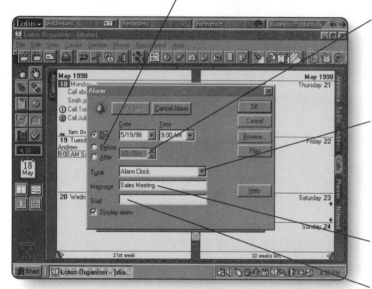

✦ Click on the plus and minus buttons to set the amount of time before or after the appointment you want the alarm to go off.

✦ The preselected tune that plays is Alarm Clock. To select a different tune, click on the down arrow at the right of the Tune list box and select from the list.

✦ Type a message in the Message text box.

✦ Organizer can start an application for you. Type the application in the Start text box.

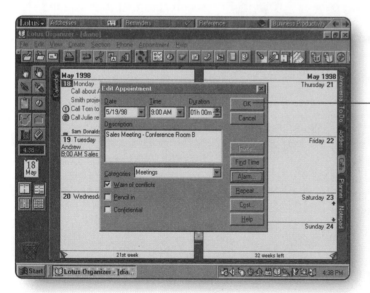

4. Click on **OK**. The alarm will be set, and the Edit Appointment dialog box will reappear.

5. Click on **OK**. The Edit Appointment dialog box will close.

NOTE

To have an alarm display in the calendar, click on View, Calendar Preferences, and place a check beside the alarm Show box (a yellow bell).

CREATING A REPEATING APPOINTMENT

A repeating appointment is one that you tell Organizer to schedule at the same time every day, week, month, and so on. This saves you the effort of having to enter the appointment repeatedly.

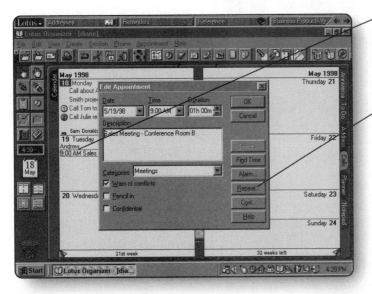

1. **Double-click** on the **appointment** you want to edit. The Edit Appointment dialog box will open.

2. **Click** on **Repeat**. The Repeat dialog box will open.

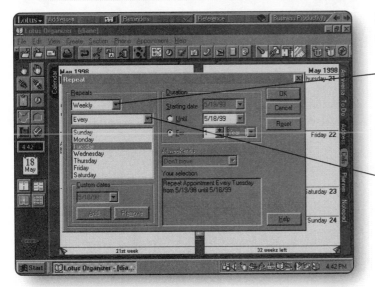

3. **Choose** from the following **options**:

+ Click on the down arrow beside the first list box in the Repeats group. Select the time period for the repeat from the list.

+ Click on the down arrow beside the second list box in the Repeats group. Select a frequency from the list.

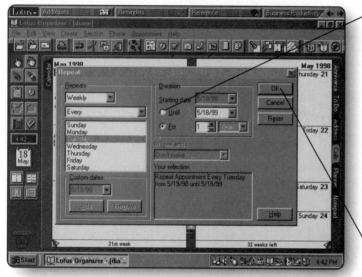

✦ To set the duration of the repeating appointment, click on either the Until or For option button. If you selected Until, click on the down arrow beside the list box and select the ending date for the repeat. If you selected For, click on the plus and minus buttons to set the numeric frequency and click on the down arrow to select the period.

4. **Click** on **OK**. The appointment will be updated and the Edit Appointment dialog box will reappear.

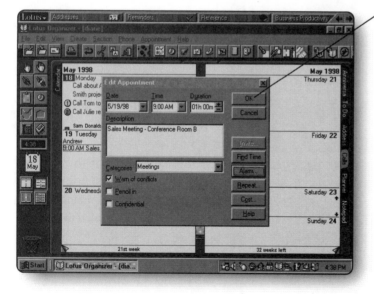

5. **Click** on **OK**. The Edit Appointment dialog box will close.

DELETING AN APPOINTMENT

If an appointment is canceled, delete it.

1. **Right-click** on the **appointment** to be deleted. A shortcut menu will appear.

2. **Click** on **Clear**. The appointment will be deleted, or if the appointment is a repeating appointment, a dialog box will appear.

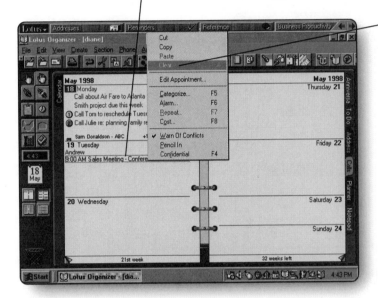

3. **Choose** an **option** from the Delete Repeating Appointment dialog box. The option will be selected.

4. **Click** on **OK**. The appointment will be deleted.

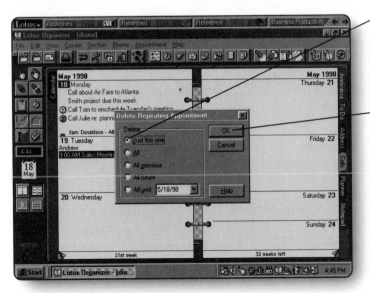

TIP

If you delete an appointment in error, click on the Undo button. The appointment will be reinstated.

PRINTING CALENDAR INFORMATION

Organizer gives you a choice of 14 different layouts for use when printing your calendar.

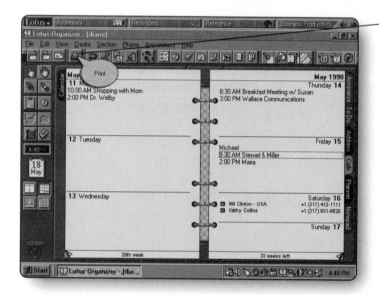

1. Click on the **Print SmartIcon**. The Print dialog box will open.

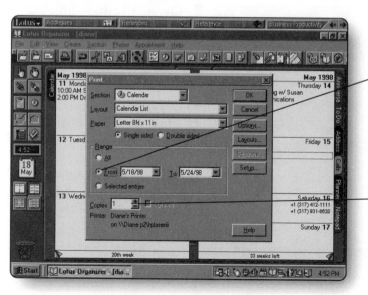

2. Choose from the following **options**:

✦ The preselected range is the current week. You can also print all your appointments or just the selected entries with the appropriate option buttons.

✦ To print more than one copy, click on the plus and minus buttons.

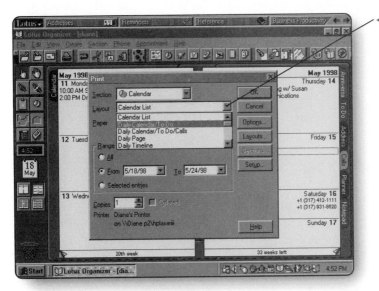

◆ To choose a different layout, click on the down arrow next to the Layout list box and make your selection.

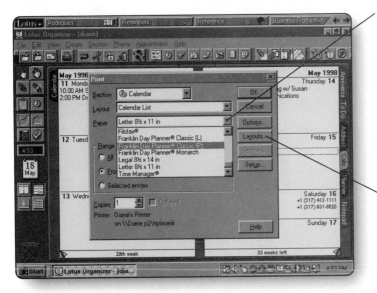

◆ If you want to print to a paper size other than the standard letter size (such as a Franklin Planner), click on the down arrow of the list box next to Paper and click on the paper size you want.

NOTE

Click on the Layouts button to modify a predefined layout to your custom specifications.

3. Click on **OK**. The appointments will be sent to the printer to print.

19 Using the To Do List

The To Do section of Organizer helps you keep track of what you want to do and when you must do it. It also allows you to assign priorities and track when a To Do task is completed. In this chapter, you'll learn how to:

✦ Enter To Do tasks

✦ Sort To Do tasks

✦ Display To Do tasks on your Calendar

✦ Print To Do tasks

ENTERING TO DO TASKS

When you create an item in your Organizer To Do list, you are creating a task. Each task can have a start and ending date associated with it as well as a priority and a category assigned to it.

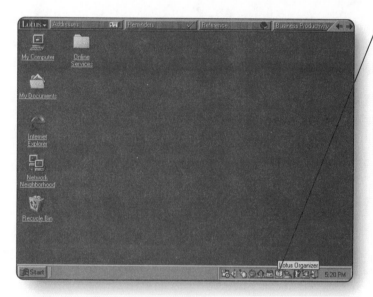

1. If Organizer is not already launched, **click** on the **Lotus Organizer** button on the SuiteStart bar. The Organizer program will begin.

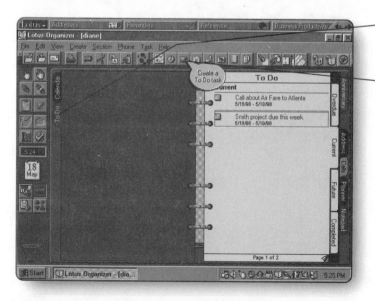

2. Click on the **To Do tab**. The To Do tab will appear.

3. Click on the **Create a To Do task SmartIcon**. The Create Task dialog box will open.

4. **Type** the **description** of the task in the Description text box.

5. **Choose** from the following **options**:

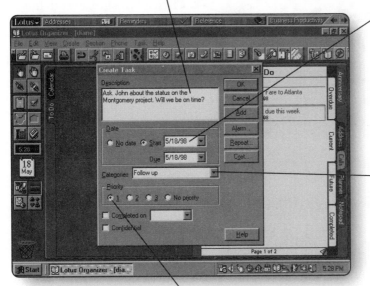

◆ You can choose to assign a date to the task. Click on No date if you do not want to assign a date. Click on Start if you do want to use dates with this task. You can select a starting and due date by clicking on the down arrow.

◆ If you want to be able to group your tasks by categories, click on the down arrow at the right of the Categories list box and select one.

◆ Tasks do not have a priority assigned to them by default. The highest priority is 1; the lowest is 3. From the Priority group, click on the priority setting you want to use with this task.

6. **Click** on **OK**. The task will be added to the To Do list.

CHANGING THE STATUS TO COMPLETED

After you are finished with a task, you'll want to mark it as completed.

Marking a Task as Completed Today

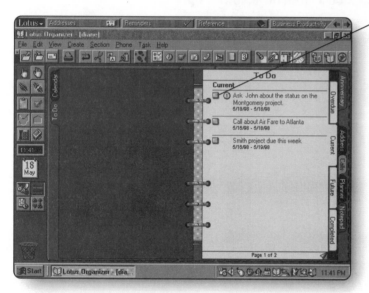

1. Click on the **box** next to the task to place a check mark in it. The task will be marked as completed as of today and will disappear from the Current page of the To Do list.

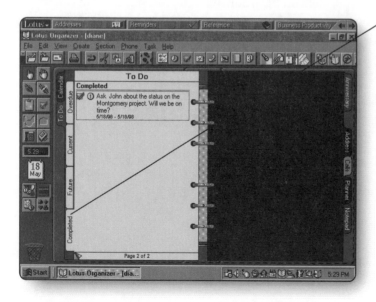

Completed tasks can be viewed on the Completed tab of the To Do list.

Marking a Task as Completed for a Day Other than Today

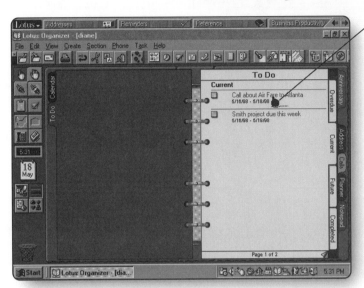

1. Double-click on the **task** you want to mark completed. The Edit Task dialog box will open.

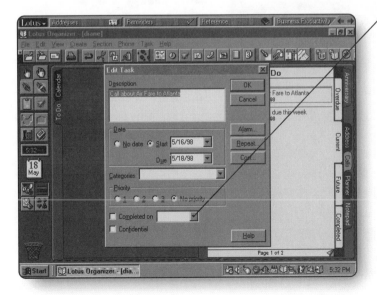

2. Click on the **down arrow** next to the Completed on text box. A calendar will appear.

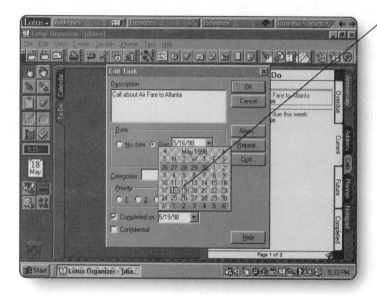

3. Click on the **date** the task was completed. The date will be entered in the Completed on text box.

4. Click on **OK**. The task will be updated.

SORTING TO DO TASKS AND WORKING WITH CATEGORIES

Organizer lets you sort your tasks by either priority, status, start date, or category. You do not have to use only the categories provided with Organizer—you can create you own.

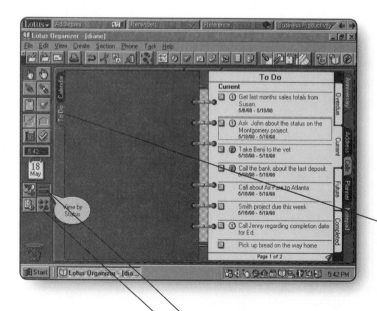

Sorting To Do Tasks Using the View Icons

The four ways the tasks can be sorted are by status, category, priority, or by start date. The default choice is to sort them by status.

1. Click on the **To Do tab**. The To Do tab will appear.

2. Choose one of the following **options**:

◆ To sort tasks by status, click on the View by Status icon.

◆ To sort tasks by category, click on the View by Category icon.

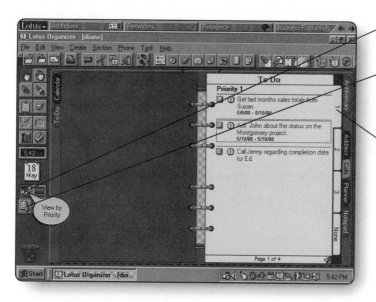

♦ To sort tasks by priority, click on the View by Priority icon.

♦ To sort tasks by start date, click on the View by Start Date icon.

Depending on the view you are using, different tabs will display vertically along the right side of the page.

Adding a New Category

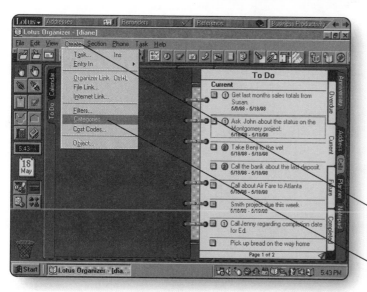

You can use categories to organize the different objects in Organizer such as tasks. If you are working on a project, for example, you may want to create a category for that project and assign the category to any appointments or tasks that you associated with that project.

1. Click on **Create**. The Create menu will appear.

2. Click on **Categories**. The Categories dialog box will open.

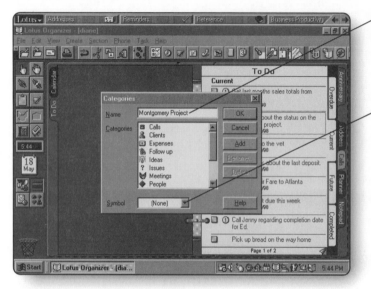

3. Type the **text** for the name of the category in the Name text box. The text will be displayed in the Name box.

4. Click on the **down arrow** at the right of the Symbol list box to select a symbol for the new category. A list of symbols will appear.

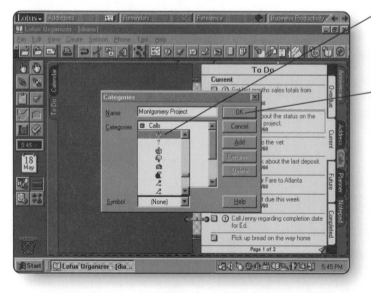

5. Click on the **symbol** you want. The symbol will be highlighted.

6. Click on **OK**. The new category will be added.

Displaying Symbols on the To Do list

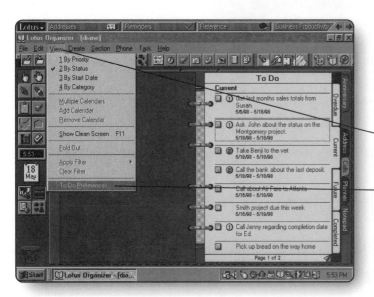

By default, the symbols you assign to different categories do not display on the To Do list. If you want to display them, you must edit the To Do Preferences.

1. Click on **View**. The View menu will appear.

2. Click on **To Do Preferences**. The To Do Preferences dialog box will open.

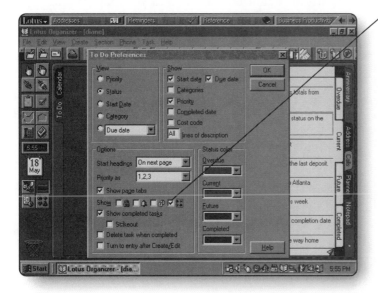

3. Click on the **Show check boxes**. A check will appear in the check boxes.

4. Click on **OK**. The To Do Preferences dialog box will close.

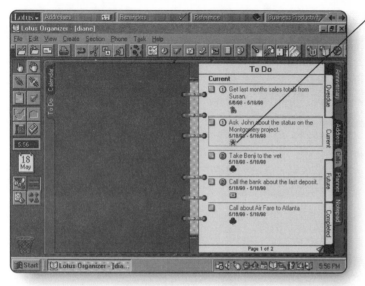

A different icon will display for each category.

DISPLAYING TO DO TASKS IN YOUR CALENDAR

Because of the nature of tasks, you may want to display them in other parts of Organizer. For example, you may want to show your To Do tasks in your Calendar.

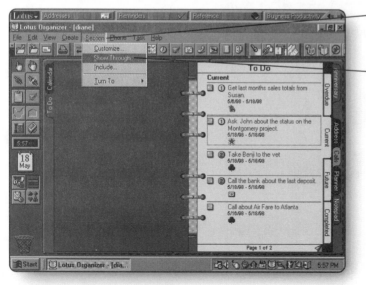

1. Click on **Section**. The Section menu will appear.

2. Click on **Show Through**. The Show Through dialog box will open.

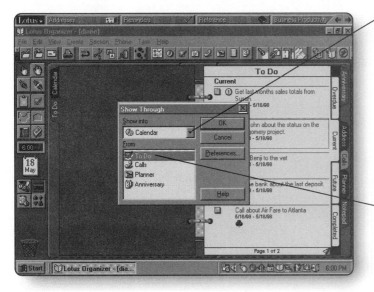

3. Click on the **down arrow** of the Show into list box. The list of available sections will appear. There are two areas that you can show into, Calendar and Planner.

4. Click on **Calendar**. The Calendar will display in the Show into box.

5. Click on a **section** in the From list box. The section will be selected.

6. Click on **OK**. The show through setting will be applied.

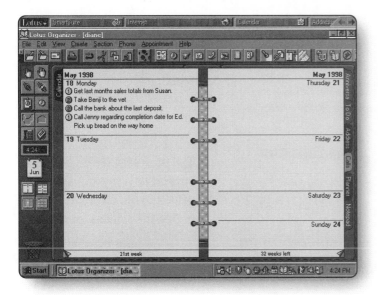

NOTE
The items will be listed in the section you selected. They integrate with the other items in that section so that you can see them all at the same time.

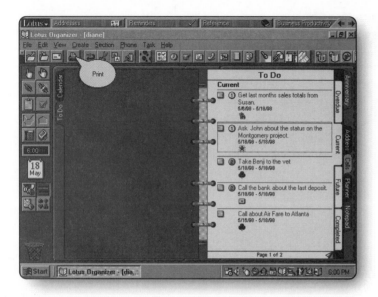

PRINTING TO DO LIST ITEMS

Organizer provides nine different page layouts for printing your To Do lists.

1. Click on the **Print SmartIcon**. The Print dialog box will open.

2. Choose from the following **options**:

♦ To choose a different layout, click on the down arrow at the right of the Layout list box and make your selection.

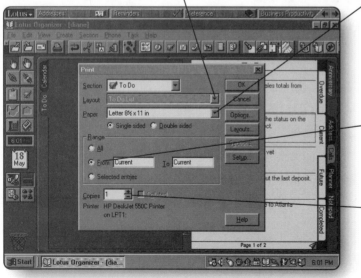

♦ If you want to print to a paper size other than the standard letter size, click on the down arrow of the Paper list box and click on the paper size you want.

♦ The preselected range is the current day. You can also print all your appointments or just the selected entries.

♦ To print more than one copy, click on the plus and minus buttons of the Copies list box.

3. Click on **OK**. The pages will be sent to the printer.

20 Tracking Addresses and Phone Calls

Two of the many advantages of Organizer are its integrated address book and call tracking features. Gone are the days when you had a separate address book and call log. Organizer's Address section lets you track a large variety of information about people, including both business and home information. The Calls section lets you create Calls entries to track your phone calls. In this chapter, you'll learn how to:

✦ Work with addresses

✦ Use Organizer's follow-up feature

WORKING WITH ADDRESSES

Organizer's Address section is much more sophisticated than a traditional paper-based address book. Beyond just using it as a repository for information, you can use it to sort and view your Address records by last name, company, category, or ZIP code.

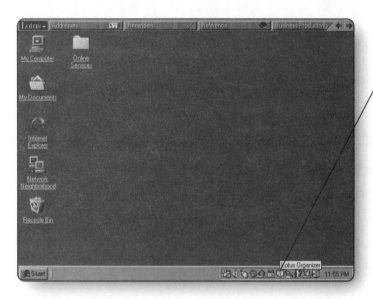

Adding an Address

1. If Organizer is not already launched, **click** on the **Organizer** button on the SuiteStart bar. The Organizer program will begin.

2. **Click** on the **Address tab**. The Address section will appear.

3. **Click** on the **Create an Address record SmartIcon**. The Create Address dialog box will appear.

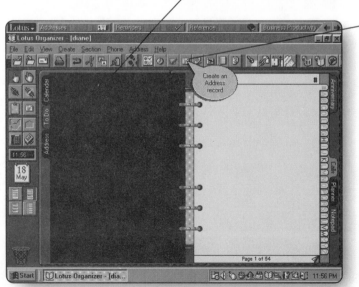

4. **Click** on the **down arrow** to select a Title. The selected title will be listed in the Title list box.

5. **Press** the **Tab key**. The First name text box will be selected.

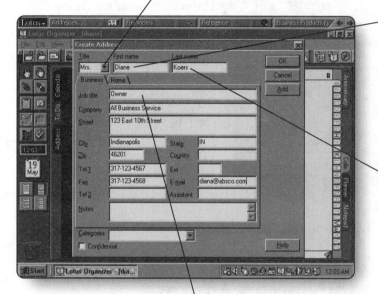

6. **Type** the **text** for the first name for the entry. The first name will appear in the First name text box.

7. **Press** the **Tab key**. The Last name text box will be selected.

8. **Type** the **text** for the last name for the entry. The last name will appear in the Last name text box.

9. If the contact is a business contact, **type** available **information** on the Business tab. Use the Tab key to move the insertion point from field to field.

NOTE

Type the information as you want it to appear when printed, including capitalization and punctuation.

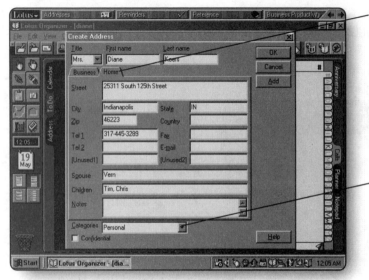

10. **Click** on the **Home** tab. The Home tab comes to the front.

11. **Type** any available **information** for the contact's home address. Use the Tab key to move the insertion point from field to field.

12. Optionally, **click** on the **Categories down arrow** and select a category for the contact. The selected category will be displayed.

13. **Click** on **OK**. The Address record will be added.

Modifying an Address

1. **Click** on the **Address tab**. The Address section will come to the front.

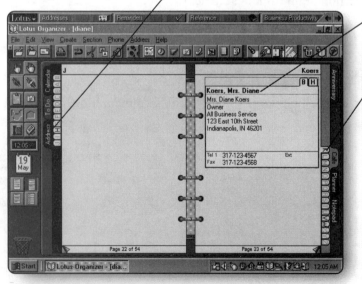

2. **Click** on the **tab** where the address record is located. The record's page will appear.

3. **Double-click** on the **record** you want to edit. The Edit Address dialog box will open.

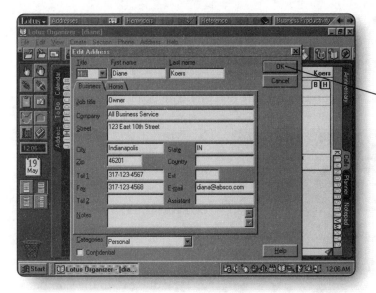

4. Enter the necessary **changes**. The changes will be reflected in the dialog box.

5. Click on **OK**. The record will be updated.

Creating Multiple Address Records for the Same Company

When you create a new address record, Organizer checks to see whether that company has been entered before. If it has, Organizer gives you the option of using the same company information for this record that was entered before. As you can imagine, this is a popular and time-saving feature of Organizer!

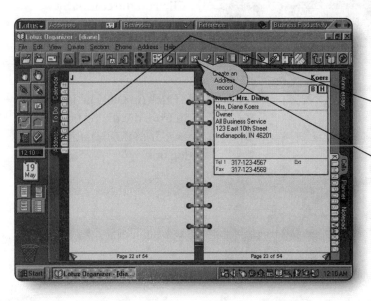

1. Click on the **Address tab**. The Address section will appear.

2. Click on the **Create an Address record SmartIcon**. The Create Address dialog box will appear.

3. **Enter** the **information** for the Title, First name, and Last name as you learned in the previous section. The information will be displayed in the appropriate boxes.

4. **Click** on the **Job title text box**. The box will be selected.

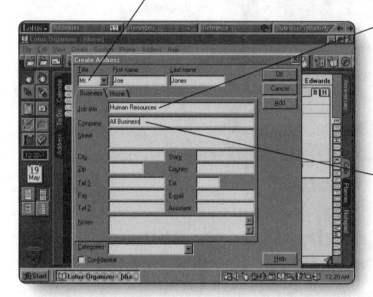

5. **Type** the **text** for the Job title. The text will appear in the dialog box.

6. **Press** the **Tab key**. The Company text box will be selected.

7. **Type** the **text** for the Company text box. The text will appear in the dialog box.

8. **Press** the **Tab key**. The Similar Address Found dialog box will appear.

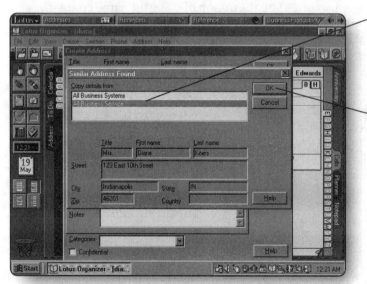

9. **Click** on the **company** you want to use. The address information for that company will appear.

10. **Click** on **OK**. The information from the dialog box will be entered into the Create Address dialog box.

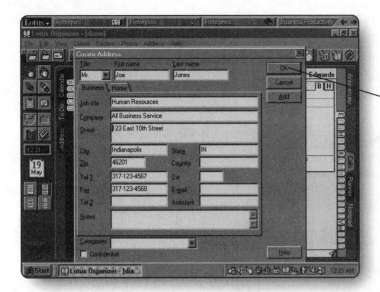

11. **Enter or edit** any **additional information** needed. The changes will be displayed.

12. **Click** on **OK**. The record will be added.

Sorting Addresses

Organizer lets you view your addresses by last name, company name, ZIP code, or category.

1. **Click** on **View**. The View menu will appear.

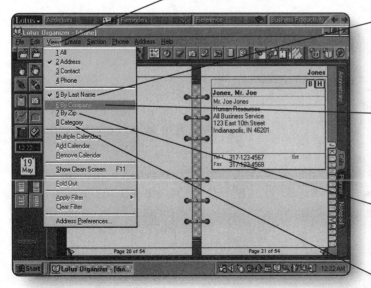

2a. **Click** on **By Last Name**. The addresses will be sorted by last name.

OR

2b. **Click** on **By Company**. The addresses will be sorted by company.

OR

2c. **Click** on **By Zip**. The addresses will be sorted by ZIP code.

OR

2d. **Click** on **Category**. The addresses will be sorted by category.

Printing Address Information

You can print your addresses using six different formats including address cards, Rolodex cards, envelopes, and phone lists.

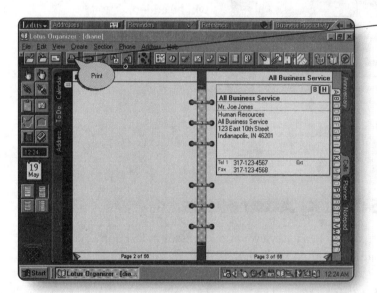

1. Click on the **Print SmartIcon**. The Print dialog box will open.

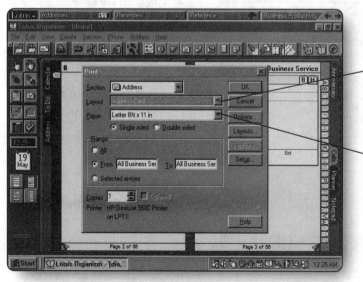

2. Choose from the following **options:**

✦ To choose a different layout, click on the down arrow at the right of the Layout list box and make your selection.

✦ If you want to print to a paper size other than the standard letter size, click on the down arrow of the list box next to Paper and click on the paper size you want.

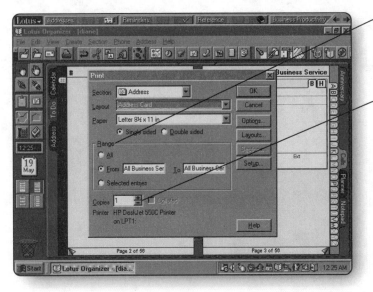

✦ The preselected range is the current record. You can also print all your addresses or just the selected entries.

✦ To print more than one copy, click on the plus and minus buttons.

3. Click on **OK**. The pages will be sent to the printer.

TRACKING PHONE CALLS

A task that many of us are required to do is to keep a call log so that we can track our calls. A call entry is easily tied to the address book because you can select from any of your address book entries when making the call.

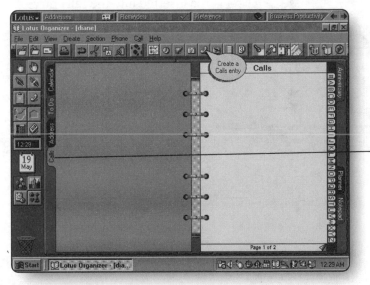

Adding a Call Entry

Call entries can be started by selecting the last name of a person from your Address Book.

1. Click on the **Calls tab**. The Calls section will appear.

2. Click on the **Create a Calls entry SmartIcon.** The Create Call dialog box will open.

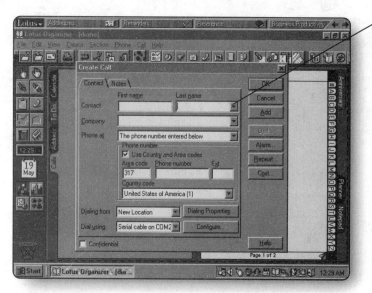

3. Click on the **down arrow** of the Last name list box. A list of names from the address book will appear.

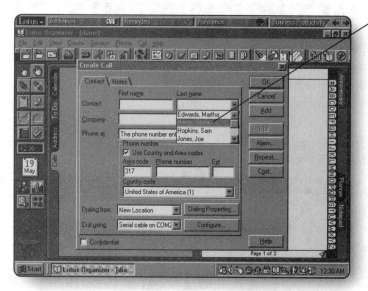

4. Click on the **name** of the person you are calling. The name will be selected. The information entered for that person when you created the address entry will automatically be inserted into the call entry.

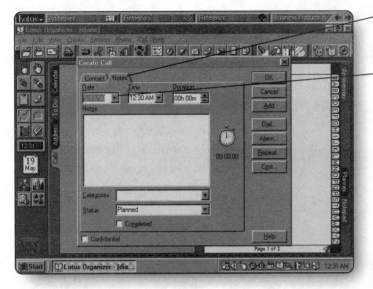

5. Click on the **Notes tab**. The Notes tab will appear.

6. Click on the **down arrow** for the Date. A calendar will appear.

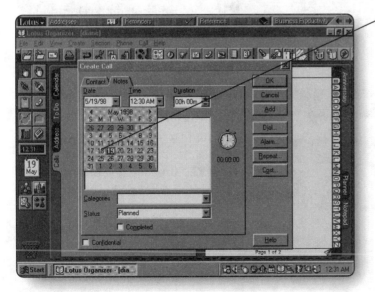

7. Click on the **date** that you made the call. The date will be entered into the form.

8. **Click** on the **down arrow** for the Time. A timeline will appear.

9. **Click** on the **time** that the call was made. The time will be entered into the form.

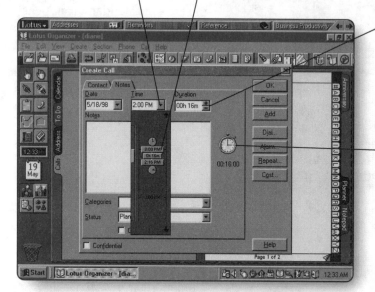

10. **Click** on the **plus** and **minus buttons** to set the Duration. The duration of the call will be increased or decreased.

TIP

Click on the stopwatch when the call is first initiated and then click on it again when the call is completed. The stopwatch will indicate total elapsed time and enter that information in the Duration text box.

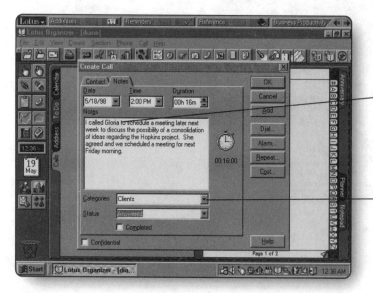

11. **Click** on the **Notes** text box. The blinking insertion point will appear in the Notes box.

12. **Type** the **text** of any notes you want to make.

13. **Choose** from the following **options:**

✦ If you want to assign a category to this call, click on the down arrow next to the Categories list box and click on the category you want to use.

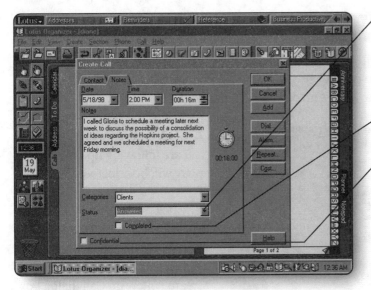

♦ To change the status of the call, click on the down arrow beside the Status list box and click on the correct status for this call.

♦ If this call topic or series is Completed, check this box.

♦ If you want to mark this call as Confidential, check this box.

14. **Click** on **OK**. The call entry will be created.

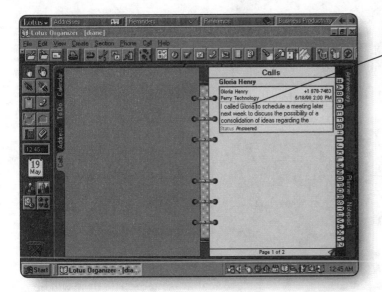

TIP

Double-click on a call entry to edit it.

Tracking Follow-up Calls

Often one call leads to another call. This second call is a follow-up call. When you create a follow-up call entry, Organizer links the follow-up call entry to the original call entry.

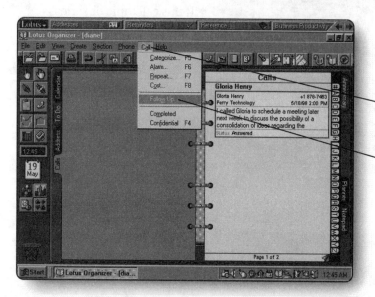

1. Click on the **Calls entry** that you are following up on. The entry will be selected.

2. Click on **Call**. The Call menu will appear.

3. Click on **Follow Up**. The Create Follow up Call dialog box will open.

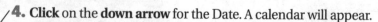

4. Click on the **down arrow** for the Date. A calendar will appear.

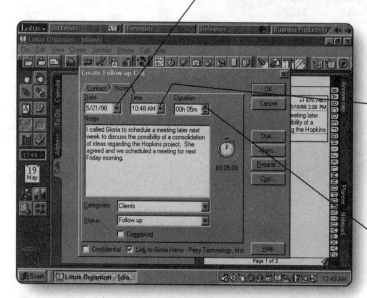

5. Click on the **date** that you made the call. The date will be entered into the form.

6. Click on the **down arrow** for the Time. A timeline will appear.

7. Click on the **time** that the call was made. The time will be entered into the form.

8. Click on the **plus** and **minus** buttons to set the Duration. The duration of the call will be increased or decreased.

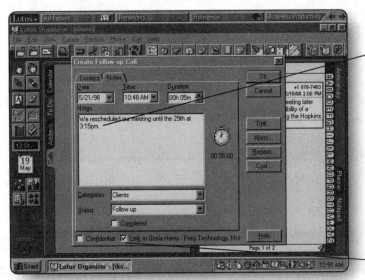

9. Click on the **Notes** text box.

10. Type the **text** of any notes you want to make.

Notice the link to the original call.

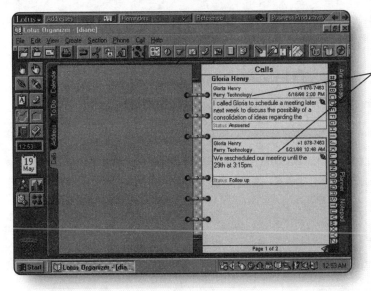

11. Click on **OK**. The follow-up call entry will be created.

Both calls are listed in the Calls list.

PART V REVIEW QUESTIONS

1. **What kind of program is Organizer?** *See "Identifying Components of Organizer" in Chapter 17*

2. **How can you make your Organizer entries save automatically?** *See "Letting Organizer Automatically Save Your File" in Chapter 17*

3. **When viewing your monthly Calendar, how is today's date displayed?** *See "Adding an Appointment" in Chapter 18*

4. **How can Organizer remind you of an appointment?** *See "Adding an Alarm to an Appointment" in Chapter 18*

5. **What is a repeating appointment?** *See "Creating a Repeating Appointment" in Chapter 18*

6. **What kind of dates can be assigned to a To Do task?** *See "Entering To Do Tasks" in Chapter 19*

7. **What are the other two areas of Organizer where you can see your To Do list?** *See "Displaying To Do Tasks in Your Calendar" in Chapter 19*

8. **What happens when you enter a company name that has been used before?** *See "Creating Multiple Address Records for the Same Company" in Chapter 20*

9. **What are the four ways you can sort address book information?** *See "Sorting Addresses" in Chapter 20*

10. **How can you edit a call entry?** *See "Adding a Call Entry" in Chapter 20*

PART VI

Using Approach

21 Creating a Database

Whether or not you realize it, you use databases every day. Your phone book is a database, your television show listing is a database, and even a cookbook is a database. A database in its most simple form is an organized list of information. Lotus SmartSuite provides a database application called Approach that allows you to create and manage databases. In this chapter, you'll learn how to:

+ **Use Approach's SmartMasters template**

+ **Work with fields and records**

+ **Enter data into a database**

+ **Move around in a database**

+ **Edit, find, and sort records**

+ **View the database in a worksheet view**

UNDERSTANDING FIELDS AND RECORDS

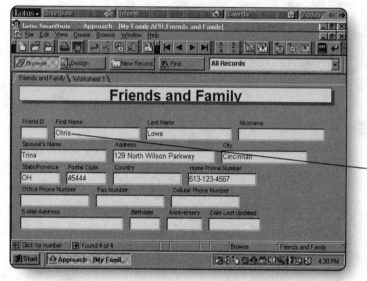

Information in a database is grouped into records and fields.

✦ A *record* is all the information about one person, product, event, and so on. Every record in a database contains the same fields.

✦ A name or address is in a *field* of the record. You can enter text, numbers, dates, or formulas in a field.

CREATING A DATABASE

There are several basic ways to create a database using Approach. One method is to use the traditional approach of starting from scratch, and another is to use a SmartMaster template. Similar to SmartMasters in other Lotus applications, Approach's SmartMasters allow you to quickly create a database with a minimum amount of work on your part.

Creating a Database Using a Template

Creating a database using a SmartMaster template saves you time because the template provides you with a predefined set of field definitions for your database file. The SmartMasters provided by Approach are designed for both business and personal use.

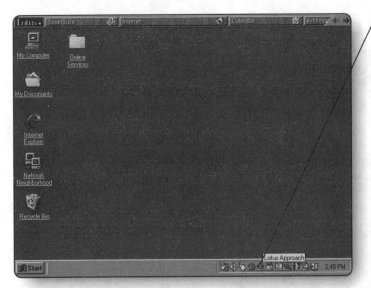

1. Click on the **Lotus Approach SuiteStart icon**. The Welcome to Lotus Approach dialog box will open.

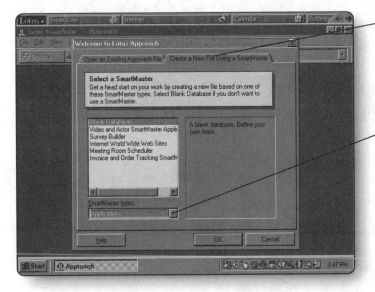

2. If necessary, **Click** on the **Create a New File Using a SmartMaster tab**. The Create a New File Using a SmartMaster tab will appear.

3. Click on the **down arrow** under SmartMaster types. A list of available SmartMaster types will appear.

4. Click on **Templates**. A list of available templates will appear.

5. Click on the **template** you want. The template name will be highlighted.

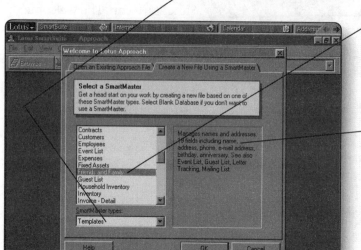

NOTE
A description of the selected template appears in the box on the right side of the dialog box. The description provides information about the use of the template, states how many fields are in the database definition, and recommends other templates to examine.

6. Click on **OK**. The New dialog box will open.

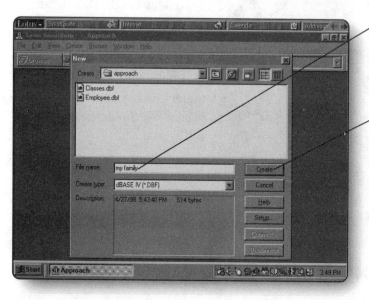

7. Type the **name** of the new file in the File name text box. The file name will appear in the text box.

8. Click on **Create**. The newly created database appears. You will notice that the fields have already been added for you. You are ready to start entering your data.

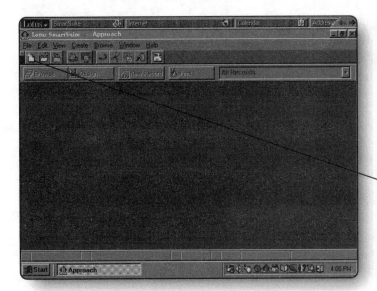

Creating a Database from Scratch

If you do not want to use a SmartMaster, you can create your own database from scratch.

1. **Click** on the **Create a new database file SmartIcon**. The New dialog box will open.

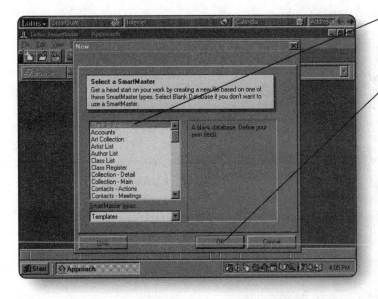

2. **Click** on **Blank Database** from the list box. The item will be selected.

3. **Click** on **OK**. The New dialog box will appear.

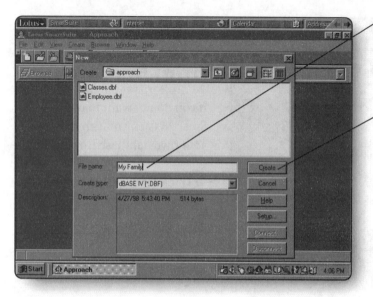

4. Type a **File name** for the database in the File name text box. The name will be assigned to the database.

5. Click on **Create**. The Creating New Database dialog box will open.

6. Type a **name** for the first field. The field will be added to the database.

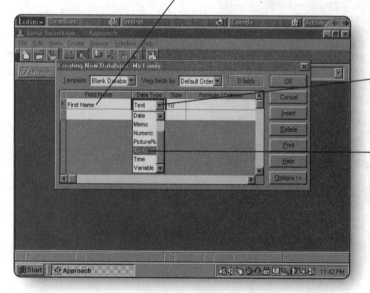

7. Press the **Tab key**. The Data Type column will be selected.

8. Click on the **down arrow** in the Data Type column. A list of available field types will appear.

9. Click on the **field type** for this field. The field type will be assigned to the field.

10. Press the **Tab key**. The Size column will be selected.

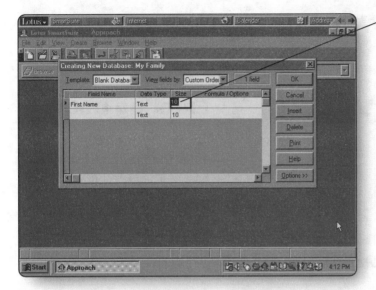

11. **Type** a **Size** for the field. The field will be made that size.

TIP

Certain field types, such as Date and Memo, will not allow you to enter a field size.

12. **Press** the **Tab key**. The Field Name column will be selected.

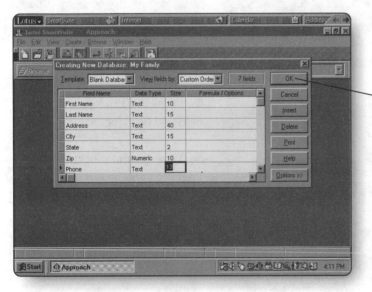

13. **Repeat steps 8** through **13** until all fields have been defined.

14. **Click** on **OK**. The database will be created.

NOTE

The database is ready for you to add data to it. Chapter 22, "Editing the Structure of a Database," will show you how to change the form.

WORKING WITH DATA

After you have created the database and form, you are ready to add and work with the data for your database.

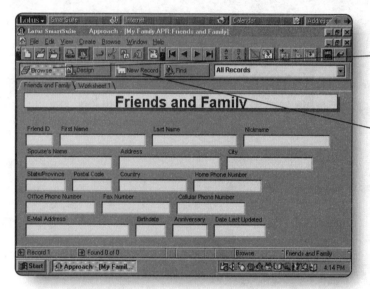

Entering Data

1. **Click** on the **Browse button**. Either the first record in the database or a blank record will appear.

2. **Click** on the **New Record button** if a blank record does not appear. A blank record will appear.

> **TIP**
> If you are working with a new database that does not contain any records, skip step 2.

3. **Type** the **data** for the first field. The data will be entered.

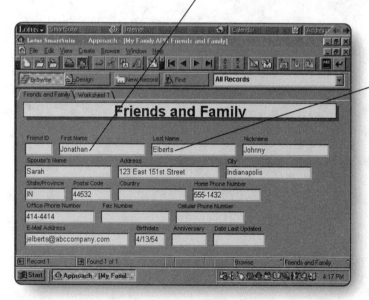

4. **Press** the **Tab key**. The next field will be selected.

5. **Type** the **data** for the field. That data will be entered.

6. **Repeat steps 4** and **5** until you have entered data for the fields on the form.

> **NOTE**
> If you want to add another record, either press the Tab key when you are finished entering data for the last field or click on the New Record button.

Moving Around in the Database

After you have inputted several records, you may need to return to a specific record to review it.

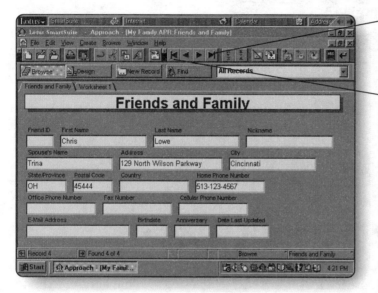

1. **Click** on the **Go to last record SmartIcon button**. The last record will appear.

2. **Click** on the **Go to first record SmartIcon button**. The first record will appear.

3. **Click** on the **Go to next record SmartIcon button**. The next record will appear.

4. **Click** on the **Go to previous record SmartIcon button**. The previous record will appear.

Editing Records

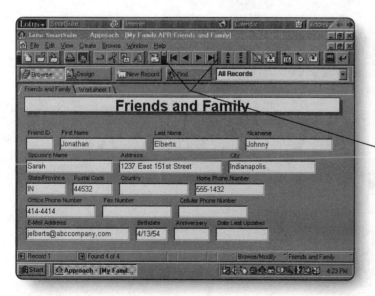

Data sometimes needs to be changed after it has been entered into your database. You may have typed something in wrong or the data needs to be updated.

1. **Click** on one of the **Go to SmartIcons**.

By using the Go to SmartIcons, you can move through the records until you locate the one you need to modify.

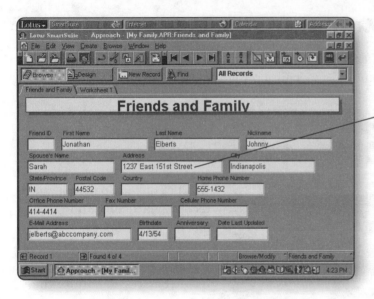

2. Click on the **field** you need to change. The blinking insertion point will appear in the data field.

3. Enter the **change**. The data will be modified.

FINDING RECORDS

You may need to locate a specific record in your database. Approach makes this easy to do using the Find button. To find records, you must create a condition to be matched. If you want to locate all the records with a certain price, Approach has a feature called the Find Assistant to assist you.

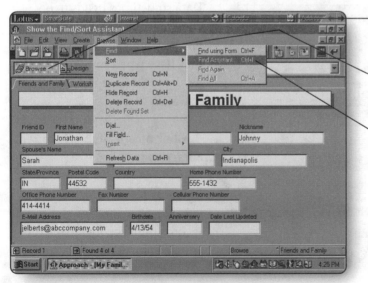

1. Click on the **Browse menu**. The Browse menu will appear.

2. Click on **Find**. The Find submenu will appear.

3. Click on **Find Assistant**. The Find/Sort Assistant dialog box will open.

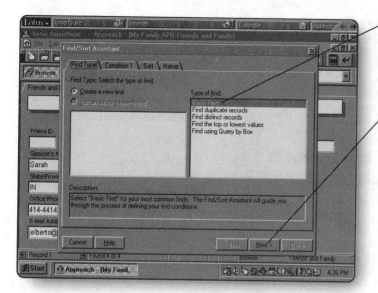

4. **Click** on the **Type of find list box**. A description of that find type will appear in the box at the bottom of the dialog box.

5. **Click** on **Next**. The Condition tab will appear.

6. **Click** on the **field** for which you want to create a condition from the Fields list box. The field will be added to the find condition.

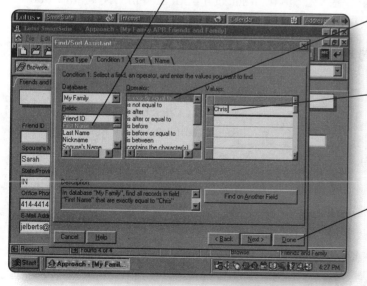

7. **Click** on the **Operator** you want. The operator will be added to the find condition.

8. **Click** on the **Values text box**. The box will be selected.

9. **Type** a **value**. The value will be added to the find condition.

10. **Click** on **Done**. The records that match the find condition will be available for you to work with.

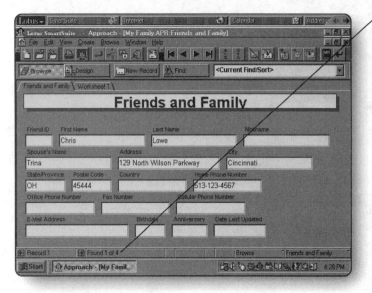

After you find the records, you can look at them and modify them just as you normally would. The status bar lets you know how many of the records in your database match the find condition.

Naming a Find

If you create a find that you want to use in the future, you can name it. You can then select it from the Find Assistant when you need it.

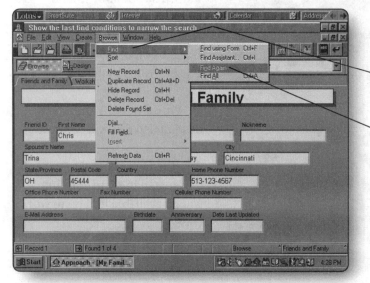

1. Click on **Browse**. The Browse menu will appear.

2. Click on **Find**. The Find submenu will appear.

3. Click on **Find Again**. The Find Assistant dialog box will open.

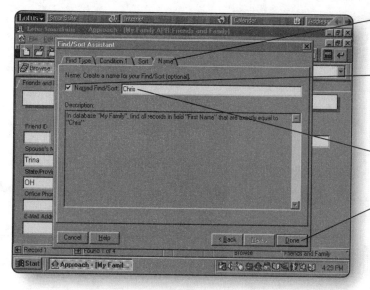

4. Click on the **Name tab**. The Name tab will appear.

5. Click on the **Named Find/Sort text box**. The text box will be selected.

6. Type the **name** of the find. A check will appear in the check box.

7. Click on **Done**. The find will be named.

TIP

To view all the records in the database, press Ctrl+A.

SORTING RECORDS

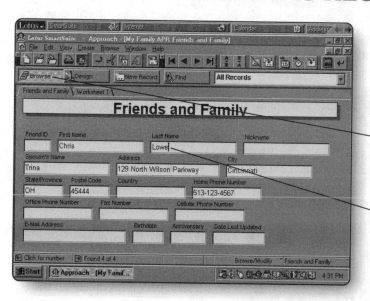

Approach provides two SmartIcons for sorting your records: Sort field in ascending order and Sort field in descending order.

1. Click on the **Browse button**. The form will be placed in browse mode.

2. Click on the **field** you want to sort on. The field will be selected.

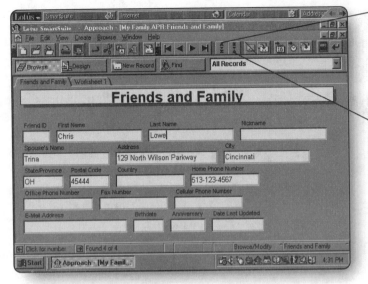

3a. **Click** on the **Sort field in ascending order SmartIcon**. The records will be sorted in ascending order.

OR

3b. **Click** on the **Sort field in descending order SmartIcon**. The records will be sorted in descending order.

LOOKING AT THE WORKSHEET VIEW

Database information can be viewed in several different perspectives. The form view you've been working with will show one record at a time, whereas worksheet view looks like a spreadsheet and will show many records at a time in a horizontal format.

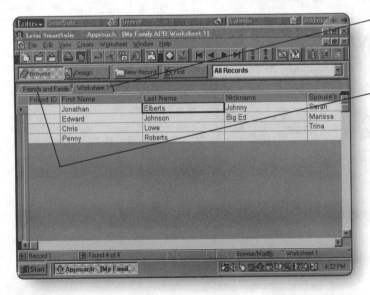

1. **Click** on a **Worksheet**. The records are displayed in a worksheet.

2. **Click** on the **"form" tab**. The database is again displayed one record at a time.

NOTE

The name of the "form" tab will vary depending on the name of your database.

22 Editing the Structure of a Database

When the newly created database appears, it displays the fields on a form. This form is used to input your data. You may want to make changes to your form (and your database), such as changing the title of the form, deleting fields, or adding fields. In this chapter, you'll learn how to:

✦ Change the title on a form

✦ Change the name of a form

✦ Add, delete, or move a field

CHANGING THE TITLE ON THE FORM

You will notice that when creating a blank database, the form has the title, "Blank Database." Changing this title requires that you use design mode.

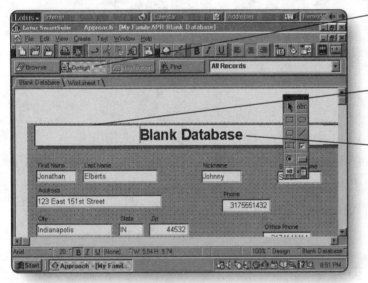

1. **Click** on the **Design button**. The form will be placed in design mode.

2. **Click** on the **title box**. The title box will be selected.

3. **Click** on the **title box** again. The title box will be placed in edit mode and a blinking insertion point will appear.

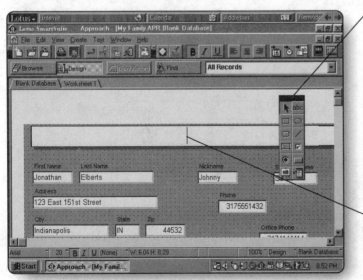

A forms toolbox will appear.

NOTE

Do not double-click on the title box. Double-clicking on it will produce the Properties dialog box, which is not required for this step.

4. **Press** the **Delete key** or the **Backspace key** until the current text is removed. The text will be deleted.

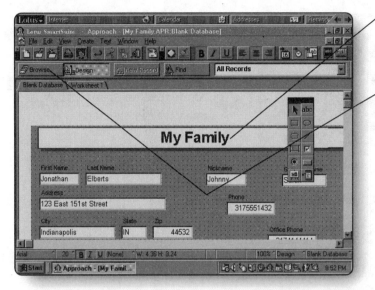

5. **Type** the **new text** for the title. A new title will be created for display on the form.

6. **Click** on **Browse**. The form will be returned to Browse mode.

CHANGING THE NAME OF A FORM

The name of a form appears on its tab. When your database is first created, its form is named Blank Database.

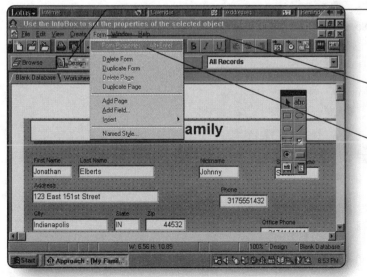

1. **Click** on the **Design button**. The form will be placed in design mode.

2. **Click** on **Form**. The Form menu will appear.

3. **Click** on **Form Properties**. The Properties for Form dialog box will open.

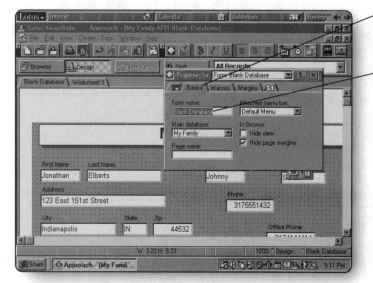

4. Click on the **Basics tab**. The Basics tab will appear.

5. Double-click on the **Form Name text box**. The text box entry will be selected.

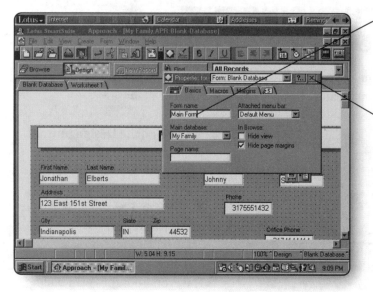

6. Type the **new name** of the form in the Form name text box. The name will be entered in the text box.

7. Click on the **Close button** of the Properties for Form dialog box. The dialog box will close, and the form's name will change.

ADDING A FIELD

You may find that you forgot a field when you were creating your database. You can add fields even after the database has been created.

1. Click on the **Design button**. The form will be placed in design mode.

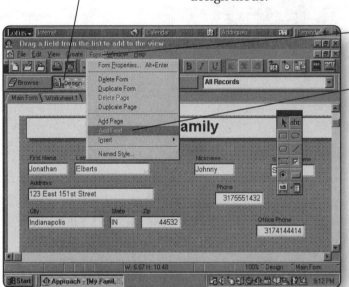

2. Click on **Form**. The Form menu will appear.

3. Click on **Add Field**. The Add Field dialog box will open.

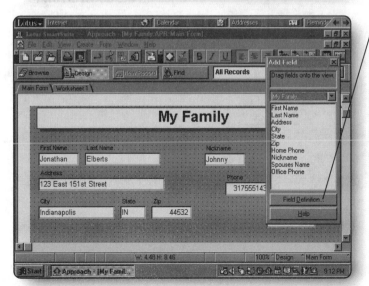

4. Click on **Field Definition**. The Field Definition dialog box will open.

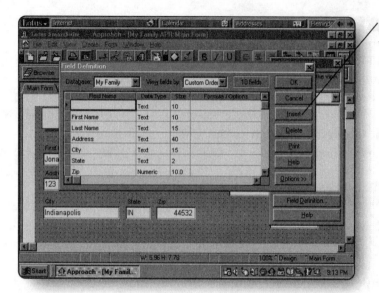

5. Click on **Insert**. A blank row will be inserted.

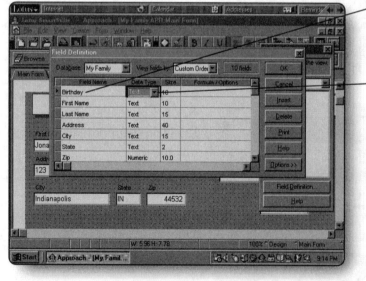

6. Type a **name** for the new field. The name will appear in the Field Name column.

7. Click on the **down arrow** in the Data Type column. A list of available field types will appear.

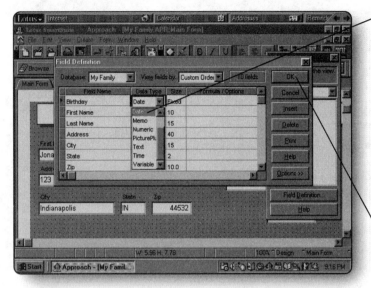

8. **Click** on the **field type** for this field. The field type will be assigned to the field.

9. **Press** the **Tab key**. The Size column will be selected.

10. If necessary, **type** a **Size** for the field. The field will be made that size.

11. **Click** on **OK**. The field will be added, and the Field Definition dialog box will close.

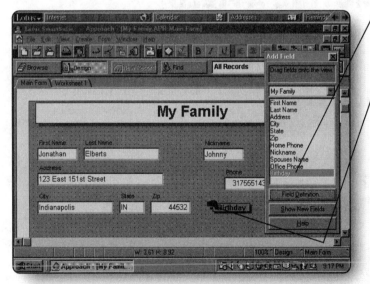

12. **Click** on the added **field** from the list box. The field will be selected.

13. **Drag** the **field name** from the list box to a new location on the form.

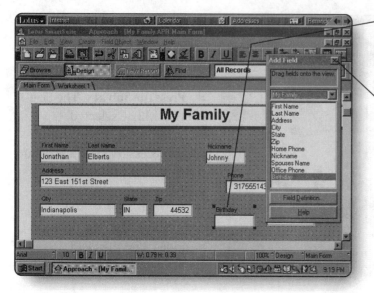

14. **Release** the **mouse button**. The field will be added to the form.

15. **Click** on the **Close button** of the Add Field dialog box. The Add Field dialog box will close.

MOVING A FIELD

When you move a field to a different location on the form, the descriptive title of the field moves along with it.

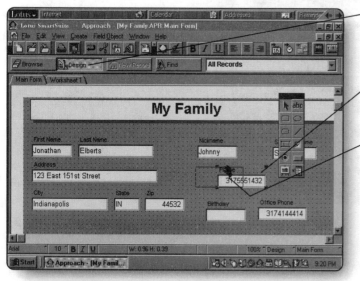

1. **Click** on the **Design button**. The form will be placed in design mode.

2. **Click** on the **field** to be moved. The field will be selected.

3. **Drag** the **field** to the new position. A small hand will appear to drag the field.

NOTE

Click on a field to be moved and use the keyboard arrow keys to nudge the field into a new location.

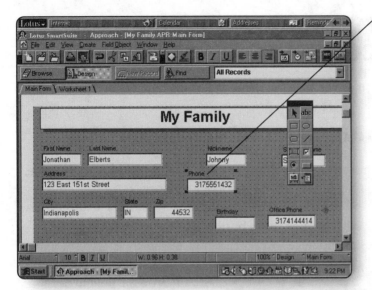

4. Release the **mouse button**. The field and its title will be moved.

DELETING A FIELD

If you do not want a field to appear on the form, you can delete it.

1. Click on the **Design button**. The form will be placed in design mode.

2. Click on the **field** to be deleted. The field will be selected.

3. Press the **Delete key**. The field will be deleted.

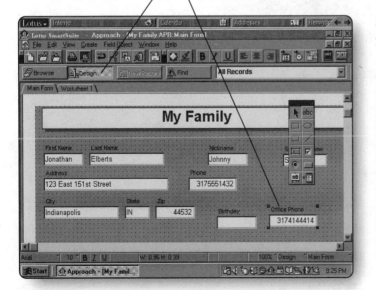

NOTE

If you have entered data into the field you deleted, you have not lost that data. Deleting a field from a form does not delete data from the database. You've only lost the ability to display the data on the current form.

FORMATTING FIELD CONTENTS

You can change the numeric format, font, or color of any field.

Adding Numeric Formatting

Change the display of a numeric field to currency, percentage, or even format it for a telephone number.

1. Click on the **Design button**. The form will be placed in design mode.

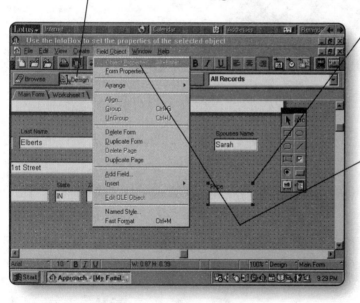

2. Click on the **field** to be formatted. The field will be selected.

3. Click on **Field Object**. The Field Object menu will appear.

4. Click on **Object Properties**. The Properties for: Field box will open.

5. Click on the **Numeric formatting tab**. The Numeric tab will come to the front.

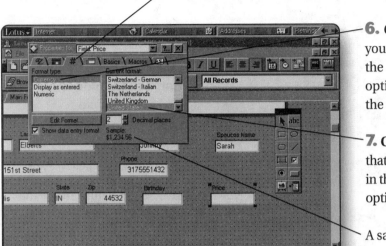

6. Click on the **format type** that you want for the selected field in the Format type list box. The options available will appear in the Current format list box.

7. Click on the **current format** that you want for the selected field in the Current format list box. The option will be highlighted.

A sample representation of your selection is displayed.

8. Click on the **Close box**. The Properties dialog box will close.

Adding Font Formatting

Add color or font attributes to any field or field label.

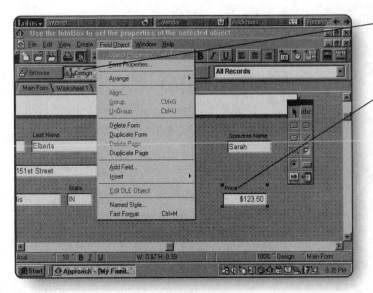

1. Click on the **Design button**. The form will be placed in design mode.

2. Click on the **field** to be formatted. The field will be selected.

3. Click on **Field Object**. The Field Object menu will appear.

4. Click on **Object Properties**. The Properties for Field box will open.

5. Click on the **Font and Style tab**. The Font and Style tab will come to the front.

6. Choose from the following **options**:

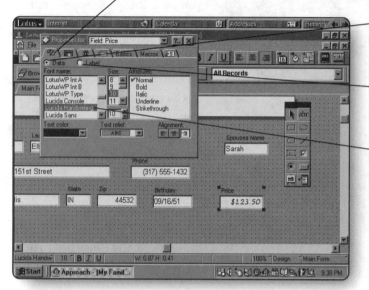

✦ Click on Data to change the formatting for the contents of the selected field.

✦ Click on Label to change the formatting for the descriptive label for the selected field.

7. Click on the **font name** that you want to use for the selected field in the Font name list box. The option will be highlighted.

8. Click on the **size** that you want to use for the selected field in the Size list box. The option will be highlighted.

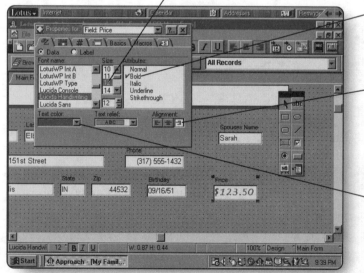

9. Click on any **attributes** you want to use for the selected field. The options will be highlighted.

10. Click on the **alignment** you want to use for the selected field. The option will be selected.

TIP

Click on the down arrow at the right of the Text color list box and select a color for the field.

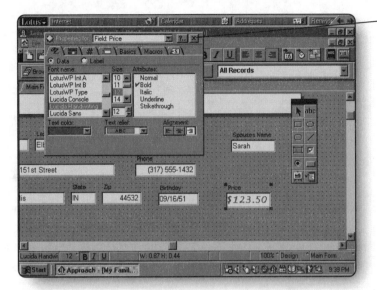

11. Click on the **Close button**. The Properties dialog box will close.

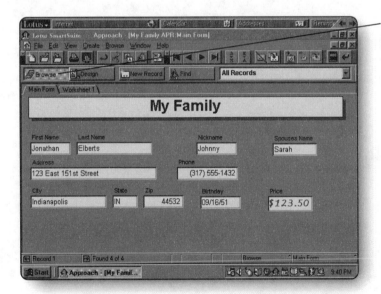

12. Click on the **Browse button**. The selected attributes will appear on the designated field.

23 Creating Database Reports

Approach allows you to decide how your printed data should look by letting you create reports. Using reports, you can control the format of the report, which fields are included in the report, and whether you want totals. In this chapter, you'll learn how to:

✦ Create a report

✦ Print a report

✦ Save a database

CREATING A REPORT

To create a report, you will use the Report Assistant.

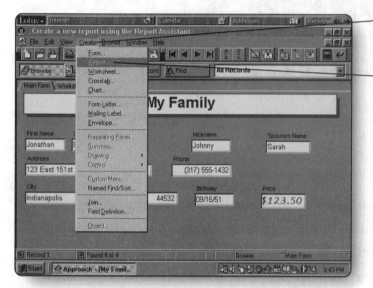

1. **Click** on **Create**. The Create menu will appear.

2. **Click** on **Report**. The Report Assistant will open.

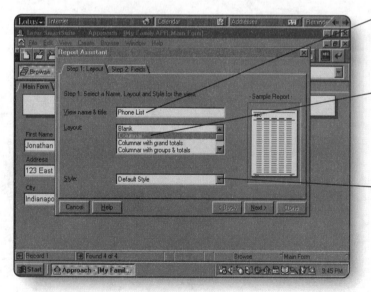

3. **Type** a **name** for the report in the View name & title text box. The report will be named.

4. **Click** on a **Layout** for the report in the Layout list box. The layout will be previewed in the Sample Report box.

5. **Click** on the **down arrow** by the Style list box. A list of available styles will appear.

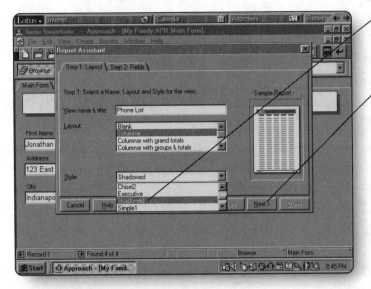

6. Click on the **style** you want. The style will be previewed in the Sample Report box.

7. Click on **Next**. The Step 2 tab will appear.

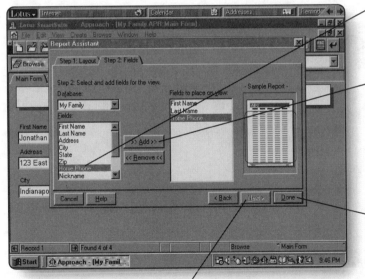

8. Click on a **field** you want in the report. The field will be selected.

9. Click on the **Add button**. The field will be added to the report.

10. Repeat steps 8 and **9** until all the fields you want in the report are added.

11a. Click on **Done**. The report will be created.

OR

If in step 1 you opted for a layout that included totals, a third tab will appear. If you did choose a layout with totals, proceed to steps 11b through 14.

11b. Click on **Next**. The Step 3 tab will appear.

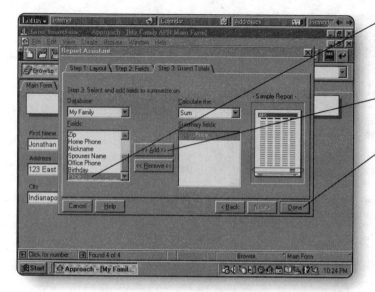

12. Click on the **field** for which you want to create a total. The field will be selected.

13. Click on **Add**. The field will be added as a summary field.

14. Click on **Done**. The report will be created.

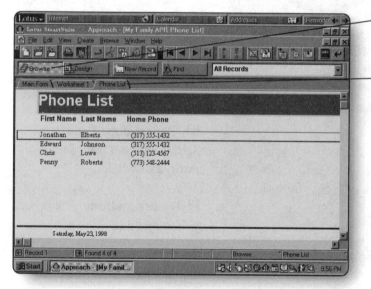

15. Click on **Browse**. The report will be displayed.

A new report tab appears along with the form and worksheet tabs.

PRINTING THE REPORT

After you create the report, you can print it.

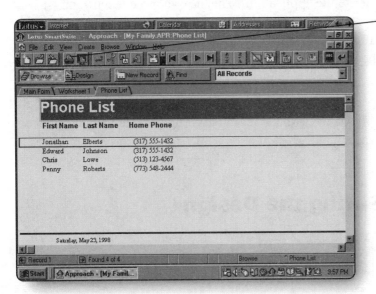

1. **Click** on the **Print SmartIcon**. The Print dialog box will open.

2. **Choose** from the following **options**:

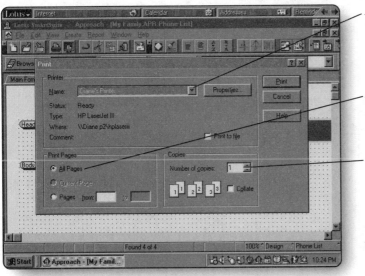

◆ To choose a different printer, click on the down arrow by the Name list box and make your selection.

◆ The preselected range is All Pages. You can also select a different range of pages.

◆ To print more than one copy, click on the plus and minus buttons in the Copies area.

3. **Click** on **Print**. The report will be sent to the printer.

SAVING THE DATABASE

Saving an Approach database is a little different from other SmartSuite applications. The file was saved when you first created it. After that, Approach will save your data automatically. You only need to save the file when you change the design of it.

> **NOTE**
> The data is saved in the database file the moment you enter a record, move to another record, or change to a different view.

Saving the Design

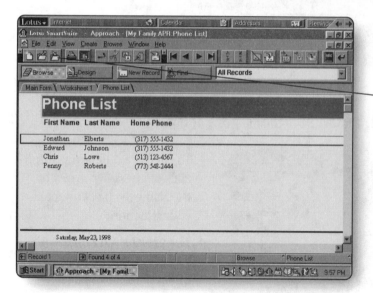

If you change the design by working in Design mode, you do need to save the file.

1. Click on the **Save SmartSuite button**. If this is the first time you have clicked on the Save SmartSuite button, the Save As dialog box will open. If you've saved the file previously, the saved file will be updated. If you have not made any changes that need to be saved, the Save SmartSuite button is not available.

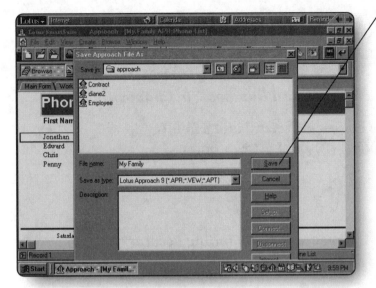

2. If the Save As dialog box opens, **click** on **Save**. The file will be saved.

PART VI REVIEW QUESTIONS

1. **What is a database?** *See "Creating a Database" in Chapter 21*

2. **What is the difference between a record and a field?** *See "Understanding Fields and Records" in Chapter 21*

3. **What button do you click to get a blank record?** *See "Entering Data" in Chapter 21*

4. **What must you do to find records?** *See "Finding Records" in Chapter 21*

5. **What two methods can you use to sort records?** *See "Sorting Records" in Chapter 21*

6. **What is the difference between form view and worksheet view?** *See "Looking at the Worksheet View" in Chapter 21*

7. **What mode must you be in to change a database title?** *See "Changing the Title on a Form" in Chapter 22*

8. **When moving a field, what moves along with it?** *See "Moving a Field" in Chapter 22*

9. **What do you use to create a report?** *See "Creating a Report" in Chapter 23*

10. **When should you save an Approach database file?** *See "Saving the Database" in Chapter 23*

Appendixes

oruary

$27,540.00

$31,212.75

$18,400.00

$11,235.50

$88,388.25

$12,000.00

$12,000.00

Installing SmartSuite

When installing the SmartSuite software, you'll be able to choose which components of the software you want to install. In this chapter, you'll learn how to:

✦ **Install SmartSuite**

✦ **Uninstall SmartSuite**

SYSTEM REQUIREMENTS

To use SmartSuite, you'll need the following equipment:

✦ IBM PC or compatible 80486/50 or higher

✦ VGA Adapter or higher resolution adapter and monitor

✦ Mouse or other pointing device

✦ Microsoft Windows 95, Windows 98, or Windows NT 4.0

✦ 8X or greater CD-ROM Drive

✦ Memory: 8MB minimum, 12MB recommended, and 16MB minimum for Windows NT 4.0

✦ Disk space: Minimum hard disk of 96MB

INSTALLING SMARTSUITE

When you place the SmartSuite CD in the drive, the SmartSuite window opens and displays available options.

TIP

If the SmartSuite window does not automatically appear, you'll have to start the installation process yourself. Click on Start, choose Run, and type **D:\install**. (Substitute D for the drive letter of your CD-ROM drive.) Press Enter.

There are four types of installation selections available:

✦ **Install**. Click on this choice to tailor where, how, and which applications you want to install.

✦ **Quick Install**. Click on this choice to quickly install the product. You'll be able to specify where you want the program, but you cannot select which components to install.

✦ **Run from CD-ROM**. Click on this choice for a minimum installation of files to your hard disk. The SmartSuite CD must be in the disk drive at all times to use the SmartSuite applications.

✦ **Extras**. Click on this choice to install the extra application "freebies" that come with SmartSuite.

TIP

Position the mouse pointer over any of the pictures on the bottom row for information about that feature.

The fastest method is to use the QuickInstall.

1. Click on **QuickInstall**. The QuickInstall dialog box will open. You'll need to specify the size of installation and the desired folder for the applications.

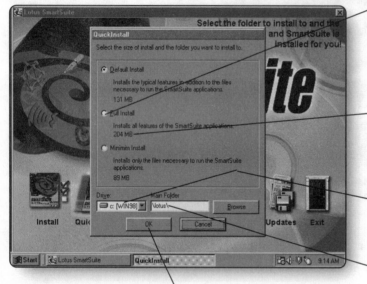

2. Click on the **type of installation** you want for the Lotus SmartSuite. The installation type will be selected. For this book, I did a Full Install.

Each option discusses the differences and the disk requirements for the various types of installation.

The product installs to the C drive unless you choose a different disk drive.

The product installs into a default folder of \lotus\ unless you type a different location.

3. Click on **OK**. The Lotus Software Agreement dialog box will open.

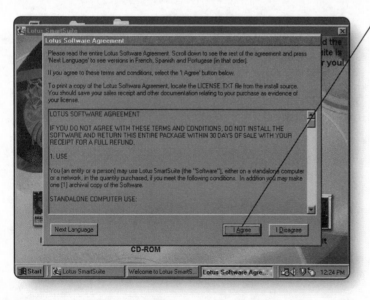

4. After reading the agreement, **Click** on the **I Agree button**. The installation process will begin.

A progress indicator shows the status of the installation.

The information screens that display will change during the course of the installation process.

When the installation process is complete, the screen returns to the opening SmartSuite window.

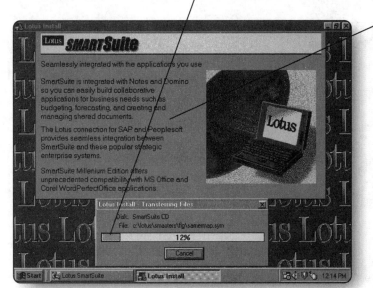

5. **Click** on **Exit**. The SmartSuite window will close.

6. **Restart** your **computer**. The installation process will be complete.

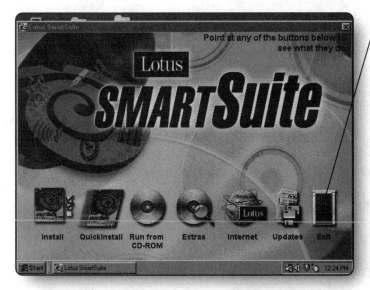

UNINSTALLING SMARTSUITE

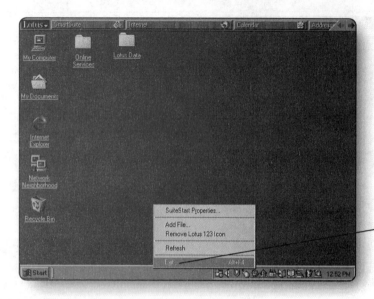

If you no longer want SmartSuite or any of its components on your computer, you can easily remove it. All Lotus applications must be closed prior to uninstallation.

1. **Right-click** on the **SuiteSmart bar**. A shortcut menu will appear.

2. **Click** on **Exit**. The SuiteSmart bar will close.

3. **Right-click** on the **Lotus button** of the SmartCenter. The SmartCenter main menu will appear.

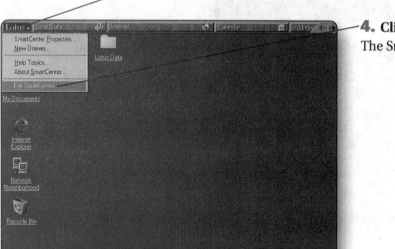

4. **Click** on **Exit SmartCenter**. The SmartCenter will close.

5. **Click** on **Start**. The Start menu will appear.

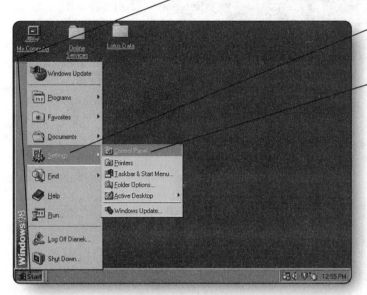

6. **Click** on **Settings**. The Settings submenu will appear.

7. **Click** on **Control Panel**. The Control Panel window will open.

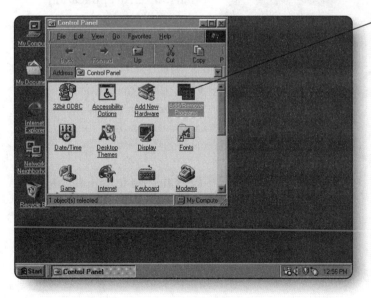

8. **Click** on **Add/Remove Programs**. The Add/Remove Programs Properties dialog box will open.

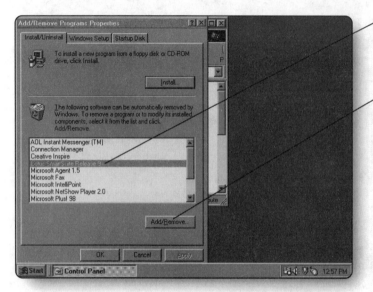

9. Click on **Lotus SmartSuite Release 9**. The item will be highlighted.

10. Click on the **Add/Remove button**. The Select Lotus SmartSuite Applications dialog box will open.

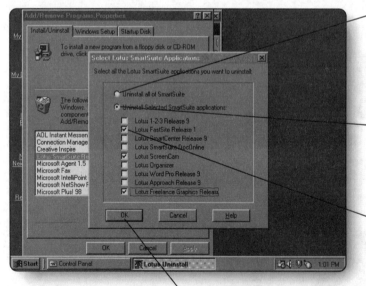

11a. Click on **Uninstall all of SmartSuite**. All application names will have a check mark by them.

OR

11b. Click on **Uninstall Selected SmartSuite applications**. The option will be selected.

12. Click on the **applications** you want to uninstall. The application names you selected will have a check mark by them.

13. Click on **OK**. The Lotus Uninstall box will open.

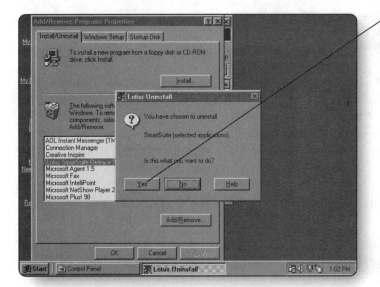

14. **Click** on **Yes**. The applications will be uninstalled.

When the uninstall is complete, a confirmation box appears.

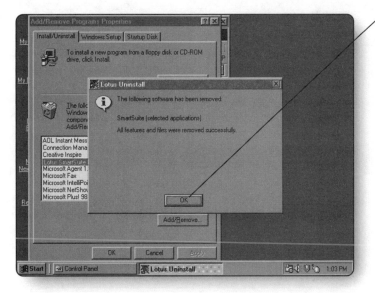

15. **Click** on **OK**. The confirmation box will close.

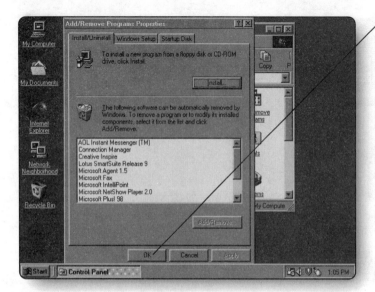

16. **Click** on **OK**. The Add/Remove Programs Properties box will close.

17. **Click** on the **OK button**. The Control Panel window will close.

18. **Restart** your **computer**. The uninstallation process will be complete.

B Working with ViaVoice Gold

Do you talk to your computer? Most of us do. ViaVoice is a product that will allow you to talk to your computer without feeling like you've gone crazy! You can dictate text right into your document without typing. In this chapter, you'll learn how to:

✦ **Install ViaVoice Gold**

✦ **Set up and test your microphone**

✦ **Use enrollment to teach ViaVoice how you speak**

✦ **Use ViaVoice with Word Pro**

✦ **Correct Errors**

INSTALLING VIAVOICE GOLD

If you installed Lotus SmartSuite using the QuickInstall, you'll need to install the ViaVoice product separately.

The hardware recommended for ViaVoice Gold includes a minimum Pentium processor of 150MHz.

1. Place the **SmartSuite CD** in the CD-ROM drive. The SmartSuite window will open and display available options.

2. Click on **Extras**. An Extras window will open.

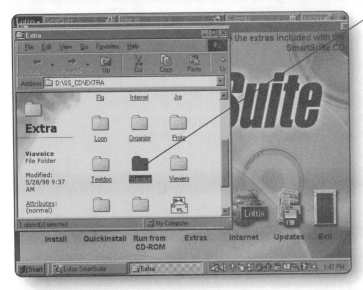

3. Double-click on the **Viavoice folder**. The Viavoice folder will open.

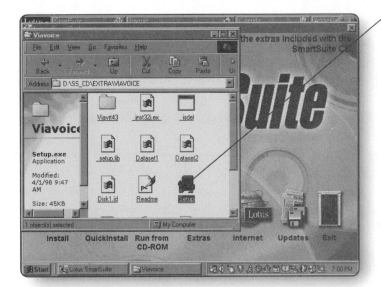

4. Double-click on **Setup**. The Install Wizard will begin.

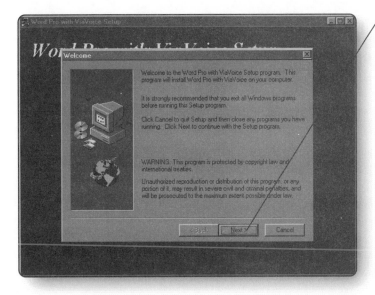

5. Click on **Next**. A message box will appear.

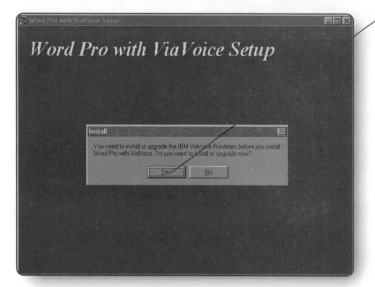

6. Click on **Yes**. The ViaVoice runtime setup program will begin.

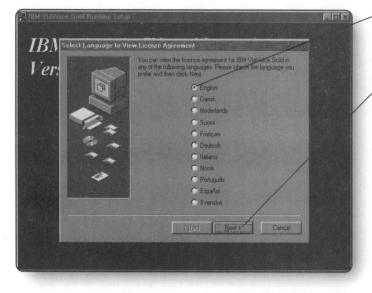

7. Click on the **Language** you prefer to use. The option will be selected.

8. Click on **Next**. The License Agreement box will appear.

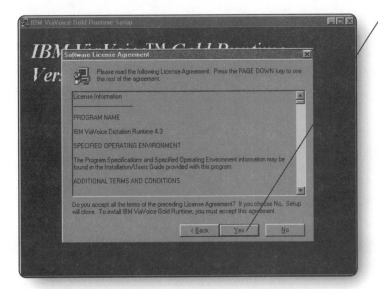

9. After reading the agreement, **click** on **Yes**. The Welcome box will appear.

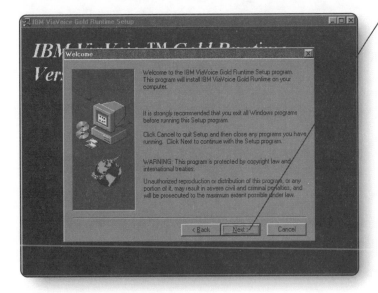

10. Click on **Next**. A voice will come across your speakers welcoming you to ViaVoice Gold.

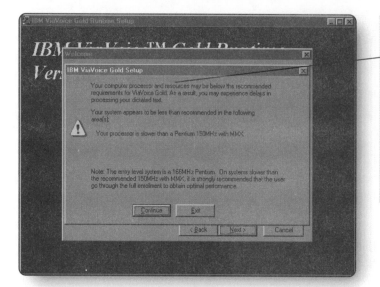

If your hardware is less than the recommended settings, a warning box will display. You can continue to install ViaVoice, but be warned that you may experience delays when using the product. Click on Continue.

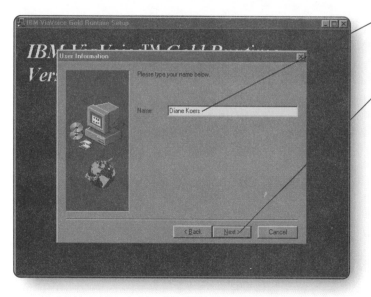

11. Type your name in the Name: text box. The text will appear in the text box.

12. Click on **Next**. The Choose Destination Location box will appear.

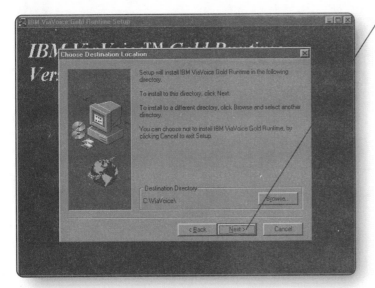

13. **Click** on **Next** to accept the default folder location (recommended). The Select Program Folder box will open.

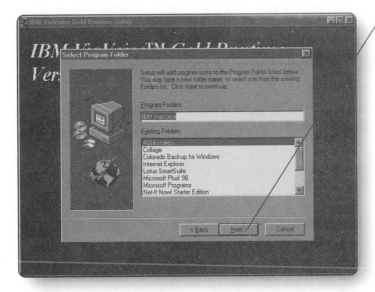

14. **Click** on **Next** to accept the default folder. The Start Copying Files dialog box will open.

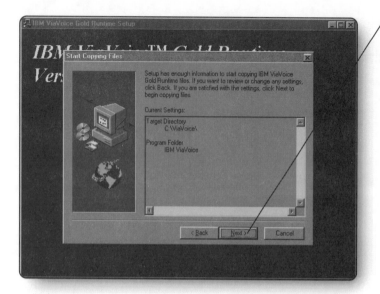

15. **Click** on **Next**. The ViaVoice Gold program will be installed. When the installation process is complete, the Setup Complete dialog box appears.

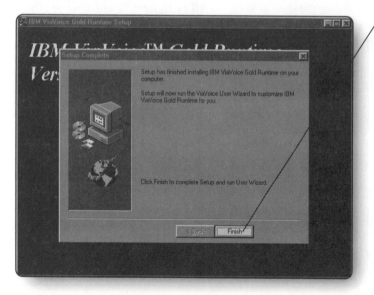

16. **Click** on **Finish**. The Word Pro portion of ViaVoice setup will begin.

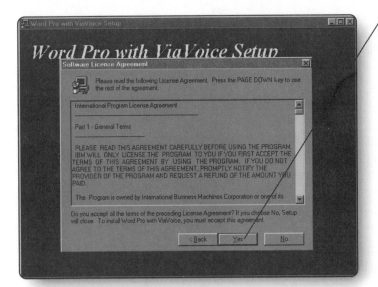

17. After reading the license agreement, **click** on **Yes**. The Choose Destination dialog box will open.

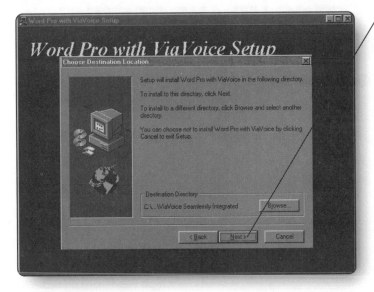

18. Click on **Next**. Program files will be copied to your system.

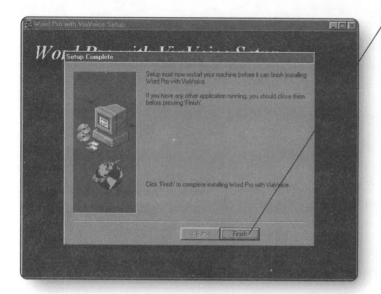

19. **Click** on **Finish**. Your computer will restart.

SETTING UP AND TESTING YOUR MICROPHONE

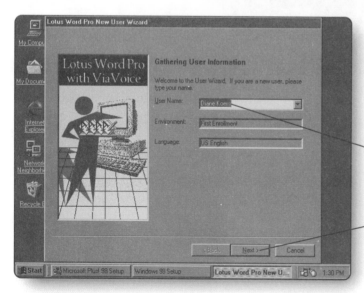

After your computer restarts, the New User Setup Wizard will resume. This is where your information will be stored and the microphone settings will be determined.

1. **Type your Name** in the User Name: text box. The text will appear in the text box.

2. **Click** on **Next**. The next page of the Wizard will appear.

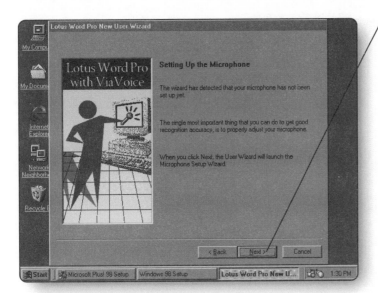

3. Click on **Next**. The Microphone Setup Wizard will begin.

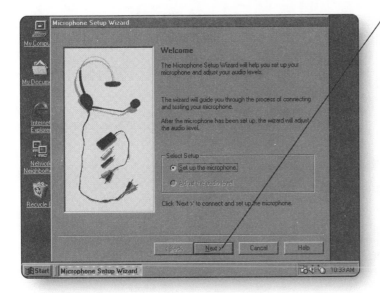

4. Click on **Next**. The Wizard will continue and you'll be prompted to identify the components of your microphone.

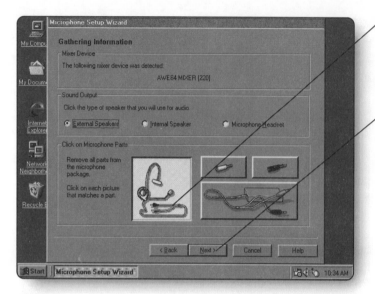

5. **Click** on the **picture** that matches your microphone components. The selection will turn bright.

6. **Click** on **Next**. The Audio test will be next.

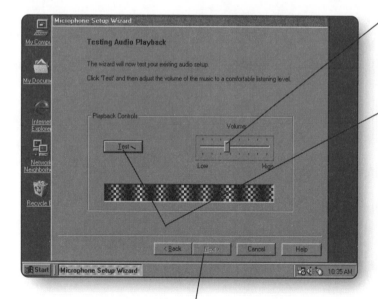

Now is the time to test the speakers or audio portion of your setup. Make sure your speakers are turned on.

7. **Click** on **Test**. Music will be played.

TIP

If necessary, drag the volume slide control to adjust the volume.

8. **Click** on **Next**. ViaVoice will adjust to your microphone.

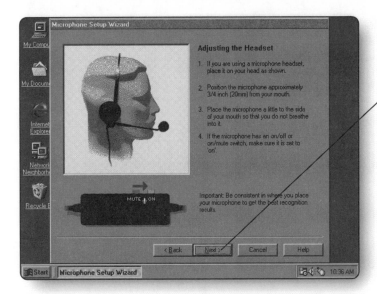

9. **Place** the **headphone set** on your head as displayed in the picture.

10. **Click** on **Next**. Make sure the microphone is plugged in and in position.

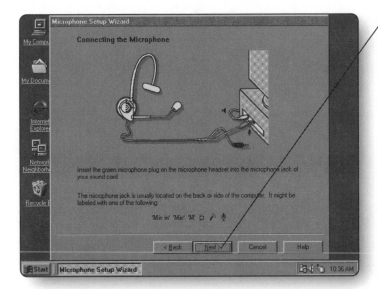

11. **Click** on **Next**. ViaVoice will test the room for background noise.

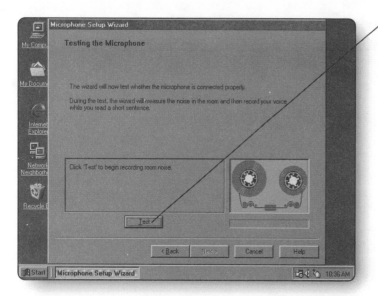

12. **Click** on **Test**. Be silent while testing the room for background noise.

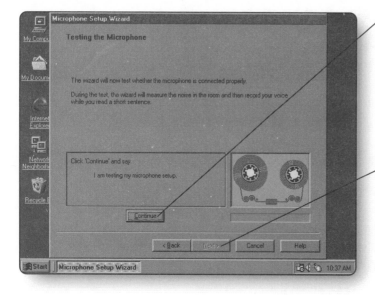

13. **Click** on **Continue**. Now ViaVoice must test your voice and the microphone together.

14. **Speak** the displayed **phrase** into the Microphone. Your voice will be recorded.

15. **Click** on **Next**. The next page of the Wizard will appear.

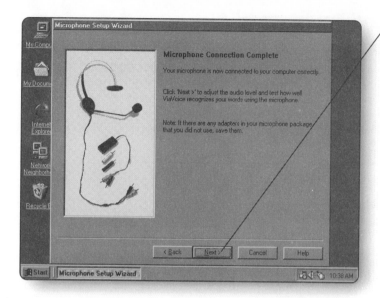

16. **Click** on **Next**. The next step of the speech recognition process will begin.

17. **Click** on **Start**. Each word will be outlined by a blue box.

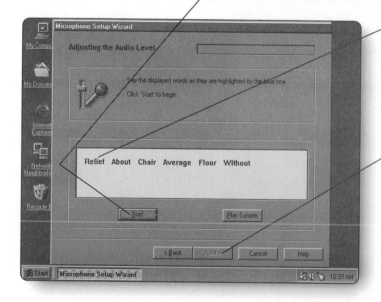

18. **Say** the **first word** into the microphone. The next word will be highlighted.

19. **Say** the **next word** until all words have been spoken.

20. **Click** on **Next**. The next page of the Wizard will appear.

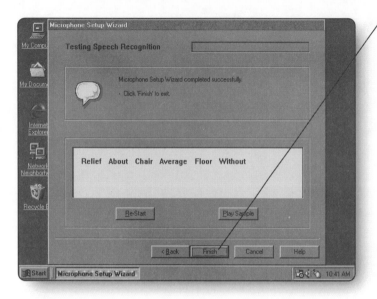

21. Click on **Finish**. The Microphone Setup Wizard is complete.

QUICK TRAINING VIAVOICE

ViaVoice will record some of your speech patterns with Quick Training. There are three dictation screens you must read.

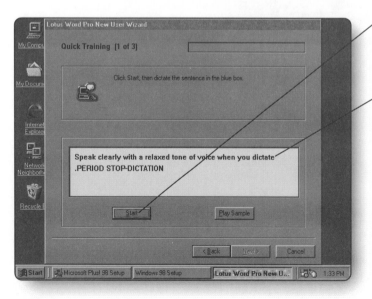

1. Click on **Start**. The text of the first screen will be outlined in blue.

2. Slowly, **speak** the displayed **words**. The second screen will appear.

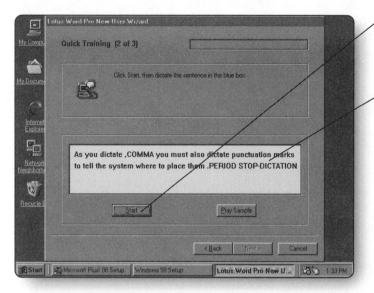

3. Click on **Start**. The text of the second screen will be outlined in blue.

4. Slowly, **speak** the displayed **words**. The third screen will appear.

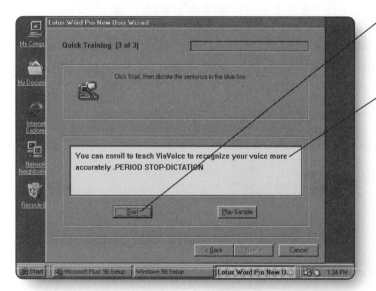

5. Click on **Start**. The text of the third screen will be outlined in blue.

6. Slowly, **speak** the displayed **words**. A Getting Help screen will be displayed.

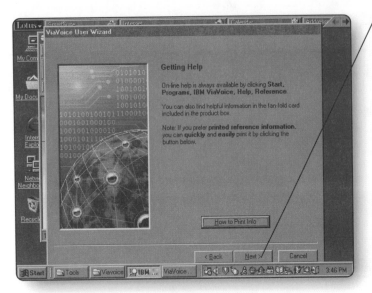

7. Click on **Next**. The What Next screen will display.

ENROLLING VIAVOICE

It's not required, but you'll want to go through the enrollment process to improve the speech recognition accuracy. The purpose is to teach ViaVoice to better recognize your personal speech patterns.

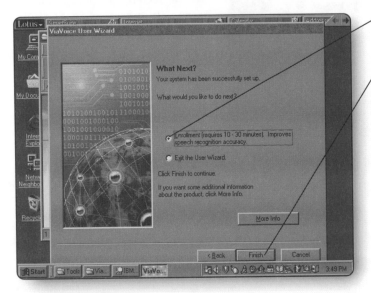

1. Click on **Enrollment**. The option will be selected.

2. Click on **Finish**. A Welcome to Enrollment help screen will be displayed.

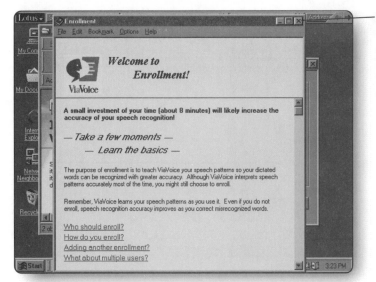

3. Click on the **Close button**. The Welcome to Enrollment help screen will close and the enrollments box will be displayed.

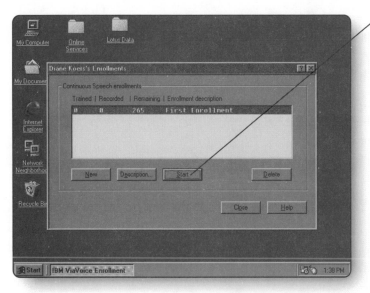

4. Click on **Start**. An Enrollment Sample box will be displayed.

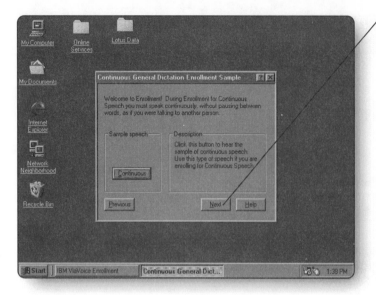

5. **Click** on **Next**. A message box will be displayed.

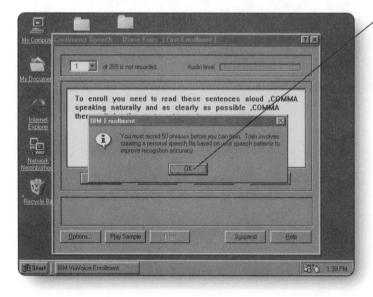

6. **Click** on **OK**. The Enrollment process will begin.

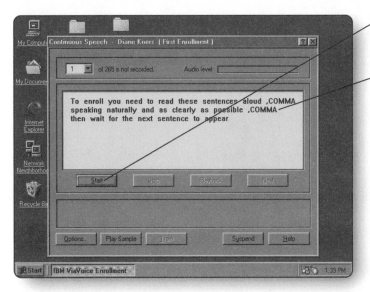

7. Click on **Start**. The beginning phrase will be displayed.

8. Read each displayed **phrase** exactly as shown. As you complete each phrase, the next one will be displayed.

There are approximately 50 sentences you need to read. When the process is complete, a message box will display.

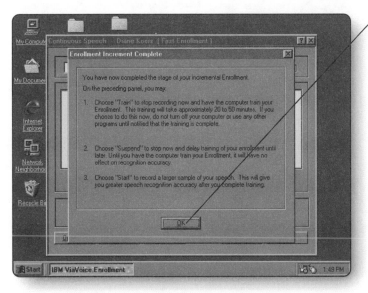

9. Click on **OK**. The Continuous Speech dialog box will reappear.

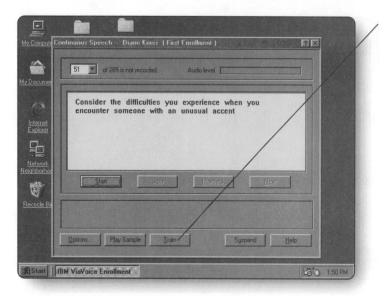

10. Click on **Train**. The Enrollment Increment Complete dialog box will be displayed.

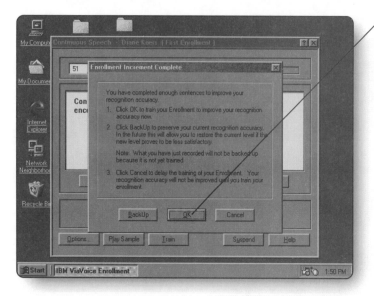

11. Click on **OK**. ViaVoice will go through an analysis of the dictated words and learn how you pronounced them. This process may take anywhere from fifteen minutes to an hour.

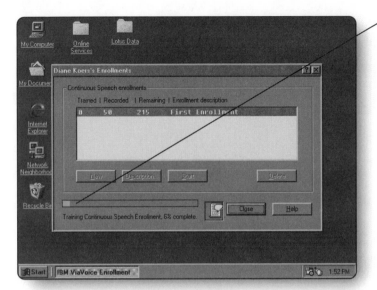

A status bar indicates the progress. When the training is complete, an IBM Enrollment dialog box will appear.

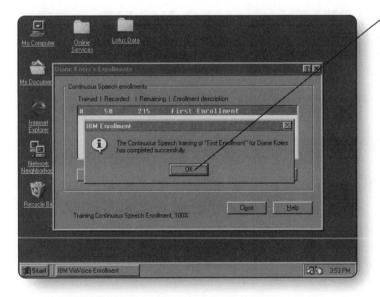

12. Click on **OK**. The dialog box will close and the Enrollment box will be redisplayed.

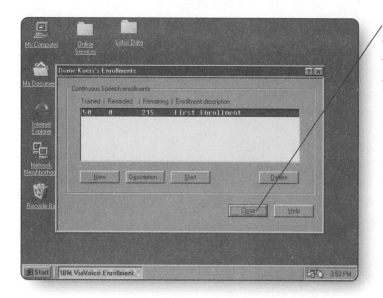

13. **Click** on the **Close button**. The Enrollment box will close. You're ready to use ViaVoice with your Lotus SmartSuite software.

DICTATING INTO WORD PRO

At the present time, the only SmartSuite application that ViaVoice works with is Word Pro.

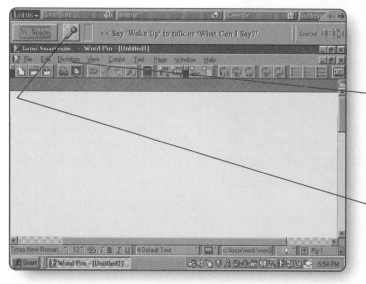

1. **Start** the **Word Pro** application with a blank document displayed.

Dictation appears on the menu bar.

A ViaVoice toolbar displays at the top of the screen.

2. **Click** on the **microphone picture** to awaken the microphone. The background on the button will turn green.

3. Say the words "**Start dictation**." The computer speaker will say "Start dictating," and the text "Begin Dictating" will appear on your document.

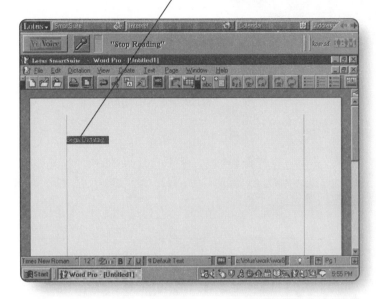

4. Speak a **sentence** into the microphone.

5. Say the word **"period"** at the end of a sentence.

6. Say the words "**Stop dictation."** The computer will say "Dictation stopped" and the words will appear on your document.

CORRECTING ERRORS

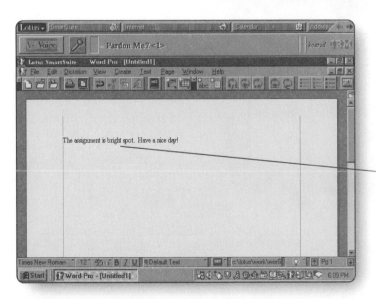

Speech recognition technology is still very new. The words you spoke may come out on the screen entirely different. You'll need to keep teaching ViaVoice until it recognizes your speech patterns.

In this example, "The sun is bright. Have a nice day!" was spoken, but it came out, "The assignment is bright spot. Have a nice day!"

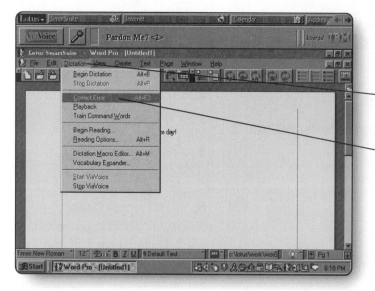

1. Highlight the **text** translated in error. The text will be selected.

2. Click on **Dictation**. The Dictation menu will appear.

3. Click on **Correct Error**. The error box will open.

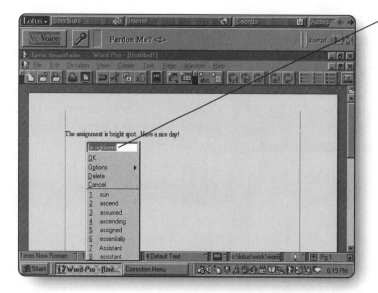

4. Highlight the text in the **error text box**. The text will be selected.

5a. **Type** the **correct word or phrase.** The correction will appear in the error text box.

OR

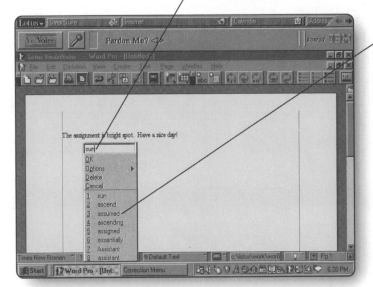

5b. **Choose** from the **suggestions** at the bottom of the list. The selection will appear in the error text box.

6. **Press** the **Enter key.** The highlighted text will be replaced with the text you typed.

7. **Repeat steps 1 through 4** for each dictation error in the document.

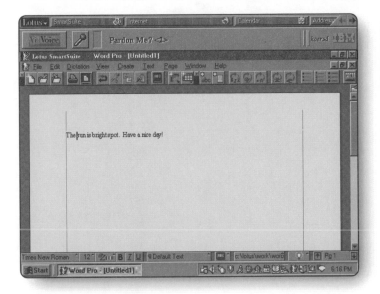

TIP

It would have been faster to manually type the correction of this error, but using the above method also teaches ViaVoice for future occurrences of the misinterpreted word.

Speech recognition is still a new technology. Be patient with this product. It does get better with time and usage. Just keep working with it and don't give up! The more you teach it, the better it will respond to you.

Glossary

A

@AVG. A 1-2-3 function that calculates the average of a list of values. SYNTAX: @AVG(*list*)

@COUNT. A 1-2-3 function that counts the nonblank cells in a list of ranges. SYNTAX: @COUNT(*list*)

@Function. A series of predefined formulas used in Lotus spreadsheets.

@MAX. A 1-2-3 function that finds the largest value in a list. SYNTAX: @MAX(*list*)

@MIN. A 1-2-3 function that finds the smallest value in a list. SYNTAX: @MIN(*list*)

@SUM. A 1-2-3 function that adds a range of cells. See also *SmartSum*. SYNTAX: @SUM(*list*)

Absolute reference. In a formula, a reference to a cell that does not change when you copy the formula. An absolute reference always refers to the same cell or range. It is designated in a formula by the dollar sign ($).

Active cell. The selected cell in a worksheet. Designated with a border surrounding the cell.

Address Book. Stores names, addresses, and phone numbers in one handy location.

Alignment. The position of data in a document, cell, range, or text block; for example, centered, right-aligned, or left-aligned. Also called *justification*.

Append. To add text to the end of the clipboard instead of replacing its contents.

Attributes. Items that determine the appearance of text such as bolding, underlining, italics, or point size.

Audience Handout. A paper copy of a presentation with representation of the slides and an area for taking notes.

Axes. Lines that form a frame of reference for the chart data. Most charts have an x axis and a y axis.

B

Bar chart. A type of chart that uses bars to represent values. Normally used to compare items.

Bold. A font attribute that makes text thicker and brighter.

Border. A line surrounding paragraphs, pages, table cells, or objects.

Browser. A software program especially designed for viewing Web pages on the Internet.

Bullet. A small black circle or other character that precedes each item in a list.

C

Cell. The area where a row and column intersect in a worksheet or table.

Chart. A graphic representation of data. Also called *graph*.

Choose. To use the mouse or keyboard to pick a menu item or option in a dialog box.

Circular reference. A cell that has a formula that contains a reference to itself.

Click on. To use the mouse or keyboard to pick a menu item or option in a dialog box.

Clip art. Drawings that can be inserted into a Lotus SmartSuite application.

Clipboard. An area of computer memory where text or graphics can be temporarily stored.

Close button. Used to shut down or exit a dialog box, window, or application.

Column. A set of cells that appear vertically on a worksheet. A single 1-2-3 worksheet has 256 columns.

Columns. Vertical divisions of text on a page.

Comment. To add annotations to a document or spreadsheet cell. Comments do not print.

Copy. To take a selection from the document and duplicate it on the clipboard.

Cut. To take a selection from the document and move it to the clipboard.

D

Data. The information to be entered into a spreadsheet.

Database. A file composed of records, each containing fields together with a set of operations for searching or sorting.

Default. A setting or action predetermined by the program unless changed by the user.

Desktop. The screen background and main area of Windows where you can open and manage files and programs.

Dialog box. A box that appears and lets you select options, or displays warnings and messages.

Document. A letter, memo, proposal, or other file that is created in the Word Pro program.

Drag-and-drop. To move text or an object by positioning the mouse pointer on the item you want to move, pressing and holding the mouse button, moving the mouse, then releasing the mouse button to drop the material into its new location.

E

Export. The ability to copy data from one program to another.

F

FastFormat. A feature that enables you to easily copy formatting applied to text.

Field. A piece of information used in a database.

File format. The arrangement and organization of information in a file. File format is determined by the application that created the file.

File. Information stored on a disk under a single name.

Fill Data. A function that allows 1-2-3 to automatically complete a series of numbers or words based on an established pattern.

Fill. The changing of interior colors and patterns.

Font. A group of letters, numbers, and symbols with a common typeface.

Footer. Text repeated at the bottom of each page of a document or spreadsheet.

Footnote. Reference information that prints at the bottom of the page.

Form. A type of database document with spaces reserved for fields to enter data.

Format. To change the appearance of text or objects with features such as the font, style, color, borders, and size.

Formula bar. The location where all data and formulas are entered for a selected cell.

Formula. A formula is an entry in a worksheet that performs a calculation on numbers, text, or other formulas.

Freezing. The preventing of sections of a worksheet from scrolling offscreen when you move down the page.

Function. Built-in formulas that perform specialized calculations automatically.

G

Go To. A feature that enables you to jump to a specific cell or worksheet location quickly.

Graphs. See *Charts*.

Greater than. A mathematical operator that limits the results of a formula to be higher than a named number or cell.

Gridlines. The lines dividing rows and columns in a table or worksheet.

H

Handles. Small black squares that appear when you select an object that will enable you to resize the object.

Header. Text entered in an area of the document that will be displayed at the top of each page of the document.

Hide. To temporarily turn off the display of certain cells, rows, or columns.

Hypertext link. Used to provide a connection from the current document to another document or to a document on the World Wide Web.

I

Icon. A small graphic image that represents an application, command, or a tool. An action is performed when an icon is clicked or double-clicked.

Import. The ability to receive data from another.

Indent. To move a complete paragraph one tab stop to the right.

Internet Publisher. Feature that lets you create and edit documents for the Web and launch Web browser software to browse the Web.

J

Justification. See *Alignment.*

L

Label. Any cell entry you begin with a letter or label-prefix character.

Landscape. Orientation of a page in which the long edge of the paper runs horizontally.

Legend. A box containing symbols and text, explaining what each data series represents. Each symbol is a color pattern or marker that corresponds to one data series in the chart.

Less than. A mathematical operator that limits the results of a formula to be lower than a named number or cell.

Line Spacing. The amount of space between lines of text.

M

Mail Merge. A feature that uses data from a data file and combines it with a document called a form file to produce personalized letters.

Margin. The width of blank space from the edge of the page to the edge of the text. All four sides of a page have margins.

Mouse pointer. A symbol that indicates a position onscreen as you move the mouse around on your Desktop.

O

Object. A picture, map, or other graphic element that you can place in a Lotus application.

Open. To start an application, to insert a document into a new document window, or to access a dialog box.

Operator. The element of a formula that suggests an action to be performed, such as addition (+), subtraction (–), division (/), multiplication (*), greater than (>) or less than (<).

Orientation. A setting that designates whether a document will print with text running along the long or short side of a piece of paper.

P

Page break. A command that tells the application where to begin a new page.

Paste. The process of retrieving the information stored on the clipboard and inserting a copy of it into a document.

Patterns. Predefined shading and line arrangements used to format cells in a worksheet.

Pie chart. A round chart type in which each pie wedge represents values.

Point size. A unit of measurement used to indicate font size. One point is 1/72 inch in height.

Point. To move the mouse until the tip of the mouse pointer rests on an item.

Portrait. The orientation of the page in which the long edge of the page runs vertically.

Presentation. The representation of information, such as sales figures and stock prices, in a series of charts rather than as lists of numbers.

Print area. The portion of a worksheet you designate to print.

Print Preview. Shows you how your printed document will look onscreen before you print it.

Properties. The characteristics of a text, objects, or devices. Text properties might include font, size, or color.

R

Range name. An English name that identifies a range and that can be used in commands and formulas instead of the range address.

Range. A collection of cells, ranging from the first named cell to the last.

Record. The collection of field information about one particular element. For example, Joe Smith's record might include field information such as name, address, and phone number.

Redo. To reverse the last Undo action.

Reference. In a formula, a name or range that refers the formula to a cell or set of cells.

Relative. In a formula, a reference to a cell or a range that changes when you copy the formula. A relative reference refers to the location of the data in relation to the formula. A relative reference can be an address or range name.

Right align. To line up text with the right side of a cell, tab setting, or document margin, as with a row of numbers in a column.

Row. Cells running from left to right across a worksheet.

Ruler. A feature that lets you easily change page format elements such as tabs and margins.

S

Save As. To save a previously saved document with a new name or properties.

Save. To take a document residing in the memory of the computer and create a file to be stored on a disk.

Script. A series of commands and keystrokes stored in a file that can be replayed by a few keystrokes or a mouse click. Sometimes called a *macro*.

Scroll bars. The bars on the right side and bottom of a window that let you move vertically and horizontally through a document.

Shape. Item such as a circle, rectangle, line, polygon, or polylines in your document.

SmartIcons. Lotus SmartSuites' name for a toolbar.

SmartMasters. A series of predefined layouts that might include text as well as formatting.

Sort. To arrange data in alphabetical or numerical order.

Speaker Note. A note that is associated with a presentation page. Used as prompts while giving a presentation to store supporting facts, sources, or reminders.

SmartSum. A function that adds a row or column of figures by clicking on the SmartSum button on the toolbar. Same as *@SUM*.

Spell Check. A feature that checks the spelling of words in your document against a dictionary and flags possible errors for correction.

Status bar. The line at the bottom of a window that shows information, such as the current formatting of a cell.

Style. A way to format similar types of text such as headings and lists.

Symbols. Characters that are not on your keyboard, such as iconic symbols, phonetic characters, and characters in other alphabets.

Syntax. The exact structure of functions and formulas.

T

Table. A set of rows and columns of cells that you fill in with text, numbers, or graphics.

Tabs. Settings in your document to determine where the insertion point moves when you press the tab key or use the indent feature.

Template. A file with customized formatting, content, and features.

Thesaurus. A feature used to find synonyms (words that are alike) and antonyms (words that are opposite).

Titles. Descriptive pieces of text. Used in charts and spreadsheets.

Toolbars. Appears at the top of the application window and is used to access many of the commonly used features of Lotus SmartSuite.

Transitions. Special effects assigned to a slide show as one slide moves to the next.

U

Undo. To reverse the last editing action.

Unhide. To display cells, rows, or columns previously hidden in a worksheet.

Uppercase. A capital letter.

V

Value. An entry that is a number, a formula, or an @function.

Views. Ways of displaying documents to see different perspectives of the information in that document.

W

World Wide Web. A series of specially designed documents—all linked together—to be viewed over the Internet.

Word Wrap. To let text in a paragraph automatically flow to the next line when it reaches the right margin.

Workbook. A single 1-2-3 file containing a collection of 1-2-3 worksheets.

Worksheet. One of several pages in a 1-2-3 workbook.

Wrapping. A function that causes text to automatically wrap to the next line when it reaches the right edge of a cell.

X

X-axis. In a chart, a reference line marked in regular intervals to display the categories with descriptive labels.

y

Y-axis. In a chart, a reference line marked in regular intervals to display the values of a chart.

z

Zoom. To enlarge or reduce the way the text is displayed on the screen. It does not affect how the document will print.

Index

Prima's *fast & easy*™ Series

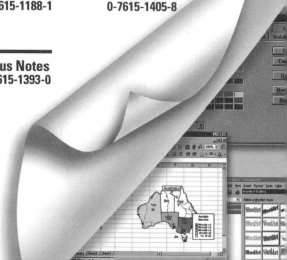